THE SCIEN

FOR GCSE

5 MAINTENANCE OF LIFE

There are many obvious differences between an oak tree and a clump of grass, an insect and a person. Yet they are all living organisms and they all carry out the same processes to stay alive. This module will help you to understand the processes of life that all plants and animals need to survive and reproduce.

Relevant National Curriculum Attainment Target: 3

5.1 Maintaining life

What is a living organism?

What features distinguish living organisms from non-living things? You can find the answer to this question by examining what living organisms *do*, and the *processes* that take place inside them. Look at these photographs. How can you tell which are living organisms and which are not?

What does this marmot have in common with the flower it is eating? In what ways do they differ?

Are these pebbles or beans? How can you tell which could be living material?

This crystal grows by using the materials that surround it. Is it living?

What changes take place when something dies?

Features of living organisms

All living organisms have *seven* important features in common. Each feature is needed to maintain life. Some of these features are easier to detect than others – but they are *all* characteristics of living organisms.

All living organisms release energy by **respiration**.
All living organisms **excrete**.
All living organisms **move**.
CAT LIT
All living organisms **respond to changes in their surroundings** . . . the sight of food!
All living organisms **reproduce** . . . and **grow**.
All living organisms **feed**.

Clear signs of life

You can usually see an animal move – **movement** is one of the clearest signs of life. As well as being able to move from place to place, there are also movements taking place inside your body, such as your heart beat, your lungs expanding and contracting – clear signs that you are alive! Movements in plants are less obvious. Their movements are so slow that you cannot see them happening.

Movements often take place as a result of changes in the surroundings of a living organism – like running away from a predator. By **responding to change**, an organism *increases* its chance of survival.

Some flowers open and close depending on the amount of light. The opening and closing is too slow for your eye to detect.

Making new life

Living organisms do not live for ever. Each type of organism continues to *maintain* the life of its **species** by producing offspring through **reproduction**. Only *living* organisms can reproduce. Most organisms start life as a single cell which then divides many times during growth to produce thousands of cells. As new cells are formed, they become *specialised* to carry out different jobs. So organisms become more complex as they grow and increase in size and mass.

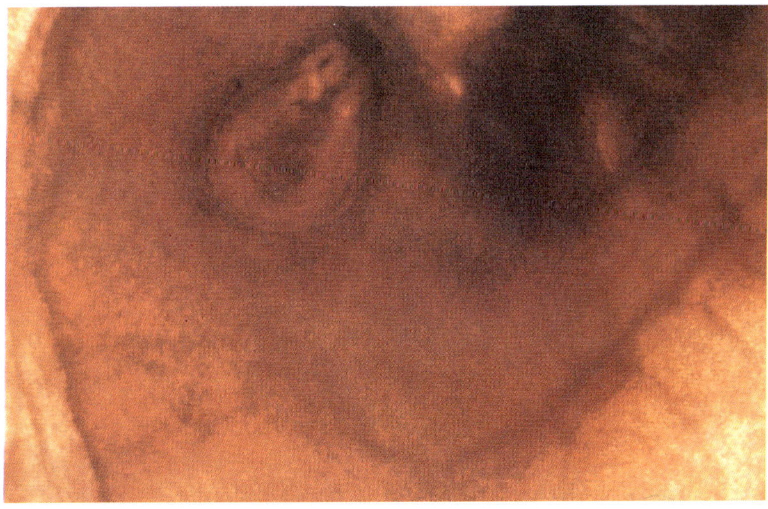

Liko all organisms, you began your life as a single cell which grew to form a complex living organism. This picture shows a human embryo after 4 weeks growth. Its cells are becoming more specialised – the oval outline (to the left) will form the head, and the faint red line (curving from left up to the right) will form the spine.

Life from chemical reactions

All living organisms need a supply of **food** to stay alive. Animals take in ready-made food. Green plants make their own food using energy from sunlight. Food substances are then changed by chemical reactions which take place inside cells. Food is changed to produce substances needed to make new cells for **growth**, and to release energy during **respiration**. Chemical reactions in cells also form waste products which are removed by the process of **excretion**.

These seven features of living organisms – movement; response to changes; growth; feeding; respiration; excretion; reproduction – are all essential for the *maintenance of life*. You can read more about living organisms and their functions throughout this module.

1 Which features does a robot have in common with a human? How does it differ?

2 Which of the seven features are you doing all the time?

Getting in food supplies

Making and using food

All living organisms need food to provide the *raw materials* they need to grow and the *energy* they need to stay alive. Green plants are **producers** – they are able to make their own food from carbon dioxide and water by using the energy in sunlight. This process is called **photosynthesis** (*see 5.3*). In contrast, animals, most micro-organisms and some non-green plants, cannot make their own food. They have to feed on other organisms – plants, animals or dead matter. The organisms that cannot make their own food are called **consumers.**

A bit of plant matter and a bit of animal meat – a consumer's delight!

This fungus is a decomposer, feeding off dead matter in this tree.

Consuming waste

Soil bacteria and some fungi feed on dead or waste matter. They are types of consumers called **decomposers.** They use substances in dead leaves, fallen logs and even animal droppings as a source of food. These bacteria and fungi produce chemicals called **enzymes** which they release from their cells to react with the dead matter. The enzymes break down (digest) this matter into soluble products which can then be absorbed into the cells of the bacterium or fungus. Digesting dead matter in this way causes the dead matter to decay (decompose). So, as well as getting the food they need, these organisms play an important role in the environment.

A variety of feeding methods

All animals, from insects to elephants, are consumers. They use a very wide variety of ways to obtain food from plants or other animals. There are many different food substances and many different animals, all of which have particular features which help them to get at the food they need. Some animals have very specialised feeding methods.

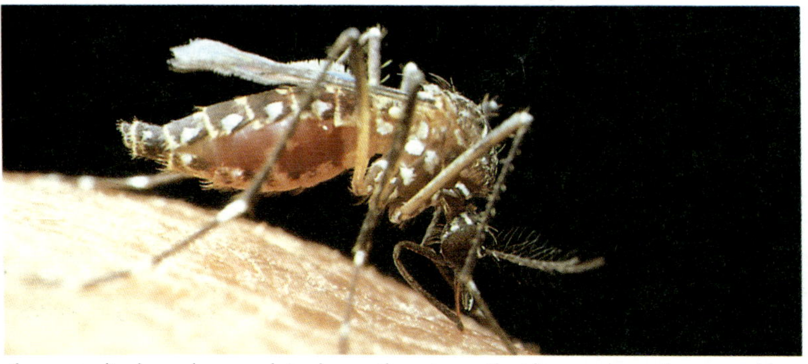

A mosquito has sharp pointed mouthparts so that it can pierce human skin and then suck up blood for food.

A butterfly sucks up sugary nectar from a flower using a long coiled tube called a **proboscis**.

Jaws!

Animals such as sheep and wolves have teeth and jaws to suit their food. The teeth of plant-eating animals (**herbivores**) such as sheep are used to cut grass close to the soil surface – and then grind it into a pulp so that it can be more easily digested.

A wolf is a meat-eating animal – **a carnivore**. Its teeth and jaws are very different from a sheep's. A wolf's teeth need to hold its prey, cut through flesh and even crush bones.

You may be an **omnivore** – eat meat and vegetables – or you may be a vegetarian. How do all your different teeth help you cut and chew your food?

1 Bottom jaw **moves up** to *cut* grass by pressing sharp incisors against hard pad.

2 Bottom jaw then **moves sideways** to *grind* grass using enamel ridges on broad cheek teeth.

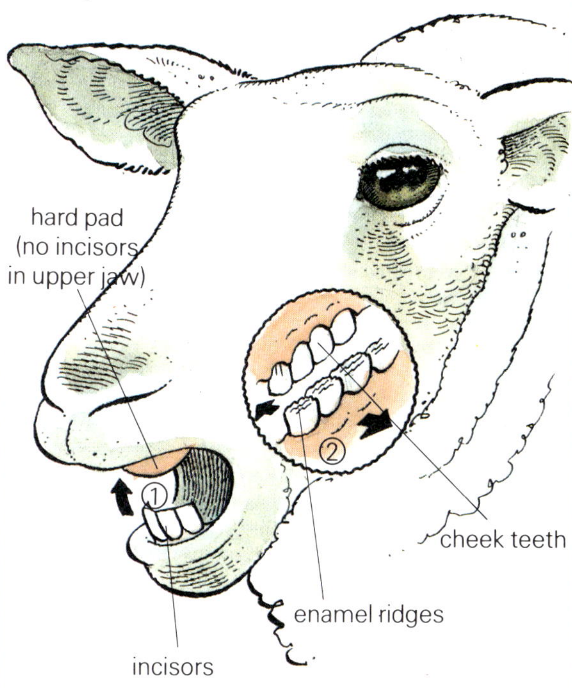

Helpful bacteria

Grass is hard to digest, even after it has been chewed into a pulp! This is because plant material contains **cellulose**, a tough substance that is used to make cell walls. Animals cannot make an enzyme to digest cellulose. They depend on bacteria in their gut to break it down. When a sheep or a cow eats grass it is swallowed into part of the stomach called the **rumen**. There the cellulose is digested by bacteria. After a while, the food in the rumen is sent back into the mouth – where it is chewed again. This is called 'chewing the cud'. When the cud is swallowed again, it goes to the main part of the stomach, and then to the rest of the gut, to complete the digestion process.

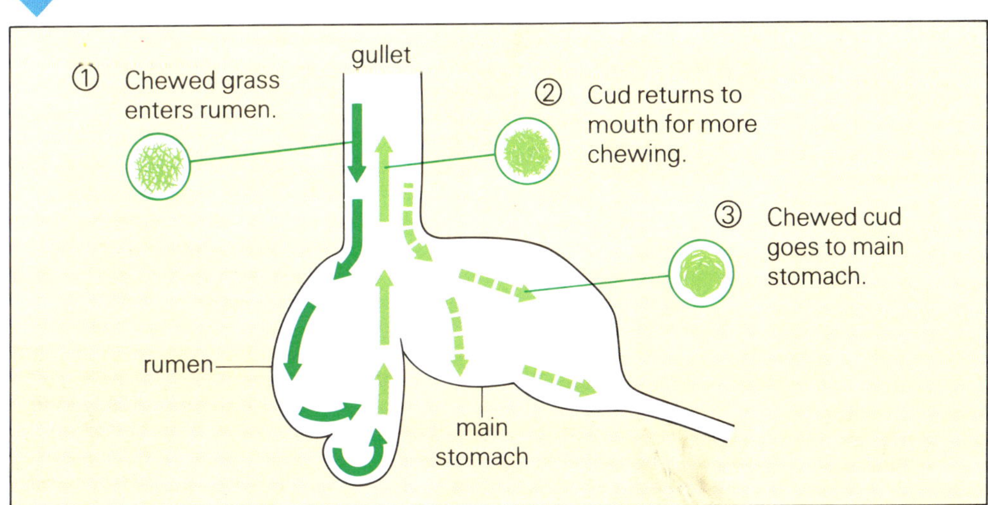

1 Suggest an explanation for the following;

- **a** Humans cannot digest cellulose.
- **b** A sheep's jaw moves from side to side when it feeds.
- **c** The gut of herbivores is very long.
- **d** The entrance to the rumen is closed in young lambs.

2 Suggest what happens to the cellulose you eat in the vegetables in your diet.

3 Houseflies feed on solid food such as sugar. They have a **proboscis** that acts like a vacuum cleaner. Food is sucked up very tiny tubes in the proboscis into the mouth.

- **a** Suggest a reason why flies secrete a liquid onto their food as they feed.
- **b** Why is this method of feeding a danger to health?

YOU CAN READ MORE ABOUT DIGESTION ON SPREADS 3.5, 3.6.

5.3 Capturing the sun's energy

Energy for all living things

The sun is the source of energy for *all* forms of life. Plants use the sun directly to make their food. Animals use it indirectly, getting their energy by eating plants or herbivores. Green plants use the energy in sunlight and convert it into sugars – which can then be used to store chemical energy in food substances, such as starch. This process of **photosynthesis** is the key to the whole food chain of life. So let's look at what plants need to photosynthesise.

Investigating photosynthesis . . .

A group of students thought that the following 'ingredients' were needed for photosynthesis:

- light • carbon dioxide • chlorophyll – the green pigment in plants

■ Do you agree with their list? What else do you think might be needed?

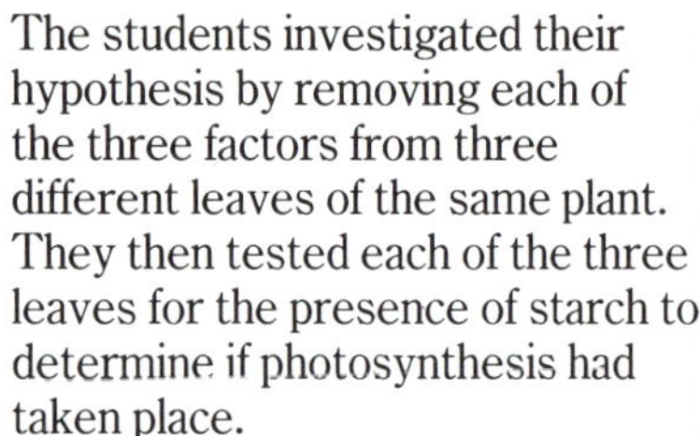

The students investigated their hypothesis by removing each of the three factors from three different leaves of the same plant. They then tested each of the three leaves for the presence of starch to determine if photosynthesis had taken place.

First they chose a plant which had *variegated* (different coloured) leaves. The absence of a green colour indicates that there is no chlorophyll in that part of the leaf (e.g. Leaf 1). They then put the plant into a cupboard for two days. One of the leaves was covered with aluminium foil (to block out the light) and another was placed in a flask containing soda-lime (a chemical which absorbs carbon dioxide). The plant was left in bright sunshine for 24 hours. The diagram shows the results the students obtained when they tested the three leaves for starch.

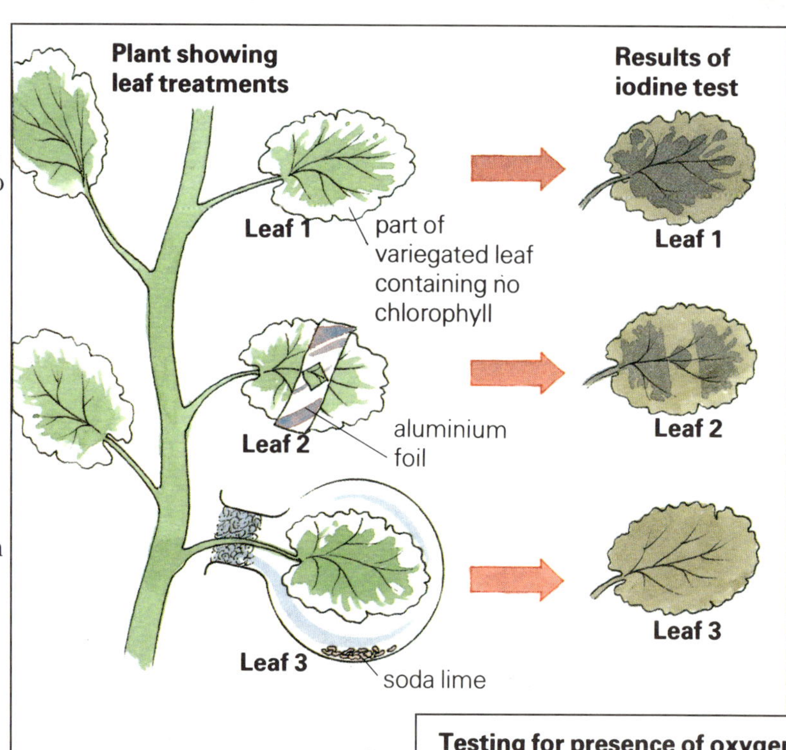

Each of the three differently treated leaves were tested with iodine solution to see if starch had been produced. What do you think these results show?

The students then tested to see if oxygen is given off during photosynthesis. How would you make sure this test was fair?

. . . and its products

The students then began to wonder what other things might be made during photosynthesis, besides sugars for food. They already knew that *oxygen* and *carbon dioxide* are exchanged during respiration – so they wondered if these two gases might be exchanged *in reverse* during photosynthesis. They decided to test if oxygen is given off from plants during photosynthesis.

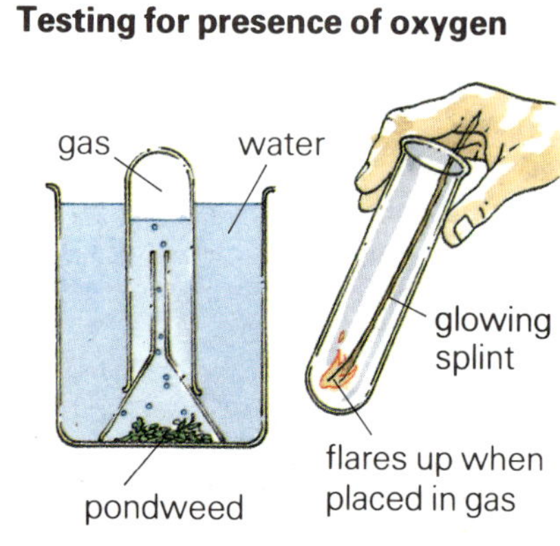

YOU CAN READ MORE ABOUT PHOTOSYNTHESIS ON SPREADS 4.6, 4.7.

Simple . . . isn't it?

The students were able to conclude from these, and other, investigations that **carbon dioxide** and **water** are the *raw materials* of photosynthesis, **sugars** and **oxygen** are the *products*; **light energy** and **chlorophyll** are *also* needed for the process to take place. But the process is quite complex – the plant is a bit like a tiny chemical factory!

Chlorophyll is present in the **chloroplasts** of leaf cells. The chloroplasts absorb energy from sunlight and use it to split the molecules of water (taken in by the plant) into oxygen and hydrogen. Oxygen is lost as a by-product and hydrogen is added to carbon dioxide (taken in from the air) to form glucose and other sugars. *Adding hydrogen* to (or *removing oxygen* from) a chemical is called **reduction**. So during photosynthesis, we can say that *carbon dioxide is reduced to form glucose*. This is not a simple reaction – it involves many stages, each requiring a special enzyme, before carbon dioxide and water can be transformed into useful sugars.

PHOTOSYNTHESIS

WATER + CARBON DIOXIDE

① **Chloroplasts** absorb **sunlight energy**

② Chloroplasts use energy from sunlight to *remove hydrogen* from water

③ Oxygen produced when hydrogen removed from water

④ Enzymes *add hydrogen* (from water) to carbon dioxide, forming glucose (by a chemical reduction)

OXYGEN + GLUCOSE

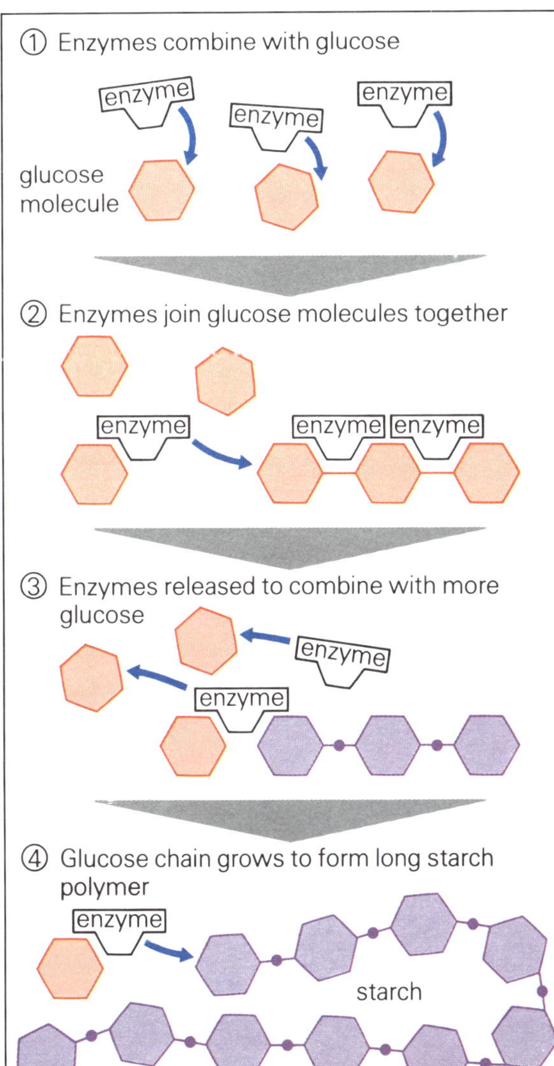

Building up stores

Some of the glucose produced by photosynthesis will break down right away to release its stored energy. The process of *releasing* stored energy is called **respiration**. The rest of the glucose is turned into starch and stored. To form starch, individual glucose molecules react together (in the presence of enzymes) to form a long chain molecule. Any molecule made up of a series of repeated units is called a **polymer**. Starch is a polymer containing hundreds of glucose units.

Some plants store starch in the cells of leaves, stems or roots. Other plants have special storage organs. For example, the potato tuber is a storage organ which holds large reserves of starch. The plant can turn starch back into glucose when it is needed.

Plants also use glucose to make another polymer called **cellulose**. Cellulose is needed to make the cell walls of a plant. The plant cannot turn cellulose back into glucose, so it cannot be used as a storage substance.

1 Explain how light energy is used during photosynthesis.

2 Explain how you would use iodine to test a leaf for starch.

3 **a** Make a large copy of the table below. Use the headings to show the students' observations and the interpretation of the results of their first investigation.

Leaf treatment	Diagram of leaf after starch test	Interpretation of results

b Why did the students use a plant which had been kept in a dark cupboard for two days?

Exchanging substances

In and out of cells

Many chemical reactions are taking place in any living cell – all the time! Raw materials for these reactions pass into cells, and waste materials pass out. For example in plants, during photosynthesis carbon dioxide moves into cells and oxygen moves out. During respiration (in animals *and* plants), oxygen moves into cells and carbon dioxide moves out. This exchange of oxygen and carbon dioxide occurs because the molecules of each gas are moving about in all directions which causes them to spread out evenly (when this is possible). This process is called **diffusion**. Diffusion occurs when molecules in a *highly concentrated* region are able to move to a *less concentrated* region.

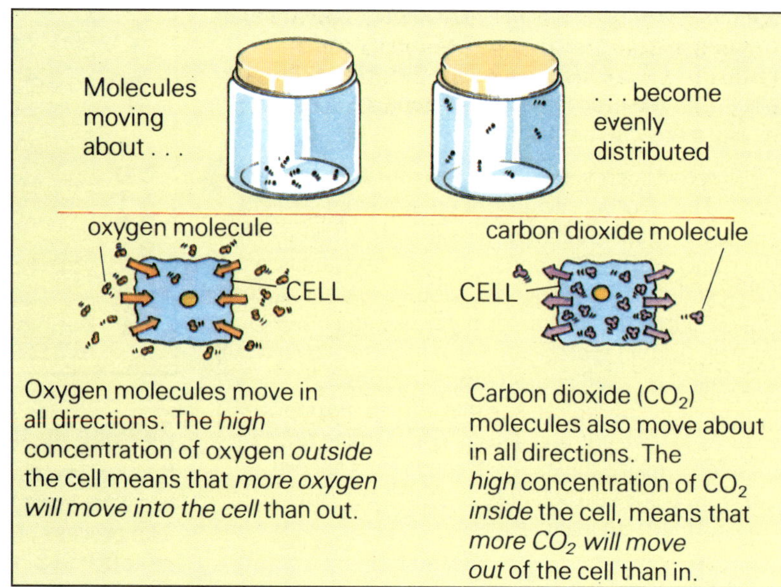

Molecules moving about . . .
. . . become evenly distributed
oxygen molecule
CELL
carbon dioxide molecule
CELL
Oxygen molecules move in all directions. The *high* concentration of oxygen *outside* the cell means that *more oxygen will move into the cell* than out.
Carbon dioxide (CO_2) molecules also move about in all directions. The *high* concentration of CO_2 *inside* the cell, means that *more CO_2 will move out* of the cell than in.

During respiration in a living cell, oxygen diffuses into the cell and carbon dioxide diffuses out.

Gas exchange in animals

As animals respire, they exchange oxygen in the air (or in water) for expelled carbon dioxide. Very small animals, such as earthworms, obtain oxygen and get rid of carbon dioxide by diffusion through their skin. This is possible because *small* animals have a large area of skin, but a small body mass. Once oxygen has been absorbed at the skin surface, it needs to diffuse over *only a short distance* to reach all the body cells.

Large animals cannot get the amounts of oxygen they need by diffusion through their skin surface because they have a small surface area compared to their large body mass. They exchange oxygen and carbon dioxide across special **gas exchange surfaces**. Many animals have **gills** or **lungs** which act as areas of gas exchange to provide a plentiful supply of oxygen to the rest of the body.

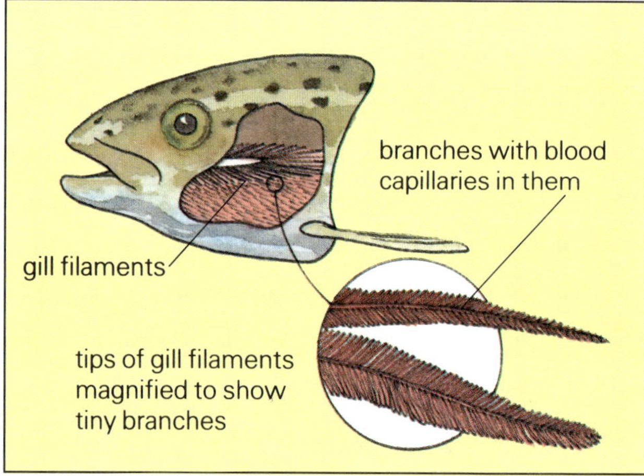

The many tiny branches of a fish's gill provide a large surface area over which gas exchange can take place.

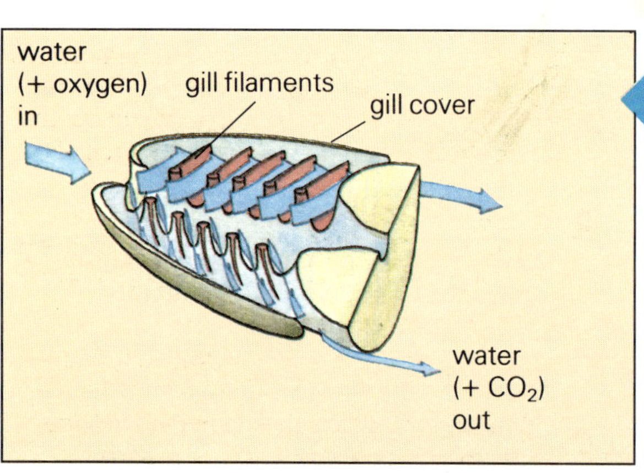

Pumping supplies in and waste out

Fish regularly take in water through their mouths and pump it across their gills. The movement of water across the gill surface is called **ventilation**, and renews the oxygen supply to the gills and removes waste carbon dioxide. Ventilation brings water which is rich in oxygen close to the gill filaments. Oxygen then passes into the blood cells in the gills by diffusion.

The breathing action in *humans* (and many other large animals) ventilates the lungs by sucking in air containing fresh supplies of oxygen into the lungs and pushing out air containing carbon dioxide.

YOU CAN READ MORE ABOUT DIFFUSION ON SPREAD 3.8.

Gas exchange in insects

Insects have a branching series of tubes, called **tracheae,** running through their bodies. The tubes open to the outside through holes called **spiracles.** Oxygen diffuses into the spiracles and along the tracheae to reach the insect's cells. As the cells respire, carbon dioxide is produced and diffuses out.

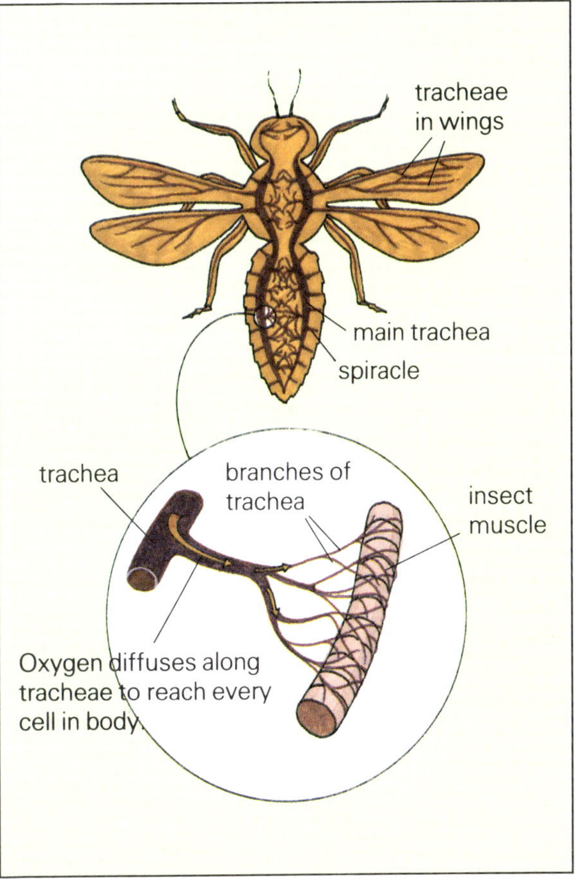

Oxygen entering the insect's trachea is able to diffuse right up to its cells.

Gas exchange in plants

Plants rely only on **diffusion without ventilation** to achieve exchange of gases. Plants carry out *two* types of gas exchange: during photosynthesis (carbon dioxide in, oxygen out) and respiration (carbon dioxide out, oxygen in). In photosynthesis, carbon dioxide is taken into the plant through tiny air pores called **stomata**. The leaf is made up of two skin-like layers – the **epidermis** – between which are lots of cells. The lower mesophyll cells are loosely packed together with air spaces around them. This means the carbon dioxide can easily diffuse from the stomata into these spaces and then through the cell walls. Similarly oxygen can diffuse out.

In respiration, plant cells get their oxygen and lose their carbon dioxide by diffusion directly (all over the plant) to and from the air and soil. Often this involves gases first diffusing through neighbouring plant cells.

This microscopic picture shows the spongy layer of mesophyll cells underneath the 'skins' of a leaf. The air spaces around the cells provide plenty of space for CO_2 to diffuse into.

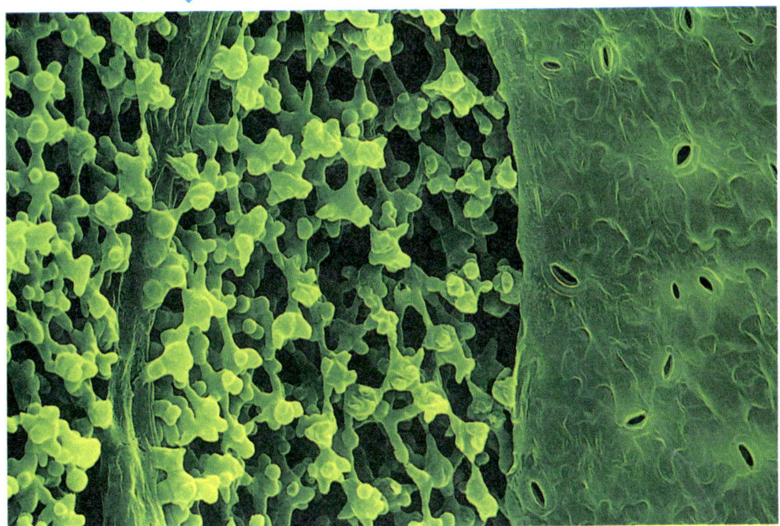

Some students observed that the abdomen of a locust moves in and out (like a pulse) and that these movements appear to increase when the locust becomes more active. They suggested that these movements were to provide more oxygen and to get rid of carbon dioxide. To test this hypothesis, the students placed a locust in a small tube filled with ordinary air and then counted the number of its pulsating movements. They then repeated the experiment but this time they blew into the tube first.

1 Why did the students repeat the experiment using their own expelled air?

2 The locust's pulsating movements increased after the students blew into the tube. Does this result support the students' hypothesis? Explain your answer.

3 To carry out their job of gas exchange as efficiently as possible, the gills of a fish bring blood and water close together over a very large area.

Use diagrams to show how this happens.

4 Why is it difficult for a large organism to get the oxygen it needs by diffusion alone?

5.5 Cleaning the bloodstream

Removing the body's waste

Like any other organism, you need to get rid of waste which is produced from the necessary chemical reactions that take place to keep your body alive. Your main organs for this process of waste removal called **excretion** are your lungs and kidneys. Your *lungs* remove **carbon dioxide** which is produced in respiration. Your *kidneys* remove **urea** which is formed when amino acids are broken down in the liver. Your kidneys also remove any excess water and salts taken in in your diet, and remove any foreign substances in the blood such as drugs and alcohol.

Within each of your kidneys there are thousands of tiny blood vessels (like this one) from which waste substances are filtered from the blood.

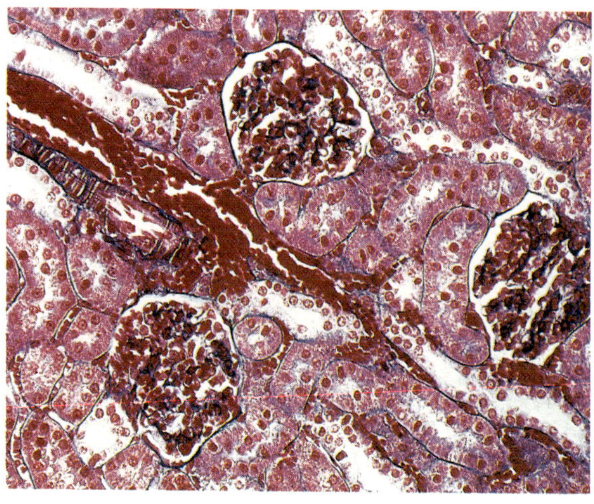

Saving and removing

Each of your kidneys contains between one and two million tiny tubes called **nephrons.** At the end of each nephron is a small cup-shaped capsule, called **Bowman's capsule** which contains a knot of capillaries called a **glomerulus.** This detailed network of the kidneys acts both to *filter* off waste substances, and to *reabsorb* important substances back into your blood. Your kidneys provide some very important functions in your body.

Blood containing waste substances flows into the glomerulus.

glomerulus

Blood is filtered into the capsule of the nephron. The cells of the capillary and the capsule act like a filter allowing only small molecules to pass through. Urea, salts, water and glucose enter the capsule.

Bowman's capsule

nephron

Useful substances such as glucose are absorbed back into the blood.

Urine containing unwanted substances flows on to the ureter and bladder.

Cleaned blood flows back to the rest of the body.

YOU CAN READ MORE ABOUT HOW YOUR KIDNEYS WORK ON SPREAD 3.10.

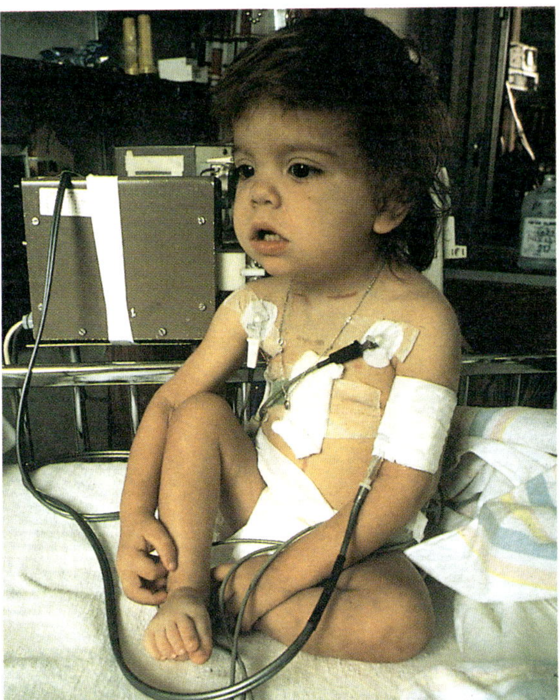

An artificial kidney – a dialysis machine – can be a life saver for some.

Kidney failure

Accidents, disease, drugs and alcohol abuse damage the kidneys' ability to function properly. Until recently, you would die if both kidneys completely failed. However, it is now possible to use a **dialysis machine** to do the job of the kidneys. Alternatively, some people are able to have a kidney **transplant** – when one kidney is transplanted from a matching donor.

Why do you think a person is only given one kidney in a transplant?

Medical machinery

A kidney machine works by removing waste substances from the blood of the patient across an artificial **dialysis membrane.** This membrane is **semi-permeable** – it allows only *small* molecules to pass through it. The membrane is surrounded by a solution, called the **dialysis fluid.** The *concentration* of substances in the dialysis fluid controls the necessary diffusion of urea out of the blood – and the diffusion of useful substances back in!

Dialysis works by imitating the processes of filtration which go on in healthy kidneys.

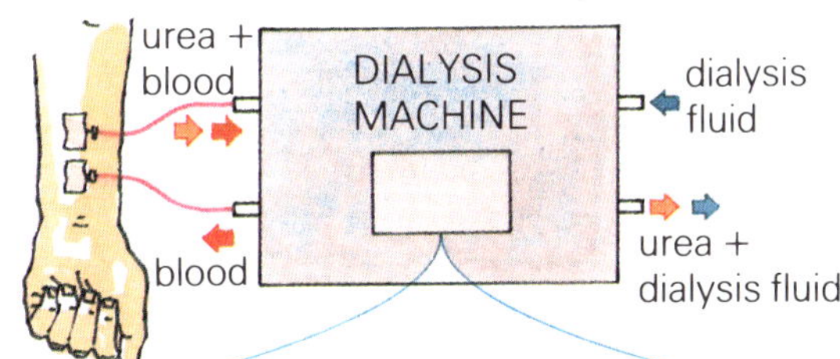

The high concentration of urea in the blood causes urea to diffuse into the dialysis fluid

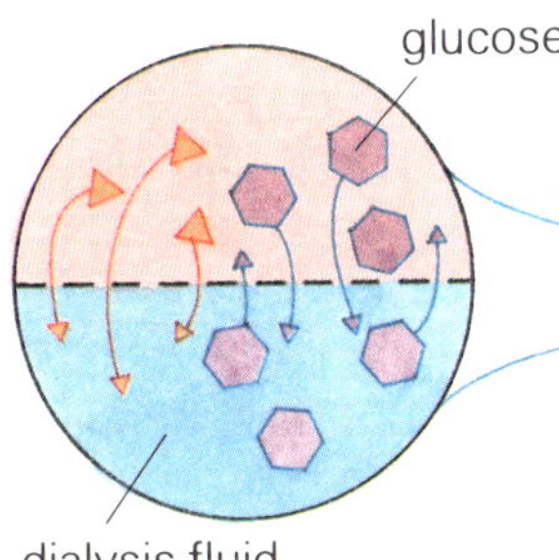

Glucose will diffuse out of blood, but . . .

. . . dialysis fluid also contains glucose which diffuses back at the same rate

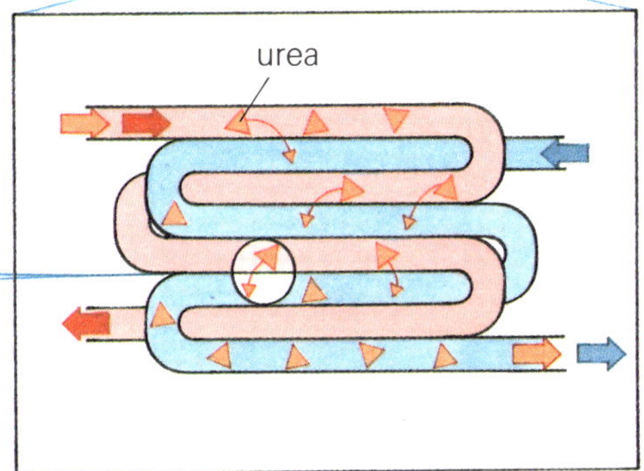

1 **a** Name one substance that is filtered into the nephron and is then reabsorbed into the blood.
b Explain why proteins are not filtered from the blood into the glomerulus.

2 Explain why the concentration of glucose in dialysis fluid is the same as in healthy blood.

3 State *one* way in which the working of a kidney machine:
a is similar to a natural kidney;
b is different from a natural kidney.

4 A firm is making some new dialysis tubing. You are the firm's chemist and have to find out if the new tubing is permeable to urea at body temperature (37°C).

You are provided with: ordinary laboratory equipment; the new tubing; urea solution; colourless dye (turns blue when mixed with urea).

Use a diagram to show how you would carry out your investigation.

What result would show that urea can pass through the tubing?

5.6 Controlling the body

Controlling conditions

There are many reactions taking place in the cells of all living plants and animals to keep them alive. All of these reactions are controlled by **enzymes** – biological catalysts which enable the chemical reactions (known as the body's **metabolism**) to take place. Any slight change (in the temperature, pH level or water content of a cell) can slow down or even stop an enzyme from working. It is therefore necessary to keep the conditions inside cells as steady as possible, so that enzymes can keep the organism working at an efficient metabolic rate.

Maintaining steady conditions inside the body is called **homeostasis**. The diagram opposite shows the major organs which regulate the conditions *inside the human body*. The **brain** has overall control of homeostatic processes. The temperature and the concentration of substances in the blood are checked as blood flows through the brain. If there needs to be any change, information will be sent to the relevant body organs along **nerves** – or by releasing chemicals called **hormones** into the bloodstream.

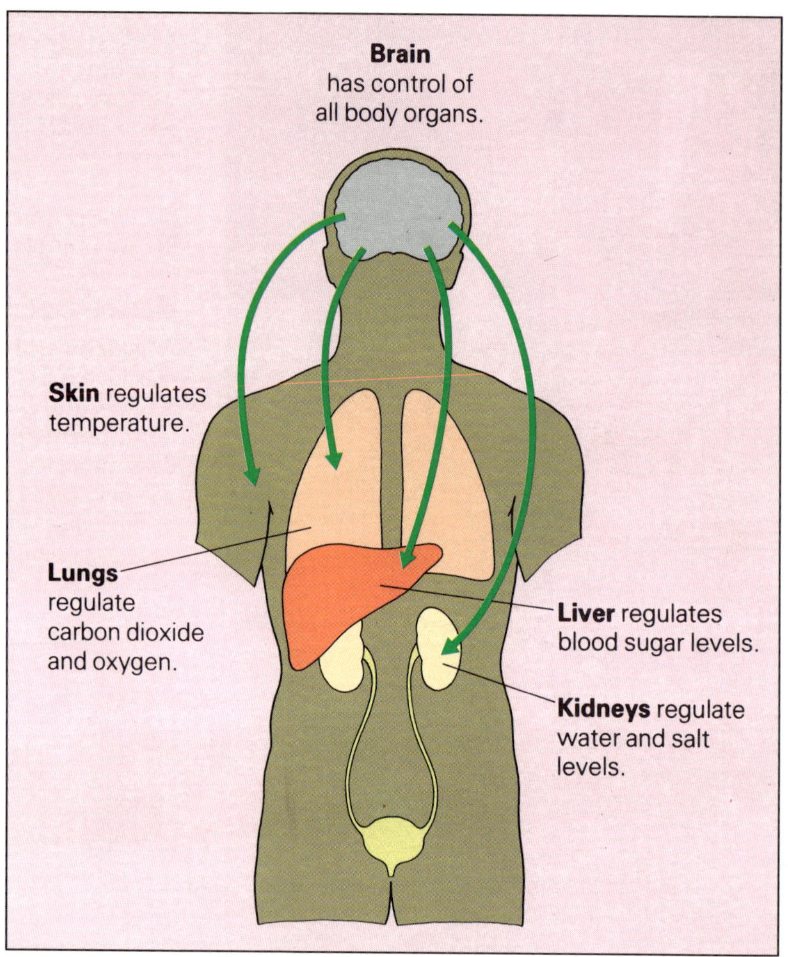

The brain acts as a centre for feedback to and from the rest of your body. It receives information – say that you are hot – and activates processes to cool your body.

Water gains

- Drink $1450\,cm^3$
- Respiration in cells $350\,cm^3$
- Food $800\,cm^3$

Total: $2600\,cm^3$

Water losses

- Faeces $100\,cm^3$
- Exhaled air $400\,cm^3$
- Sweat $600\,cm^3$
- Urine $1500\,cm^3$

Total: $2600\,cm^3$

Balancing water content

You take in (and lose) water in large amounts every day. To keep the amount of water in your body at a steady level the quantity of water you drink must be balanced by the quantity that you lost through sweating, urinating etc. These two pie charts show the typical daily water balance in the human body.

The amount of water lost by the different methods shown in the pie chart will change during very hot weather. Can you predict what these changes will be?

Kidneys as regulators

You will have noticed what happens when you drink more fluid than you need to – you urinate more than usual. Why does this happen?

As well as removing waste substances (*see* 5.5), your kidneys also regulate the amount of water in your blood. When you drink large quantities of fluids, your blood becomes diluted – *less* concentrated. Your kidneys remove this excess water by producing *large* quantities of urine to restore water balance. On the other hand, when you are short of water your blood becomes *more* concentrated, so the kidneys produce *less* urine to conserve body water.

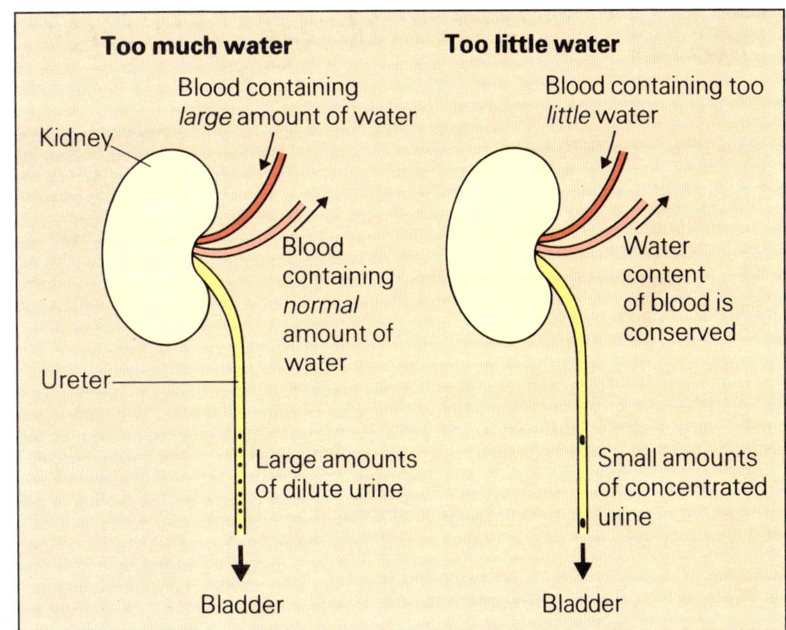

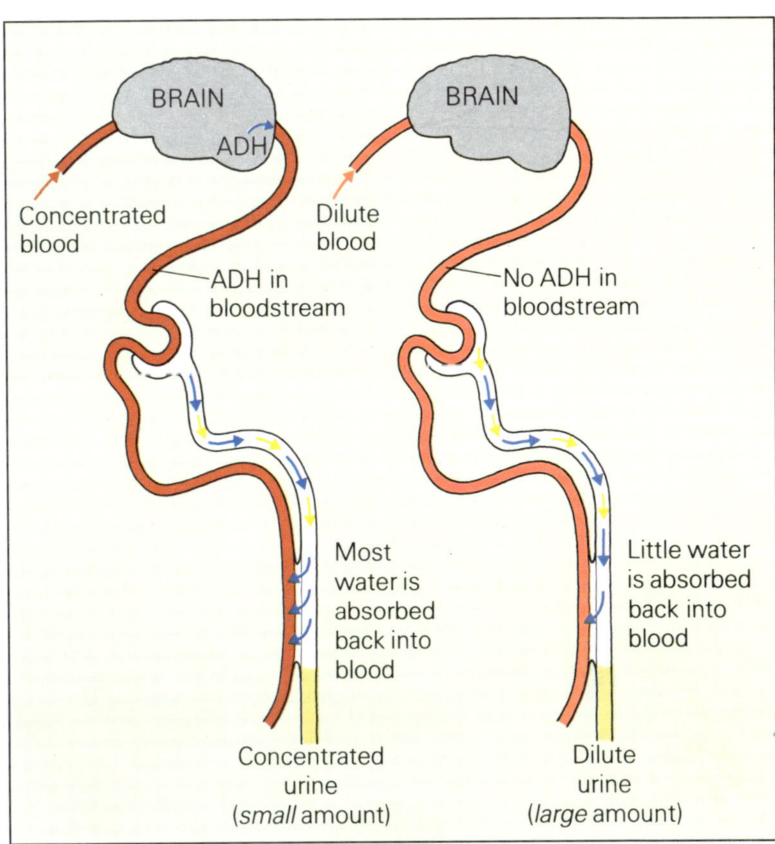

Chemical control

The amount of water you lose in your urine is controlled by a hormone called the **antidiuretic hormone** (**ADH** for short). ADH is made by a gland in your brain and it is released when your body becomes short of water and your blood becomes concentrated. The hormone makes the wall of the kidney nephron *more porous* – so water can be reabsorbed back into your blood. *Less* water then passes in urine to your bladder. If you drink a lot of fluid, however, ADH will not be released because your blood will be quite dilute. In the *absence* of ADH, less water is reabsorbed and *more* water is present in your urine passing to the bladder – hence all those trips to the toilet!

ADH is one of the many hormones your body produces to maintain its steady state. ADH controls the amount of water removed from the body.

1 **a** State four ways in which the human body loses water.
b Why does respiration cause an increase in the water content of the body?

2 Explain the effect that you think each of the following will have on the amount of urine produced:
a drinking a large amount of fruit juice.
b cold weather.
c long periods of vigorous exercise.
d damage to the gland that produces ADH.

YOU CAN READ MORE ABOUT CONTROLLING THE BODY ON SPREAD 3.14.

5.7 Sensitive to change

Responding to change

Like any living organism your body is always responding to changes in your surroundings. You will start to sweat if you are too hot; shiver if you are cold. Any change in the surroundings which affects an organism is called a **stimulus**. For example, a snake will flick out its tongue as it moves around to taste chemicals in the air. The chemicals released into the air (from other animals and plants) are stimuli that snakes can detect. The snake's tongue picks up chemicals, and carries them to **receptors** in its mouth which can detect even the slightest trace of chemicals. The ability to respond to stimuli in this way is called **sensitivity.** The snake's tongue is sensitive to chemicals produced by plants and animals. It uses this to find food, and avoid being attacked by predators – a 'whiff' of life and death for the snake!

Slow to respond

Plants cannot move from place to place to find their food, but they still need to respond to changes in their surroundings. A plant growing on a window-sill will grow towards light – so that its leaves are placed in the best position for photosynthesis.

By changing the way in which its leaves (or flowers) are positioned, or by growing its shoots or roots in certain directions, a plant can make *slow* movements that respond to its environment. A change in the direction of plant growth is called a **tropism**. For example, the growth response caused by light is called a **phototropism** (*see 5.9*).

It takes a much longer time for a plant to respond to change than it does a snake.

From stimulus to response

The following sequence is a model of the events that take place when an organism responds to a stimulus:

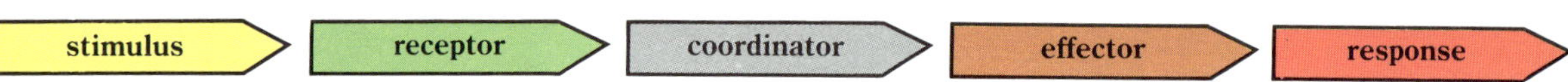

A rapid or complex response may involve several separate actions happening together. The more rapid or complex the response, the more important the coordinator stage becomes.

Look at how the snake responds to its surroundings in this sequence:

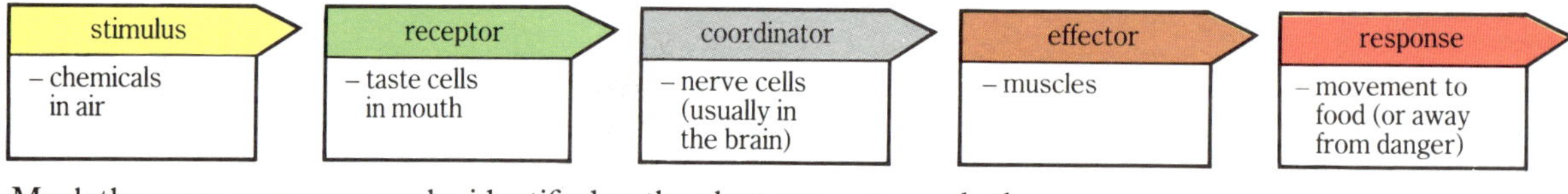

Much the same sequence can be identified as the plant grows towards the light:

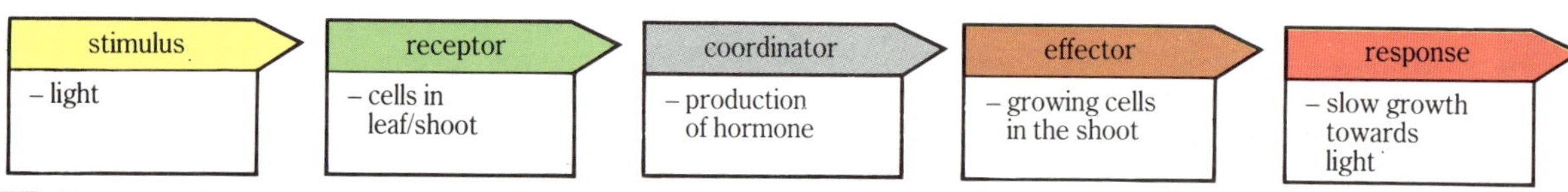

Compare these two sequences. What difference(s) do you notice? What explanation(s) can you give for the difference(s)?

Investigating animal behaviour

The behaviour of small animals such as woodlice can be observed using a **choice chamber.** You can look at how they respond to a particular stimulus – such as a change in humidity. In the investigation shown here, the chamber is divided into a humid (moist) side and a dry side. Some students observed that on placing 10 woodlice into a choice chamber, they immediately crawled about in all directions. When the woodlice found themselves on the dry side, they moved about rapidly. In contrast, the woodlice on the wet side moved slowly and eventually stopped. After 20 minutes of being in the chamber, 9 of the woodlice were on the wet side, and remaining there.

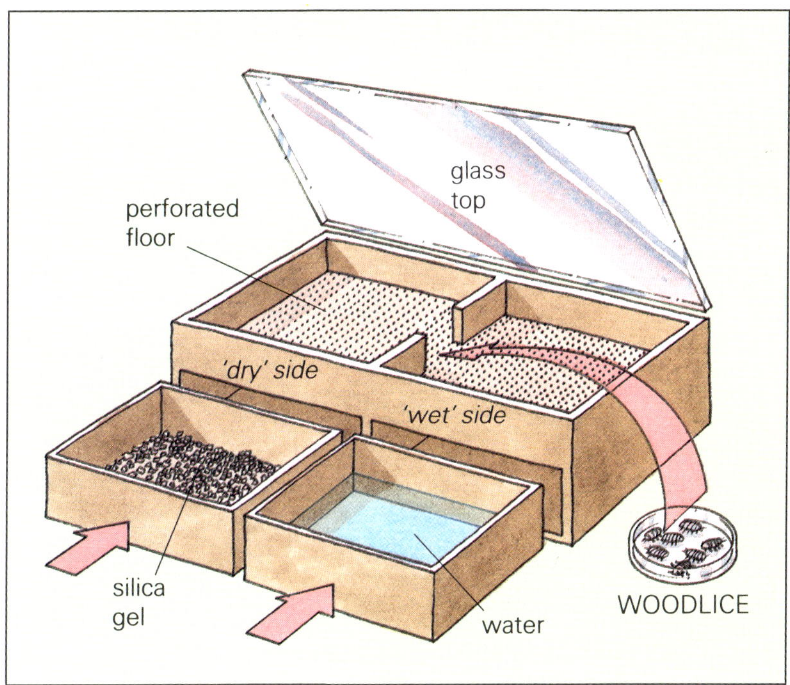

shine light on one side
turn plant on its side
place stick above tip

① Stimulus? — 3 days later — Response?

② Stimulus? — 3 days later — Response?

③ Stimulus? — 3 days later — Response?

Investigating plant behaviour

The slow responses of plants to stimuli mean that observations need to last several days. Investigations, such as the three examples illustrated here, show that plants do respond to several different stimuli.

What kind of stimulus does the plant respond to in each of these three investigations? How does it respond?

What does this investigation tell you about the production of hormone and its effect on plant growth?

1
- **a** How do woodlice respond to dry air?
- **b** How would you make sure that the woodlice in the investigation were responding to differences in humidity?
- **c** Where would you expect to find woodlice in the environment?

2
- **a** Interpret the results of the investigation into plant growth shown above.
- **b** What is the response observed in sample 1 called?
- **c** How do you think the seedling benefits from this response?

3 When the young shoots of a bean plant are stroked lightly with a match, they coil. What is the stimulus which produces this response?

How do bean plants growing in the garden benefit from this response?

5.8 Responding to change

Stimulus	Receptor	Sense
Light energy	Light sensitive cells, called rods + cones in the retina of the eye	Vision
Sound energy	Cells in the cochlea of the ear	Hearing
Gravity e.g. falling (Movement energy)	Gravity receptors in the ear	Balance
Change in temperature (Heat energy)	Temperature receptors in the skin	Temperature detection
Pressure, pain and touch	Pressure, pain and touch receptors in the skin	Touch and pain
Chemicals in the air, drink and food (Chemical energy)	Chemical receptors in the nose and tongue	Smell and taste

Detecting change

Like many animals, you have a **nervous system** that enables your body to detect and to respond quickly to stimuli. Your **senses** make you aware of changes taking place inside your body and around you. Special sense organs contain **receptors** that detect different kinds of stimuli. A stimulus, such as bright sunlight, reaches a receptor as a form of **energy** – as light energy. Receptors convert this energy into electrical energy which travels along your **nerves** as **nerve impulses**.

You have receptors in the sense organs of your body which detect different stimuli.

Linking all parts of the body

The main parts of the nervous system are shown here. The **brain** and **spinal cord** form the **central nervous system** (**CNS**) which is linked to all parts of the body by a network of thousands of branching nerves. The CNS and nerves are made up of nerve cells or **neurones**. Each neurone has a cell body with long fibres spreading from it. The long nerve fibres carry impulses from one part of the body to another. Hundreds of tiny nerve fibres are bundled together to form a single nerve.

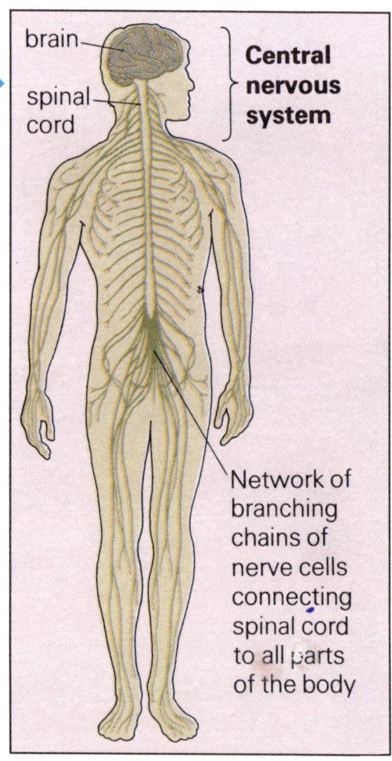

Organising the best response

When the receptors in your sense organs are stimulated, impulses are carried along **sensory neurones** to the central nervous system. Your brain or spinal cord coordinates your body's response to the stimulus by sending impulses along **motor neurones** to the part of your body that needs to react. For example, this is what happens when you accidentally touch a hot plate and then quickly pull your hand away:

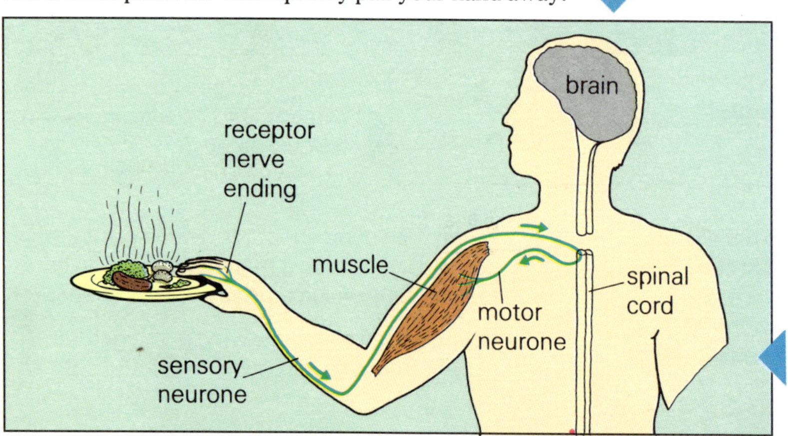

When you touch a hot plate impulses are sent from your fingertips to your central nervous system.

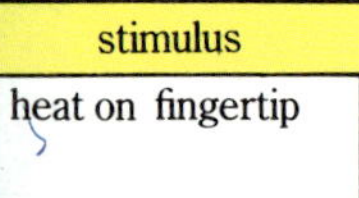

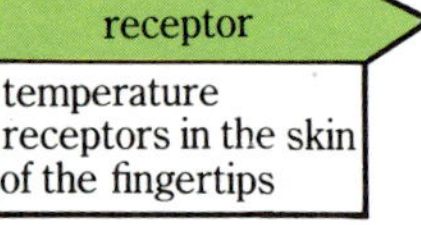

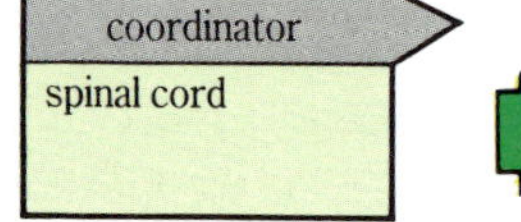

effector

muscles in the hand and arm

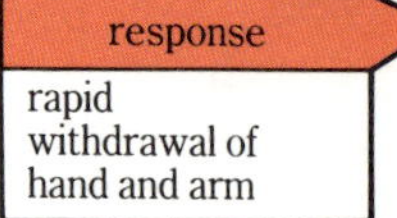

sensory nerves

motor nerves

Protecting the body from damage

Pulling your hand away from a hot plate is a **reflex action** – a rapid automatic response to a stimulus which protects the body from possible harm. *Blinking,* when dust gets into your eye; *narrowing the pupil* of your eye in bright light; *coughing* when food goes down the 'wrong way' and touches the windpipe – these are all instant reflexes. In each case you cannot help yourself from reacting – stimulation of particular receptors has caused an *involuntary response* to take place.

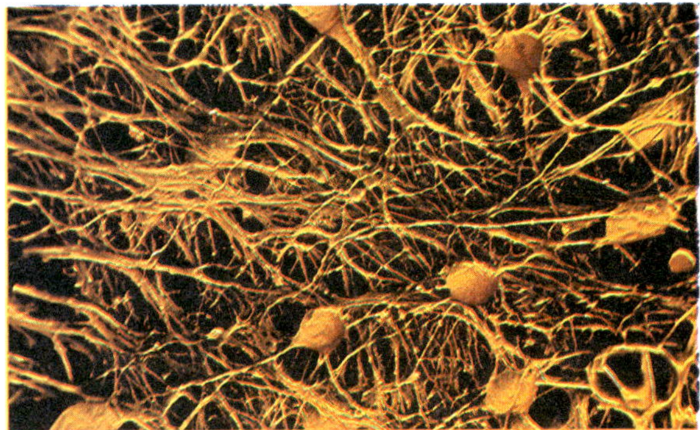

Your brain has millions of nerve cells. Magnified about 200 times, here are some of your brain's 'blob'-like nerve cells. They interact by sending electrical pulses around the brain, controlling all your thoughts and actions.

The sequence of events in a reflex action, though complex, takes place in an instant.

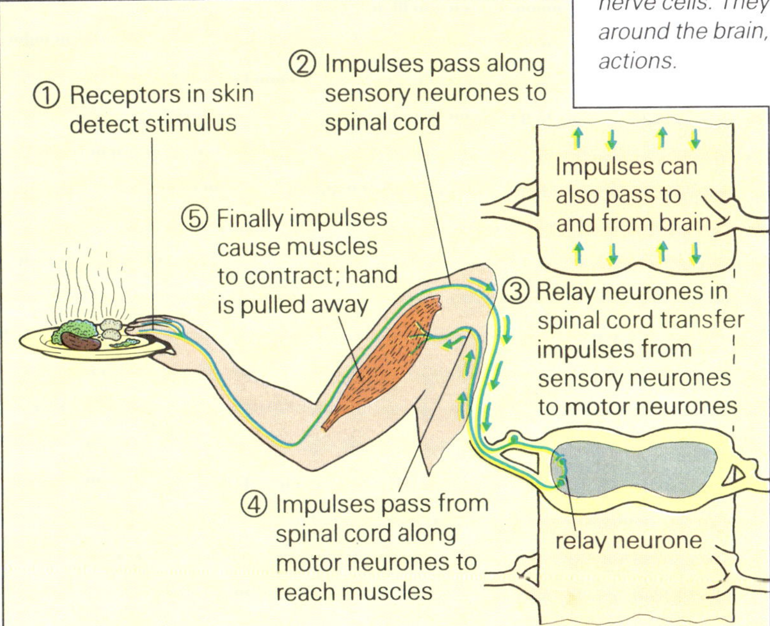

Making decisions

Nerve cells in the spinal cord also carry impulses to your brain to keep it informed about events affecting your body. The brain stores some of this information as **memory.** Unlike reflex actions, many of your other actions are *voluntary* – they are controlled by the brain. For example, after touching a hot plate you may decide to put on a kitchen glove before picking up the plate again. This is possible because you have **learned** from past experience that the plate burns and stored the information in your brain. You can then decide how to act on this information.

1 Copy and complete the following table.

Reflex	Stimulus	Receptor	Response	Purpose
Blinking	?	Retina	Eyelid muscles contract	?
Narrowing pupil	Bright light	?	Iris closes	To reduce light entering eye, improves vision
?	Dim light	?	Iris opens	?
Withdrawal of foot	Standing on a sharp nail	?	?	?

2 Use the sequence –

stimulus→receptor→coordinator→effector→response

to explain what happens when:

a you prick your finger with a needle.

b you smell tasty food.

c you accidentally pick up a hot plate and realize it is very expensive!

Plant growth responses

Slow to respond

If you look into bright sunlight you will immediately screw up your eyes. Like other animals you respond quickly to stimuli. Plants, on the other hand, do *not* usually respond to stimuli by sudden movements. Their responses normally involve very slow growth movements called **tropisms**. For example, a plant growing near a window will gradually bend towards the daylight so that its leaves get plenty of light for photosynthesis. This response, called **phototropism**, is slow and long-lasting. It is very different from rapid, short-lasting nervous responses, such as blinking, shown by humans and some other animals.

Can you catch a fly with your fingers? The venus fly trap is an unusual plant in that it responds quickly to touch.

Light

Light

ink markings (equally spaced)

Shoot tip uncovered; light from *one* side

Shoot tip covered; light from *one* side.

Appearance after 2 days

Shoot grows and bends toward light

Shoot grows straight up

Plants also respond to gravity, touch, water, chemicals and temperature. Each stimulus produces a growth response (a tropism) which places the plant in the *best position for survival.*

Investigating phototropism

What do you think actually takes place during phototropism? The investigation here shows how plants detect, and respond to, light.

The results show that when the shoot grows, it is the part just below the tip that grows most. Since no bending occurred when the tip was covered, bending will only occur when the light stimulus reaches the tip.

Other experiments led scientists to suggest that the response is controlled by a chemical *produced in the tip* which controls the growth in the region behind the tip. This hypothesis of chemical control can be summarised by the sequence:

stimulus	receptor	coordinator	effector	response
light	shoot tip	chemicals made in the tip	growing region behind the tip	bending towards light

Testing for chemical control

The following experiment was carried out to test the chemical control hypothesis. Three groups of grass seedlings were treated. Each group, consisting of 20 seedlings, was placed in a box with bright light shining on them from one side only. The appearance of the seedlings after two days is shown on the right. The lengths of the seedlings were measured at the start and at the end of the experiment. The average measurements are shown in the table below.

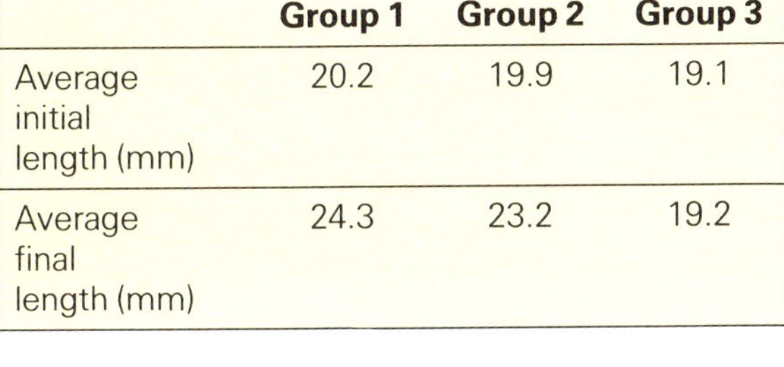

	Group 1	Group 2	Group 3
Average initial length (mm)	20.2	19.9	19.1
Average final length (mm)	24.3	23.2	19.2

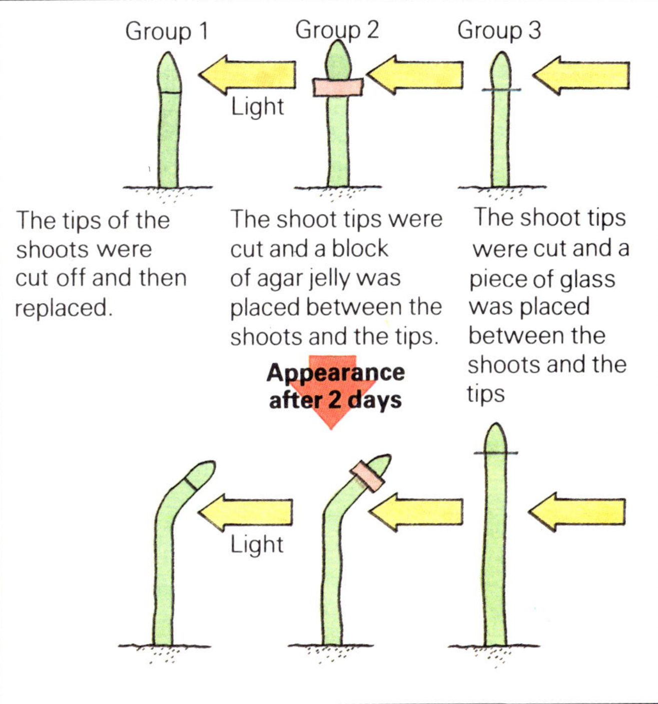

Control by hormones

This experiment supports the idea that a chemical produced in the tip of a shoot controls the growth response. Further experiments revealed this chemical as a type of hormone called **auxin**, found in plants. When a shoot is lit from above, the auxin spreads evenly down from the shoot tip. When it is lit from *one side*, more auxin collects on the far side. This causes the cells on this far side to get longer. Because the elongation of cells causes the shoot to grow, the shoot *bends* as the unlit side of it grows longer than the lit side.

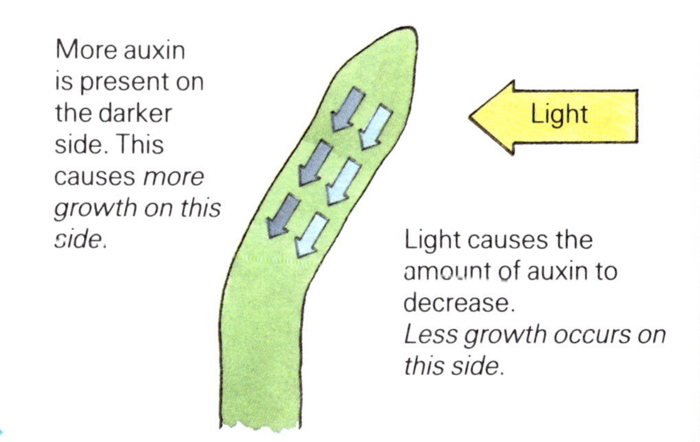

The direction of light affects the distribution of auxin in the shoot tip.

1 **a** Calculate the average change in length of each group of seedlings shown at the top of this page.
b Why was there no growth in group 3?
c Explain how these results support the hypothesis that growth responses are controlled by a chemical.
d Why were there 20 seedlings in each group instead of just one?
e Describe how you would accurately measure the lengths of the curved shoots at the end of the experiment. (Straightening them may cause them to break.)

2 You blink when dust enters your eye. How does this response differ from the way a plant shoot bends towards light?

3 Another experiment was carried out on some seedling shoots – the cut tip being pushed to one side.

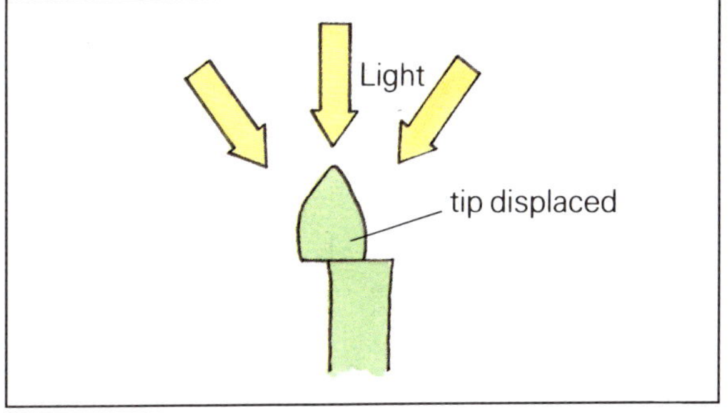

Predict what each shoot will look like in two days. Explain your answer.

Plant reproduction

Producing new offspring

Plants and animals cannot live for ever. Each type of organism needs to produce more of its own kind by the process of **reproduction**. This process may be asexual or sexual.

Many organisms – some plants and simple animals – reproduce on their own *without another individual*. We call this **asexual reproduction**. For example, cells from plant roots, stems or leaves may grow to produce new plants. (This is also called vegetative reproduction.)

Sexual reproduction involves *two* individuals and requires the production of special sex cells called **gametes** (made in the reproductive organs of the plant or animal). During the process of **fertilisation**, the male gamete fuses with the female gamete to form a single cell called a **zygote**, which then grows into a new individual.

Mosses reproduce asexually by producing spores inside a spore capsule. When ripe the capsule bursts and the spores are scattered forming more individuals.

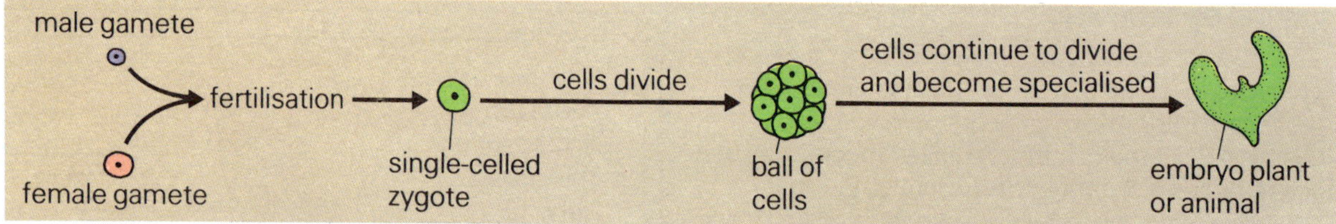

Sexual reproduction occurs in plants as well as animals. It always involves the fusion of gametes to form a zygote.

Sexual reproduction in plants

Flowers contain the reproductive organs of the plant. Their job is to produce gametes – and to bring male and female gametes close together, so that fertilisation can take place. The *male* gamete is in the **pollen grain** produced in the **anther** of a flower. The *female* gamete is in the **ovule** which lies in the **ovary**. Attached to the ovary are the **stigma** and **style**. Before fertilisation can occur, pollen from the anthers has to be *transferred* to the stigma. This process is called **pollination**. The transfer of pollen from the anther of one flower to the stigma of another flower of the same type is called **cross-pollination.** Pollen grains can be carried on the bodies of insects (insect pollination) or blown around in the wind (wind pollination).

Using the diagram, identify the features of the insect-pollinated flower which increase its chances of being pollinated.

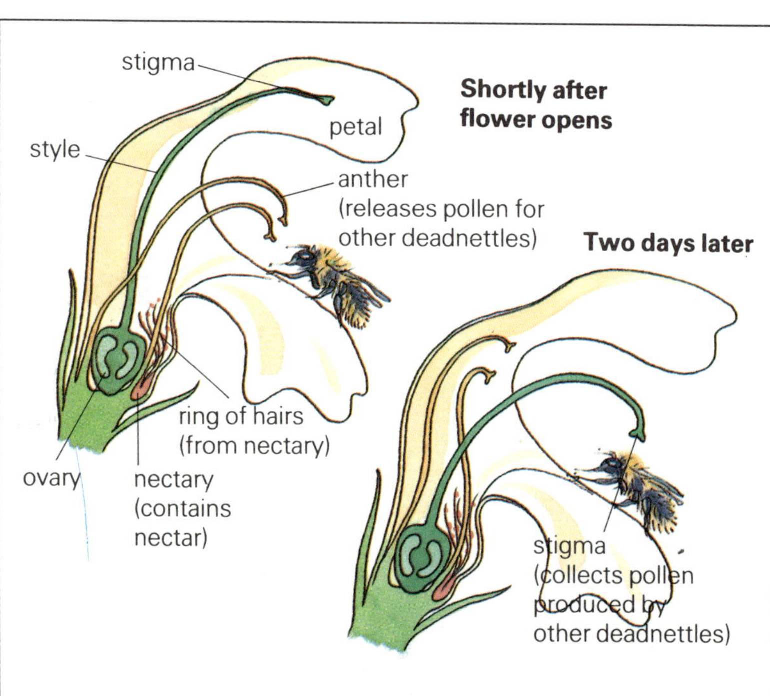

Flowering plants such as this white deadnettle are cross-pollinated by insects. Just how do you think the pollen gets from one flower to another?

A bee feeding on the nectar of one flower gets covered in pollen. When it visits another flower (to feed again!) some of the pollen from the first plant will get onto the stigma (of the second plant), thereby pollinating the second plant.

The wind will transfer the pollen from the anthers of this common alder flower to the stigma of others for cross-pollination.

Nature's way

Different plants are constructed to help pollination occur easily. *Wind*-pollinated flowers often hang down so that they are easily shaken. *Insect*-pollinated plants often have beautiful colours and scents (and supplies of sugary nectar) to attract the insects into the plant's waiting reproductive organ – the flower!

Producing seeds

Pollination is complete when pollen (from a first plant) has landed on a stigma (of a second plant) and the process of fertilisation begins. The cells of the stigma produce a sugary fluid which nourishes the pollen grains – this helps them to grow to form a **pollen tube**. The diagram shows how the pollen tube then grows towards the female gamete in the ovary. The pollen tube contains the male gamete (from the *first* plant) which fuses with the female gamete (in the *second* plant) to form a zygote. The zygote is a single cell which grows to form an **embryo** plant. The fertilised ovule grows to form a **seed**. Each seed has a hard outer coat to protect it and also contains a store of food surrounding the embryo plant.

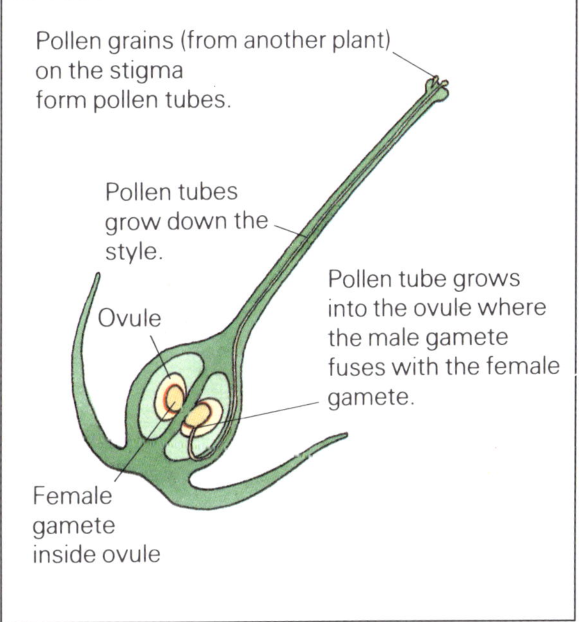

The growth of a pollen tube to the ovule carries the male gamete to the female gamete.

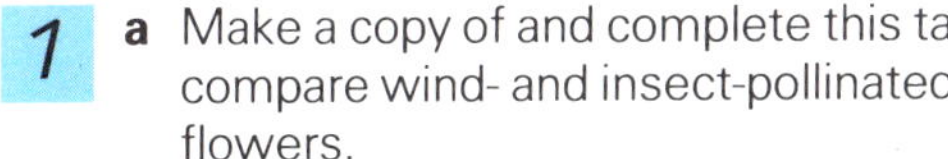

1 **a** Make a copy of and complete this table to compare wind- and insect-pollinated flowers.

	Insect	Wind
Stigma	Sticky to take pollen from insects	?
Petals	?	Small with little or no colour
Nectar and scent	?	?

b Suggest reasons for each of the differences given in the table.

2 **a** State *two* changes that you can observe in the white deadnettle opposite that take place in the two days after opening.

b Explain how these changes help to make sure that these flowers are cross-pollinated.

3 A scientist observed that some types of flowers produce small amounts of pollen grains with spiky surfaces. Other types of flowers produce very large quantities of smooth and light pollen grains.

What do these observations tell you about how these flowers are pollinated? Explain your reasoning.

5.11 Plant seeds and germination

Embryo plants

At **fertilisation** in plants, the male gamete from a pollen grain fuses with (fertilises) a female gamete to form a **zygote** (*see 5.10*). Hormones in the ovules are then released by the plants which stimulate the development of **seeds** from fertilised ovules. Each seed contains an **embryo** plant which grows from the zygote. A store of food is also formed in the seed to provide the embryo plant with the energy and chemicals it will need to survive and grow. Seeds, such as peas and beans, are a popular source of food for us. You'll come across other seeds inside fruits you eat – the pips in apples and oranges, for example. The **fruit** is the part of a plant which surrounds the seed or seeds.

Many seeds survive through bad conditions – freezing winters, drought and so on – by going into a **dormant** stage. Respiration and other chemical processes slow down to a very low level during dormancy – the seed appears to be dead, but will begin to grow in suitable conditions.

You can eat a whole variety of tasty seeds – these will contribute nutrients and vitamins to your balanced diet.

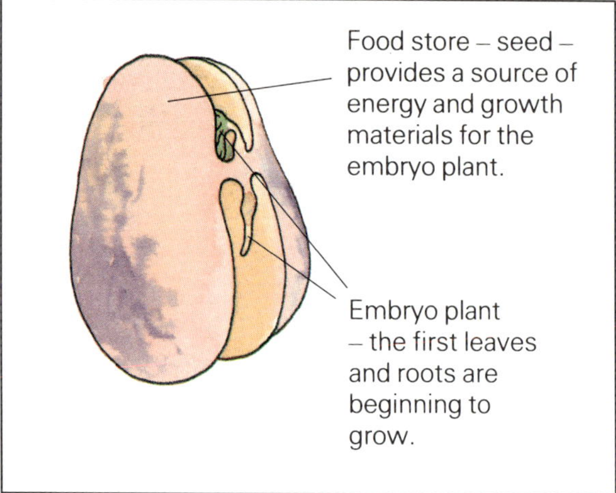

A seed contains an embryo plant and a source of food for it to use to grow.

Scattering seeds

When seeds fall from the parent plant they are scattered over a wide area. This avoids overcrowding and competition for light and water – for the right conditions in which to grow.

It also enables plants to spread into – **colonise** – new habitats. Seeds and fruits containing seeds can be dispersed by wind, animals and by 'explosive' pods. The diagrams below show how the structure of some common seeds is adapted to suit various methods of dispersal.

Study the diagrams carefully. How does the structure of each seed or fruit ensure that it is dispersed over a wide area?

Germination of seeds

Seeds which land in suitable places – where there is water and light – will begin to grow into young plants. This process is called **germination**. A number of changes take place inside the seed as germination begins. *Water* is absorbed by the seed. This makes the seed swell and softens the seed-coat so that it eventually splits. *Enzymes* in the seed become active – and break down the insoluble stored food into soluble foods (such as sugars) that can be transported to the growing embryo. Sugars are used, along with oxygen (from the air or soil), in **respiration** by the embryo to provide energy for growth. The embryo forms young roots that grow out through the split seed-coat and into the soil to keep the plant in place, absorbing water and nutrients. The young shoot grows upwards, develops leaves, and begins to **photosynthesise**. For all these changes to take place, the germinating seed needs a supply of **water** to transport food and enzymes, **oxygen** for respiration, **light** for photosynthesis, and a suitable **temperature** for enzyme activity.

From seed to shoot: (Top left) A dried-out pea seed before germination; below, a germinating pea which has soaked up water for a day. One day later, the seed coat is set to burst (bottom right). Finally the shoot and root emerge – one up, one down.

Plants without seeds

Seeds are formed as a result of sexual reproduction. New plants can also be formed by **asexual reproduction**. Strawberry 'runners' and the 'eyes' on potato tubers are products of asexual methods of forming new plants (*see 5.10*). If you take a cutting from a plant you are making a new plant artificially by using asexual reproduction. When you plant the cut end of a stem in compost or soil, roots *may* develop from the cut stem. Some cuttings will fail to form roots and so die.

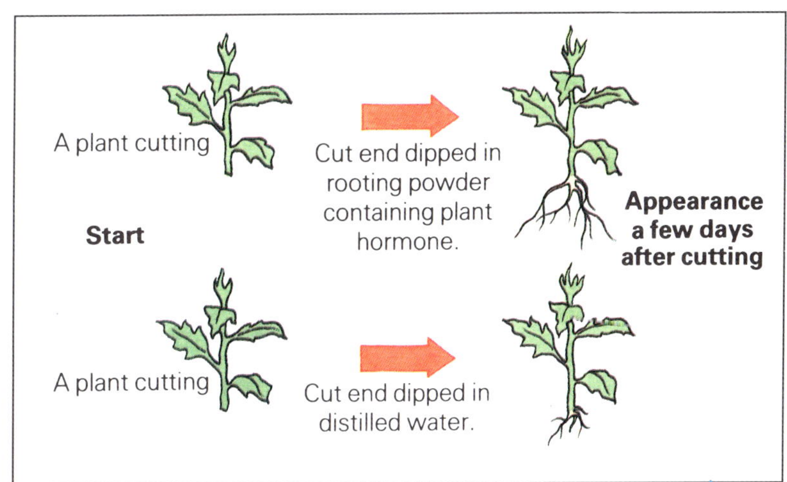

Gardeners and plant breeders use rooting powder containing plant hormones to increase the success rate of making new plants from cuttings.

1 Describe how the seeds of the following plants are dispersed:
Dandelion
Strawberry
Peas

2
- **a** Look at the diagram above. Give one difference between the two sets of cuttings two days after planting.
- **b** How does treatment with hormone powder help the cuttings to grow?

3 Some seeds were collected from the droppings of a bird which had fed on some berries. Another set of seeds was collected from berries that had fallen from the tree.

Both sets of seeds were placed in moist soil and put in a warm place. After four days the number of seeds that had germinated was counted.

	Percentage germination
Seeds from bird droppings	85
Seeds from fallen berries	40

- **a** Suggest two hypotheses to explain how seeds are affected as they pass through the bird's gut.
- **b** Describe a method of testing each hypothesis.

YOU CAN READ MORE ABOUT RESPIRATION AND PHOTOSYNTHESIS ON SPREADS 4.6, 4.7.

5.12 Animal reproduction

Sexual reproduction

During sexual reproduction male gametes fuse with female gametes to form **zygotes**. In both animals and plants, the *male* gametes are very small and can move. In contrast, the *female* gametes are fixed in one place and are larger than the male gametes. The male gametes in a plant move down the pollen tube to reach the ovule (*see 5.10*). The male gametes of an animal are the **sperm cells** or **sperm**; the female gametes are **egg cells** or **ova**. When released into a fluid, sperm can swim to reach and fertilise egg cells. Gametes in animals and plants have to be brought close together before the male gamete can move itself towards the female gamete. In plants, **pollination** brings pollen grains (containing the male gametes) close to the ovule (with its female gamete). In animals, **mating** brings sperm cells (the male gametes) close to egg cells (the female gametes).

Male gametes move down pollen tube to the egg cell.
Pollen grains on the stigma.
Ovule containing female gamete.

In plants the male gamete moves down the pollen tube to the female gamete.

Animals breeding in water

Many animals live and breed in water. The eggs of these animals, such as fish, toads and frogs, are fertilised *outside* the body of the parent-animal. First the female sheds her eggs into the water. Then the male immediately releases sperm over them – the sperm swim to the eggs and fertilise them in the water. This is **external fertilisation**. The eggs are usually left unprotected and many eggs and young get eaten by predators. Only a small number of species of animals that live in water protect their eggs while they are developing.

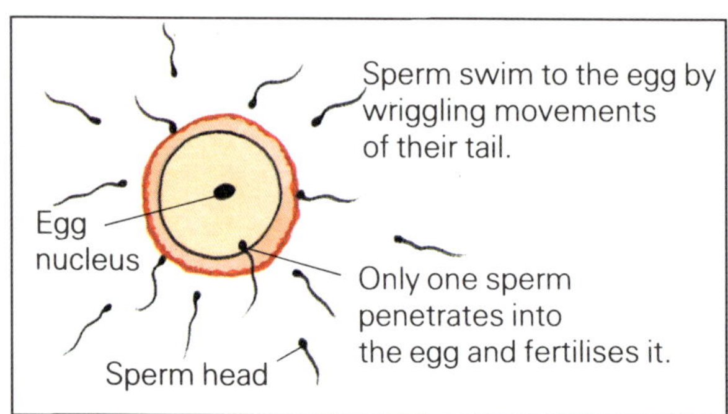

In animals the male gamete swims to reach the female gamete.

As they are laid, the eggs of a frog are surrounded by a jelly-like substance – albumen – which is much the same stuff as surrounds the yolk of a hen's eggs (the 'white' of the egg). This jelly provides some protection for the eggs and causes them to stick together to form ***frog spawn****.*

Animals breeding on land

External fertilisation is not possible on land because eggs and sperm would soon dry up. The eggs of animals which live on land are fertilised *inside* the body of the female. This is **internal fertilisation**. Reptiles, birds and mammals place sperm inside the body of the female during mating. The sperm then swim through the moist lining of the female organs to the eggs and fertilise them. In mammals, the fertilised eggs develop inside the body of the female. In contrast the eggs of reptiles and birds are laid outside the body – the hard shell formed around these types of fertilised eggs prevents them from drying up after they are laid. They continue to develop inside the shell until they are ready to hatch into young.

Gases can diffuse through the egg shell.

Embryo bird in a fluid-filled sac.

Carbon dioxide

Oxygen

Yolk sac containing food as fat and protein.

This special sac, called the **allantois**, contains blood vessels that carry oxygen from the air space to the embryo. Carbon dioxide travels in the opposite direction.

The fertilised eggs of birds develop in a hard shell outside the female's body.

Parental care

The eggs of many reptiles, such as turtles, are laid and then also left to develop on their own inside their shells. Birds lay their eggs in a nest and **incubate** them by sitting on them to keep the temperature warm. Most newly-born birds and mammals are protected, fed and kept warm by the parents. The chicks of birds which nest on the ground, such as partridges, are covered with downy feathers at birth and can run around soon after hatching. Chicks of tree-nesting birds, such as blackbirds, hatch with few feathers, closed eyes and limited powers of movement – it takes a few weeks before they can begin to look after themselves.

A blackbird feeding her young. The chicks open their mouths and the bird pushes food down their throats. In a few weeks the young birds are able to fly short distances and find their own food. Soon they can fly away for good.

Eggs for survival

Animals whose eggs have only a small chance of developing into adults need to produce large numbers of eggs to ensure that the species survives. Animals which produce fewer eggs usually provide some parental care of the developing eggs. The table opposite shows the relationship between the number of eggs and the methods of reproduction and development.

Animal	No. of eggs (average)	Development of eggs	Length of parental care (average)
Cod	7 million	in water	none
Stickleback	300	in water	2 weeks
Turtle	15–25	shelled eggs	none
Partridge	8–16	shelled eggs	3 weeks
Blackbird	3–6	shelled eggs	3 weeks
Cat	4	egg develops inside mother	5 weeks

1 Suggest reasons for the following:
- **a** the trout produces more eggs than the turtle;
- **b** the trout produces more eggs than the stickleback;
- **c** the turtle produces more eggs than the blackbird.

2 Predict which eggs in the table will have **a)** the largest store of food, and **b)** the smallest store of food. Explain your answers.

3 Suggest a hypothesis to explain why blackbirds lay fewer eggs than partridges.

4 Female birds lay eggs containing a developing embryo and food surrounded by a hard shell.
- **a** Name two substances which can pass through the shell. Why must they do so?
- **b** Why is the fat in yolk a good food to store in a closed egg?
- **c** Why do the eggs of frogs and trout not need a hard shell?

Human reproduction

Producing gametes

Sexual reproduction in humans also involves the production of gametes, like any other animal. **Sperm** are produced by the man in tiny tubes inside his **testes**. **Eggs** (or **ova**) are produced by the woman in her **ovaries**. The diagrams show the tissues involved in the production and release of gametes in humans.

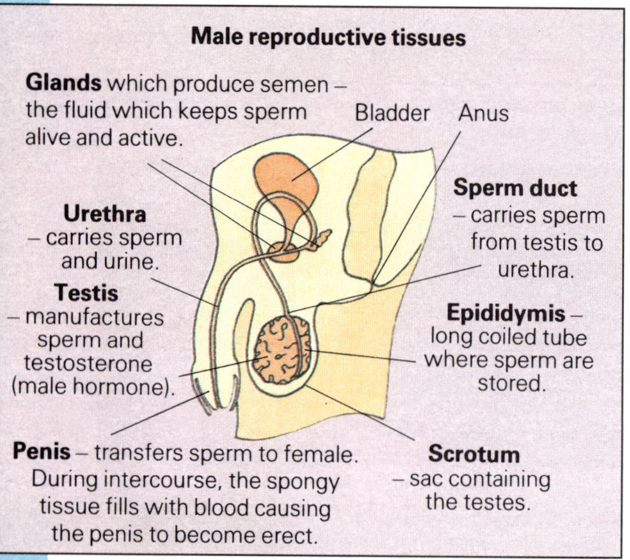

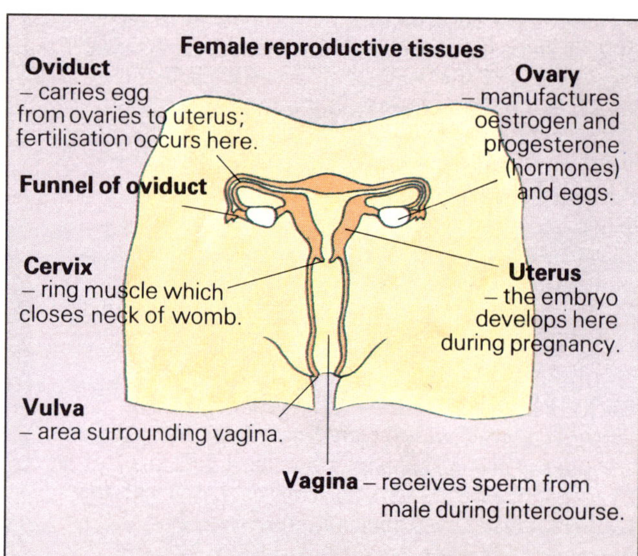

Action of hormones

The testes and ovaries of humans do not produce gametes until **puberty** is reached – usually around the age of 11–14 years. Your sex organs mature at this age because the **pituitary gland**, a small gland near your brain, releases the hormones **FSH** and **LH** into your bloodstream. These hormones are released continuously after puberty, and act on the testes and ovaries.

In *boys*, they stimulate the testes to produce sperm and to release the male sex hormone **testosterone**. This hormone controls the development of male characteristics such as growth of the penis, testes and body hair. In *girls*, the release of FSH and LH controls the production of eggs and the release of the female sex hormones, **oestrogen** and **progesterone**, by the ovaries.

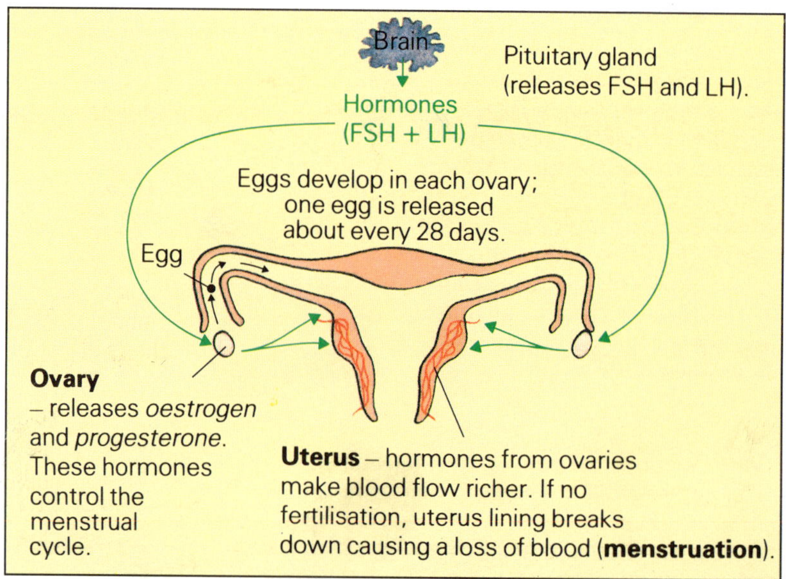

The pituitary hormones and the female sex hormones begin to control changes in a young woman's ovaries and in her uterus in her early teens. This is marked by the onset of menstruation (monthly period).

The start of life

Usually just one mature egg is released from one or other ovary during **ovulation** – once every 28 days or so. It then passes along the oviduct towards the uterus, a journey which takes about 7 days. If the egg meets a sperm within 1 to 3 days after being released, it can be **fertilised**. If it is not fertilised, it will break up as it passes along the oviduct. Sperm will only be present in the oviduct if sexual intercourse has recently taken place. **Semen** (a mixture of sperm and nutritive fluid) is **ejaculated** from the penis into the vagina at the climax of intercourse. Once inside the vagina, the sperm swim through the cervix and along the uterus towards the oviduct. Millions of sperm are released into the vagina at ejaculation, but only a few of the healthiest ones will reach the oviduct. The fusion of a sperm and an egg is called **fertilisation** (or **conception**). The cell that is formed, the **zygote**, continues to pass along the oviduct towards the uterus. As it passes along, the single-celled zygote divides several times, so that by the time it reaches the uterus, it is like a ball of cells. This ball of cells, called an **embryo**, sinks into the lining of the woman's uterus – a process called **implantation** – and the woman is now pregnant.

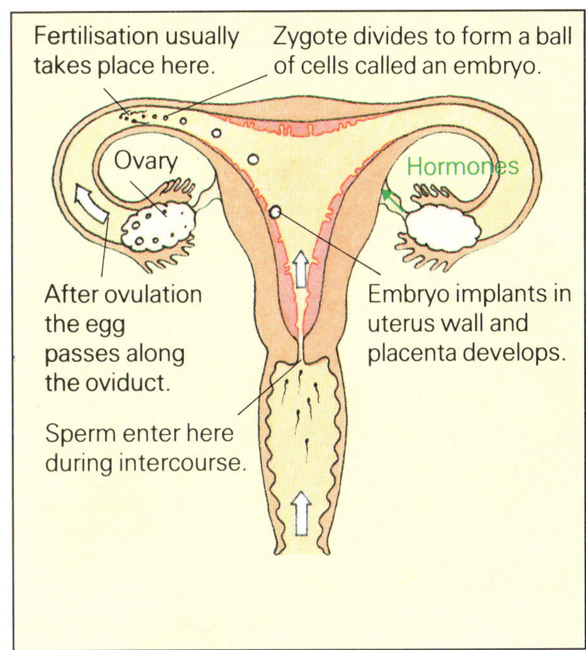

Fertilisation or conception takes place when a sperm, released during intercourse, fuses with an egg inside the oviduct of the woman.

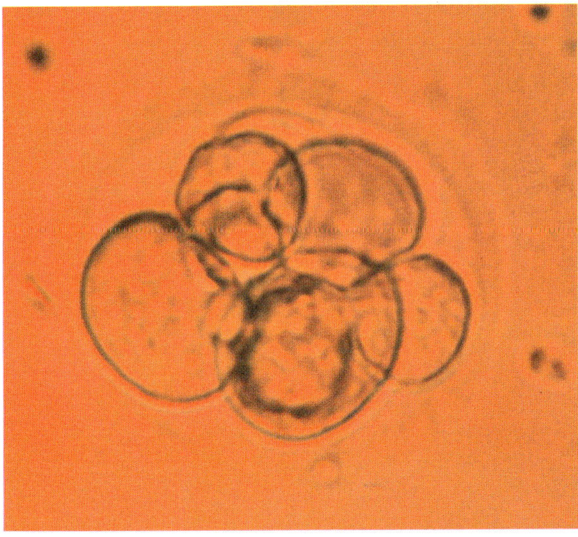

There are eight cells in this human embryo. Can you see them all? Starting from a single fertilised zygote, how many divisions have occurred to reach this stage?

Technology assisting nature

Some women have blocked oviducts. In the past women with this problem could not have children. A technique has been developed which overcomes this. The technique (often called making 'test-tube' babies) involves fertilising a human egg *outside* the body. This is known as **in vitro fertilisation**. Injections of FSH and LH are given to the woman so that she produces a mature egg. A doctor makes an incision in the abdomen wall and inserts a fine tube through it to suck the eggs from her ovary. (The hormone treatment often causes many eggs to be released at the same time.)

The eggs are placed into a solution containing a mixture of food, salts, oxygen and water. Semen (from the father) is then mixed with the eggs to fertilise them. The fertilised eggs are kept in the solution to develop into embryos for a few days. Then an embryo is implanted by the doctor into the mother's uterus.

1 Explain how changes take place in the development of boys and girls when FSH and LH are released from the pituitary gland.

2 Why do women usually release only one egg a month when many fish release millions?

3 Use the diagrams to list, in the correct order, **a** the male tissues that sperm pass along after being made in the testes, and **b** the female tissues that sperm pass along after being released in the vagina.

4
- **a** Explain why a blocked oviduct prevents fertilisation.
- **b** How are eggs and sperm kept alive outside the body during 'in vitro' fertilisation?
- **c** Explain why doctors inject FSH and LH before attempting to remove mature eggs.

5.14 Development in the womb

Warm, well-fed and protected

Your life, like every human life, started from a zygote the size of a full stop! It takes 38 weeks for this single cell to develop into the millions of cells that make up a newborn baby. This period of important rapid growth and development, called the **gestation period**, takes place inside the mother's womb or **uterus**. It is a characteristic of all mammals. By developing inside the mother's body, the young mammal is kept warm, is fed by the mother, and is protected from damage and from predators.

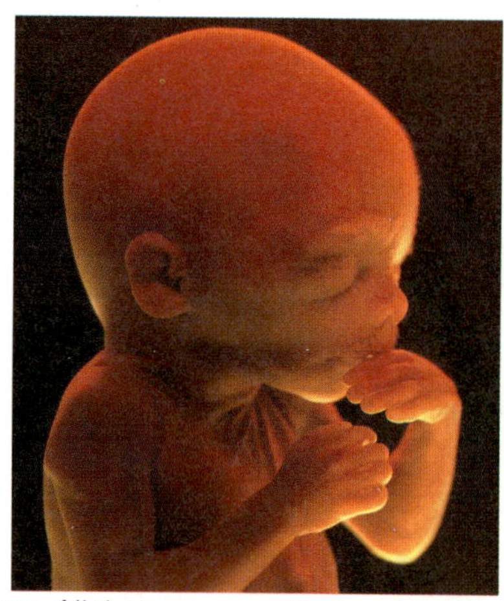

A 20-week-old foetus. All the organs and limbs of the developing baby are well formed at this stage.

Early development

The human zygote initially divides several times as it passes along the oviduct, to form a ball of cells called an **embryo** which sinks into the soft lining of the uterus. This embryo then receives food and oxygen from the blood flowing through the uterus lining of the woman. After 3 weeks, a **placenta** develops (on the lining of the uterus) from some of the cells of the embryo. The **umbilical cord** connects the developing embryo to the placenta and acts as a lifeline, bringing food and oxygen to the foetus from the mother's placenta and taking away excretory substances. After only 4 weeks in the uterus, the embryo is 46 mm long and has a beating heart! You can recognise certain human features after 8 weeks – from around this stage the embryo is known as a **foetus**. Women usually begin to feel the foetus kicking after it is about 16 weeks old. From 27/28 weeks onwards the foetus has a good chance of surviving an early – **premature** – birth, provided it is given special hospital care.

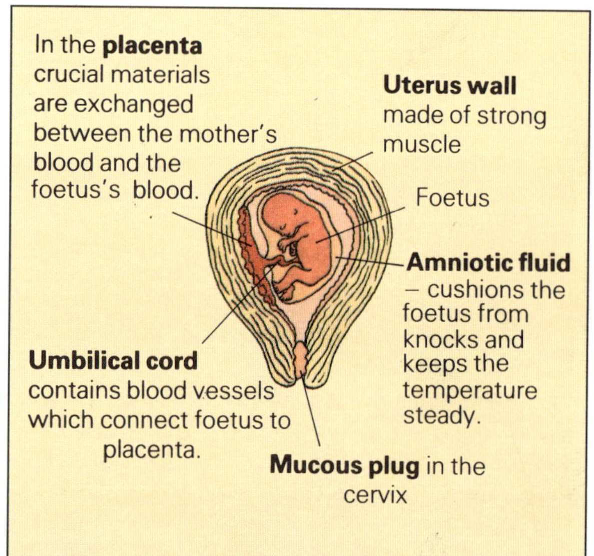

The foetus develops while being fed and protected inside the mother's womb.

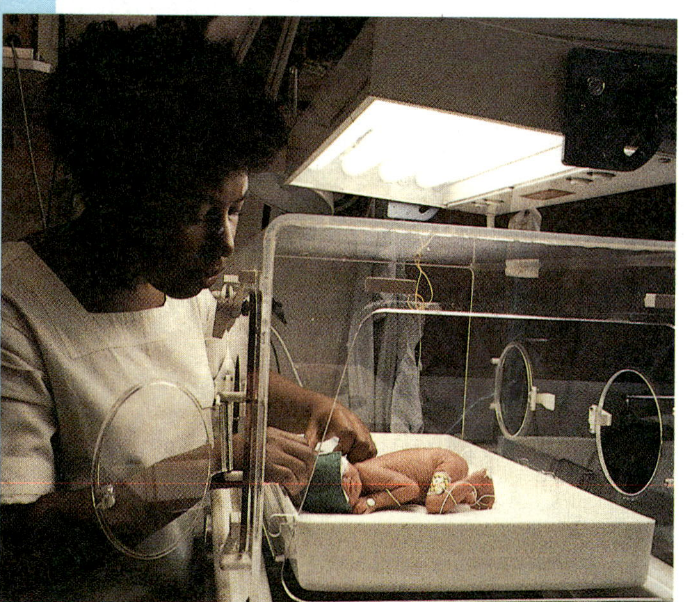

In or out – which is the best? A very premature baby can survive in an incubator which supplies the main provisions of the mother's womb – warmth, food and oxygen.

The placenta

The placenta is essential for the growth of a healthy baby. The functions of the placenta are:

- To absorb **oxygen** and **food** substances such as glucose and amino acids from the mother's blood.
- To release the hormones **oestrogen** and **progesterone** which are needed to prevent the shedding of the uterine lining.
- To excrete waste substances such as **carbon dioxide** and **urea** into the mother's blood.

The placenta is an extremely efficient organ for exchanging substances. Like other organs for exchange, such as the lungs and the small intestine, it has a *large surface area*, it is *thin*, and it has a very *good blood supply*.

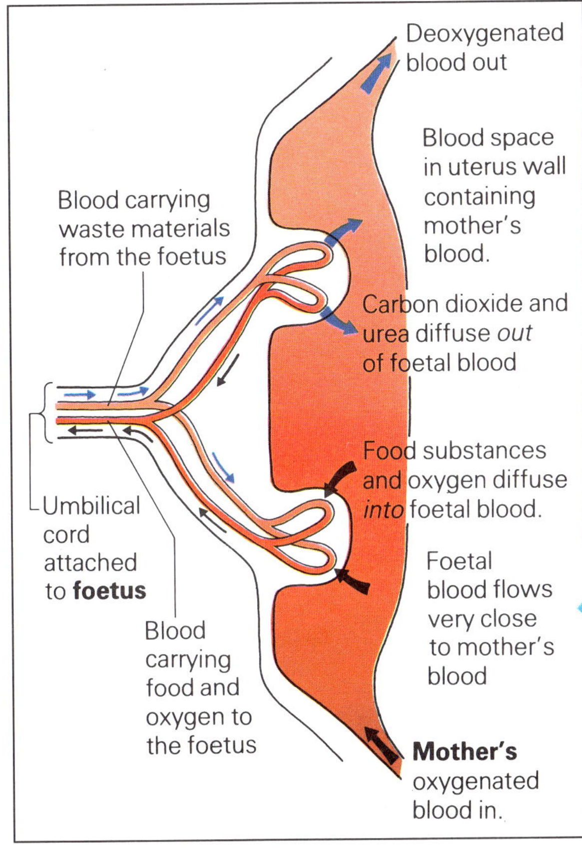

Harmful substances

Oxygen and food are not the only substances that can pass across the mother's placenta to the foetus. Women who *smoke* have **carbon monoxide** and **nicotine** in their blood. If a woman smokes during pregnancy these substances will pass to the foetus. Carbon monoxide restricts the oxygen supply to the foetus. Nicotine puts stress on the foetal heart by making it beat more quickly. **Alcohol** can also damage the foetus. Women who *drink alcohol* during pregnancy run the risk of having smaller and underdeveloped babies. Many other kinds of **drugs** can be harmful to the foetus if they are taken during pregnancy. In the 1960s, many pregnant women took a drug called thalidomide to help them sleep better and to relieve tension during their pregnancies. The drug caused many babies to be born with severely deformed limbs.

The placenta is an essential organ for exchanging materials so that the foetus continues to survive all through the gestation period.

This table shows one effect that smoking during pregnancy may have on newborn babies.

		Number of babies born to non-smoking mothers	Number of babies born to smoking mothers
Mass at birth (Kg)	Less than 2.4	4	3
	2.4 to 3.1	42	24
	3.2 to 3.5	70	44
	3.6 to 3.9	54	23
	Greater than 3.9	30	6
	Total in sample	200	100

Harmful organsims

The placenta also protects the developing foetus from disease. A bacterium or virus that causes a disease in a mother can only reach the foetus by passing across the placenta. The **rubella virus** that causes German measles is one that can. This virus can seriously damage a foetus which is infected in the first 3 months of its development. This is why *all* young women should be vaccinated against rubella *before* they are able to become pregnant. The **AIDS virus** can also be passed on by a woman to her baby. The life expectancy of a baby born with AIDS is only a few months.

1 Use the table of birth mass above to answer the following questions.

- **a** What percentage of babies had a birth mass greater than 3.5 kg in
  - **i** non-smoking mothers?
  - **ii** smoking mothers?
- **b** Use the data to give one effect of smoking on birth mass.
- **c** Suggest a possible reason for this effect.

2

- **a** Name three substances that will be more concentrated in the foetal blood flowing *into* the placenta than blood flowing *out*.
- **b** Explain how the structure of the placenta is suited to its job of exchanging substances between the foetus and mother.

3 Explain why babies born to heroin and crack addicts can suffer withdrawal symptoms after birth.

5.15 The newborn baby

A new life

Birth usually takes place in the 38th week of pregnancy. A few weeks before birth, the foetus usually comes to lie in the **birth position** – with its head nearest the woman's cervix. The woman's body begins to release certain hormones which start the birth process by bringing about regular **contractions** of the muscles in her uterus wall. This is when she goes into 'labour'.

Being born is quite an amazing experience! The first nine months of your life as a foetus are spent in the very stable, dark and fluid environment of your mother's uterus. Suddenly at birth, you are exposed to very different conditions! When inside the mother, feeding, gaseous exchange and excretion are carried out for the foetus by the placenta. After being born a baby has to start maintaining its own life – and all those complex functions!

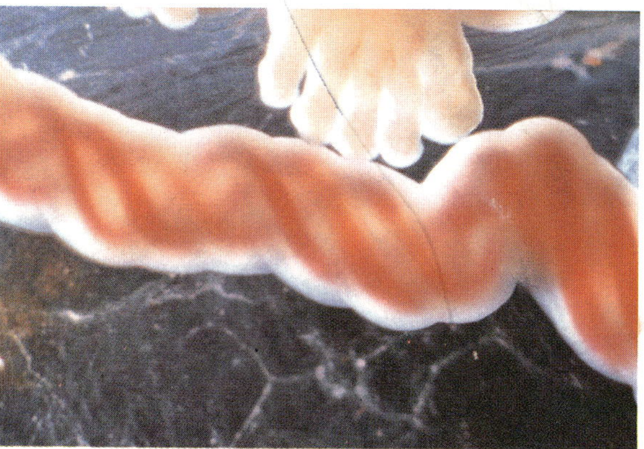

An umbilical cord – it connects the baby to the mother's placenta in the womb. After the birth, the baby begin to breathe, feed and excrete on its own. So the cord is cut – leaving us all with a belly button!

Maintaining early life

The first breath a baby takes is a **reflex action** (*see 5.8*) stimulated by the sudden fall in temperature outside the mother's body. The air entering the baby's lungs causes them to inflate for the first time and gaseous exchange begins to take place. Unlike many other animals, humans are quite helpless when they are first born. Their parents have to do a lot for them. Like all mammals, humans **suckle** (provide milk for) their young. During the first 3 to 4 months milk (breast or bottle) provides all a baby's energy needs and nutrients, except for iron. Babies obtain the iron they need to make haemoglobin from their mother during pregnancy and store it. Many mothers choose to breast-feed their babies because human milk is perfect for a baby's dietary needs. It is also produced at the right temperature, at low cost and is even hygienically packed! Breast milk also contains **antibodies** from the mother – special substances which protect the body from disease.

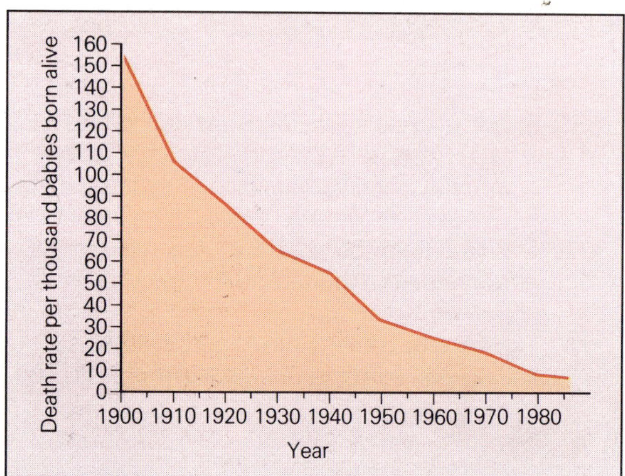

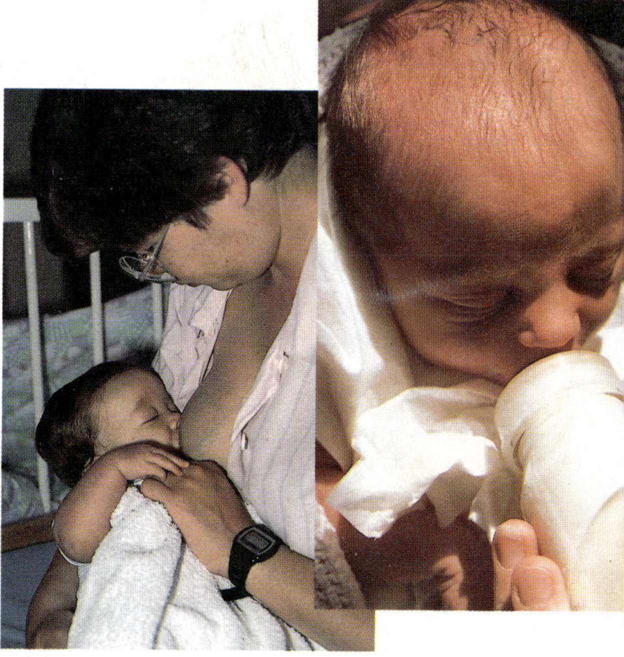

Is breast best? If you had a baby what would you prefer to do – breast feed it or bottle feed it? Think of all the pros and cons for both.

Infant mortality

The graph opposite shows how many babies (out of every thousand born) died in their first year since 1900. As you can see, there has been a very big fall in the **infant mortality rate**, but even so about 10 babies in every thousand still die before their first birthday.

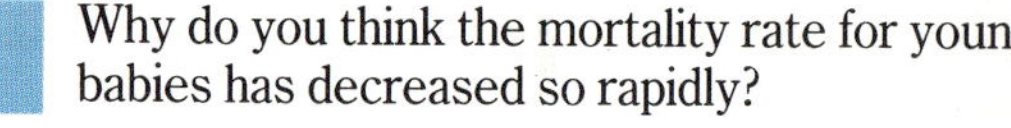

Why do you think the mortality rate for young babies has decreased so rapidly?

Fighting childhood diseases

Many babies used to die from infectious diseases caused by bacteria or viruses. Now deaths from serious diseases such as whooping cough, polio and diphtheria are much less common in this country – because babies are **immunised** against them. Once children are immune to a particular disease, they will not catch it.

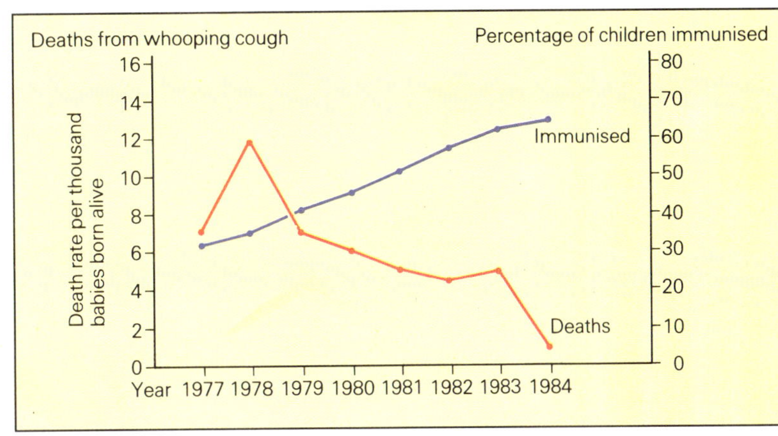

The graph shows the effects of immunising children against whooping cough in recent years. Do you think the programme has been effective?

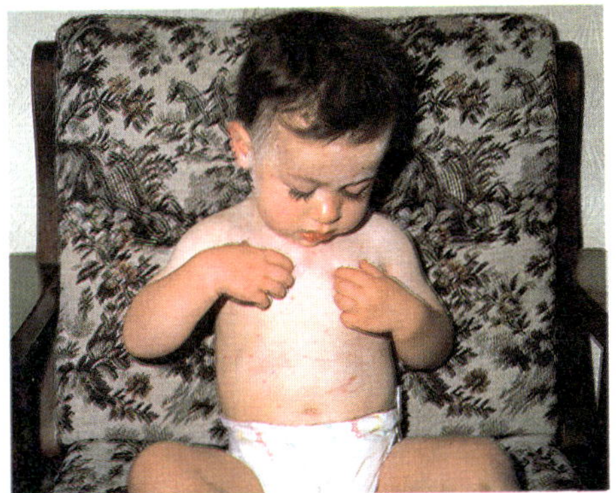

This child has chicken pox. It is a fairly harmless disease but very infectious. Once you have had it you will be immune in the future.

Age	Immunisation given
3–6 months	1 Diptheria, whooping cough, tetanus, polio
4–6 weeks later	2 Diphtheria, whooping cough, tetanus, polio
4–6 weeks later	3 Diphtheria, whooping cough, tetanus, polio
1–2 years	Measles
4–5 years	Diphtheria, tetanus, polio
10–13 years	BCG vaccination against TB if skin test negative
11–14 years	Rubella (German measles) – girls only
15 years	Tetanus and polio

Keeping your child up to date with vaccinations is an important part of your responsibility as a parent. Doctors keep records and issue reminders to help you keep a check.

Natural immunity to disease

There are many diseases which you will only catch once. This is because you develop a **natural immunity** to the disease. For example, when the virus that causes chicken pox enters your body, it grows and gives the symptoms of chicken pox. You recover from the disease because your white blood cells produce antibodies that destroy the virus. The next time the virus enters your body, you will already have the right antibodies present in your blood. A *different* type of antibody is needed to fight off *each type* of virus or bacterium.

Providing immunity

Babies and young children can be protected from many of the more serious diseases by 'persuading' their bodies to make the necessary antibodies. When you are immunised against a disease, a *harmless* form of the virus is introduced into your body deliberately. This makes your body produce antibodies that also make you immune to the *harmful* form of the virus. To protect infants and children from disease, all infants in the UK begin an **immunisation programme** when they are about three months old – this should continue until they are about 15 yrs.

1 In the early 1970s some parents became concerned about the safety of the whooping cough vaccine – they considered the side effects of the vaccine were quite risky. Some decided not to have their babies immunised. What effect did this have?

2 The World Health Organisation (WHO) try to persuade mothers in developing countries to feed their babies on breast milk rather than powdered milk. What are the advantages of breast milk for these mothers and babies?

3 Suggest reasons why infant mortality has declined so rapidly since 1900.

Index *(refers to spread numbers)*

For additional information, see the following modules:

3 Humans as Organisms
4 Environments
10 Inheritance & Inheritance

Photo acknowledgements

These refer to spread number and, where appropriate, the photo order:

Geo Science Features *5.1/1, 5.2/2, 5.3, 5.7/2, 5.10/1, 5.10/3*; Sally & Richard Greenhill *5.2/1*; NHPA (J. Shaw) *5.1/2, 5.10/2,* (S. Dalton) *5.1/4, 5.7/1, 5.9, 5.12/2,* (L. Campbell) *5.1/5,* (A. Bannister) *5.2/4,* (E. James) *5.12/1;* Science Photo Library (Dr J. Burgess) *5.1/3, 5.4, (Petit Format) 5.1/6, 5.13, 5.15/1,* (M. Dohrn) *5.2/3,* (M. Kage) *5.5/1.* (H. Morgan) *5.5/2,* (CNRI) *5.8,* (J. Hesteltine) *5.11/1,* (A. Hart-Davis) *5.11/2,* (J. Stevenson) *5.14/1, 5.15/3,* (J. Howard) *5.15/2,* (A. Bartel) *5.15/4;* J. Widel *5.14/2.*

Picture Researcher: Jennifer Johnson

6 MAKING THE MOST OF MACHINES

People have developed machines over thousands of years from simple stone tools to complex spacecraft exploring distant planets. Machines allow us to alter the force we can apply, the speed of our movements and to transfer energy. This module looks at forces, movement and energy, and how we can design machines that alter these to suit our purposes.

Relevant National Curriculum Attainment Target: 10, (11), 13

6.1 Machines – moving with the times!

An easy life?

A **machine** is anything that makes *work* easier to do. Even simple tools like a screwdriver or scissors are hand-held machines. You probably use a great many tools and machines every day to make life easier. But you are not the first person to do so! Our use of tools and machines has a long history

Which of these tools do you use most often? What do they help you to do?

Useful tools

About two million years ago, our ancestors began to use the sharp edges of broken pieces of **flint** as their first tools. These sharp flints were used to cut through the tough hides of the animals that our ancestors had caught for food.

At the sharp end

Thousands of years later, people began to make broken flints into *more useful* shapes by hitting them with other rocks. The first such tools were scrapers and hand axes. Later on, the flints were made into spear heads and arrow heads.

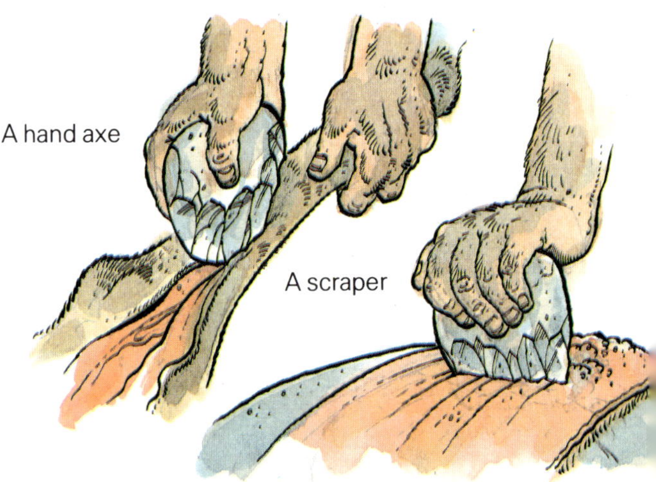
A hand axe
A scraper

Early machines

Eventually our ancestors began to devise simple machines to make their own muscle-power *more effective*. A **ramp** is a simple machine – it is easier to pull a load up a slope than to lift it straight up. Throughout history, people have devised new ways of making the most of their own strength – levers, wheels, pulleys, bearings . . . these all help in their own way.

Rolling parts help to move a load.
A ramp can be used to raise a heavy lead.
A lever can be used to lift a load.

The age of 'the elements'

Over the last few thousand years, other machines were developed that used **natural forces** (like wind and water) to provide large amounts of **energy** to operate the machines. There are two problems with using a natural force like the wind. Sometimes the wind doesn't blow! And strong winds are often only found in certain places – like the top of a hill! So, you can't always use natural force *when* you want it, nor *where* you want to.

Windmills were used to grind tonnes of cereal crops into flour – but couldn't work without a wind!

The steam age

These problems can be overcome by using the **energy** locked up in **fuels** as the source of power. The amount of energy needed for the machine can then be *controlled* – and when the machine moves, it can take its source of power along too!

The **steam-engine** was the first machine successfully to use a fuel (coal or wood) as a power source. Its invention – just 150 years ago – led to the **Industrial Revolution**, causing great changes in the way people worked and lived.

At first steam engines were stationary machines just used to provide a reliable source of power. In 1804 an engineer called Trevithick tostod out tho first mobilo stoam engine. It lead to other mechanised transport such as tractors and trains (like "Stephenson's Rocket" shown here).

The space age

Over millions of years, our ancestors changed slightly from one generation to the next. Those with larger brains were more intelligent and could invent more tools to help them survive. Nowadays, not only do we have machines that help us survive (even in space!), we also have machines like Hoovers, computers and tape recorders which help to make the things we do more convenient and enjoyable.

But our use of machines can pose problems too. The use of **robots** in factories can pose problems over job losses; many machines are powered by **electricity** – yet the generating of that electricity can often cause **pollution.** Each one of us has a *responsibility* to use machines in a sensible way. This module looks at how we can make the most of our machines!

1 Think of any machines that rely on some sort of fire or wheel. Use your ideas to explain which you think was the most important discovery in human development – fire or the wheel.

2 Which machines (that you regularly use) could you do without? How would this change your life?

3 What tasks would you like to invent a machine to do? Make up your own design for how such a machine would work.

Forces in action

Pushes and pulls

Most machines and tools work by applying forces in a helpful way. A **force** is a push or a pull of some kind. If you push or pull a stationary object (which is free to move), it will begin to move (after enough effort!). For example, a stationary shopping trolley won't move until you start to push or pull it.

Newton's laws of motion

About 300 years ago, a scientist called Sir Isaac Newton devised several laws about forces and motion. Newton's first two laws say that:

- *the motion of an object won't change unless a force changes it* (– still objects stay still and moving objects keep moving . . . unless a force acts on them).
- *when a change takes place, it does so in the direction of the overall force* and *the greater the force, the faster the change in motion.*

Newton's laws have proved pretty reliable – even after three centuries! In honour of his work, forces are measured in units called **newtons** (symbol: **N**).

A force applied to a stationary object might make it move . . . *a force applied in the* opposite *direction can make it* slow down.

Forces do not always produce movement. Forces can also act to stop *movement, or to* keep *an object stationary. Only* ***unbalanced forces*** *produce movement.*

Forces everywhere

Usually more than one force is acting on a body at any time. Any **mass** attracts another mass with a force called **gravity**. The Earth attracts everything on it with a force pulling towards the centre of the Earth. The size of this gravitational pull is about 10N (9.8N to be more precise) on every 1kg mass. The gravitational pull on an object is called its **weight**. So if you have a mass of 35 kg, your weight will be about 350 N!

Force due to gravity [N] = mass [kg] × **g**.

(where **g** is the **acceleration due to gravity** (*see 6.12*).

Balanced forces produce no movement.

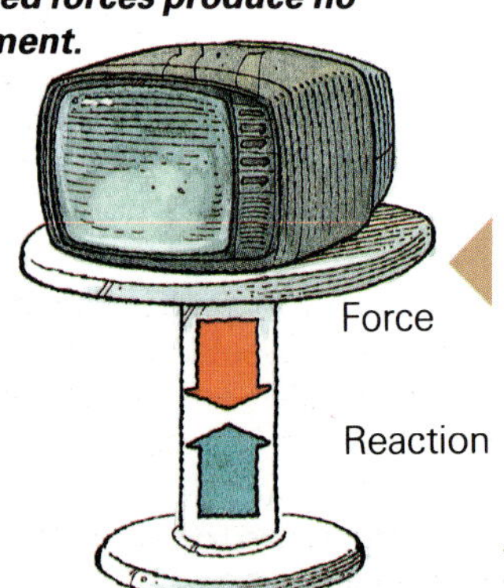

Think about a TV on a stand; its weight acts straight down. Weight is a force – and forces make things move – so why doesn't the TV move?

There must be another force acting on the TV that exactly balances the downward force of its weight. This force is called the **reaction** force – it acts in the *opposite* direction to the weight. The reaction force is supplied by the stand which holds up the TV. This is an example of how *equal forces that act along the same line but in opposite directions will cancel each other out.*

YOU CAN READ MORE ABOUT MASS AND WEIGHT ON SPREAD 2.6

Out of line

By stepping onto the centre of a small table, your weight will be balanced by an equal but opposite reaction force from the table. But when you move to the edge of the table, your weight moves *out of line* with the reaction force – and so the table *moves*. When you land, the bump you feel is the reaction force of the ground acting on you!

Avoid things that will not provide a reaction force in line with your weight.

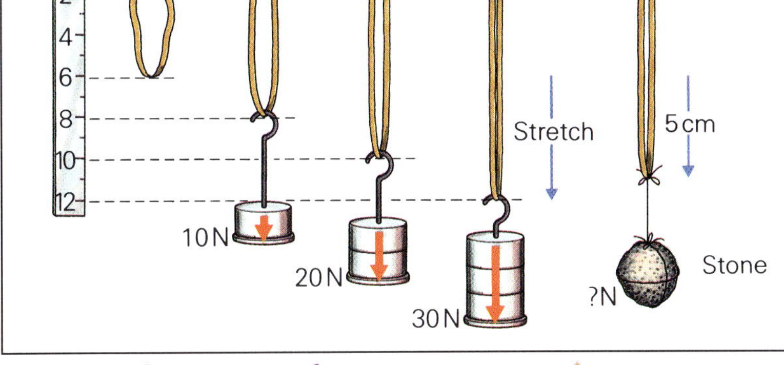

Using stretch to measure forces

Raschid and Beatrice made a simple forcemeter by fixing a single rubber band onto a stiff piece of card. When the band was used to lift or pull an object, the band stretched. To *calibrate* the scale in Newtons, they added known weights to the end of the band, and they marked the stretch caused by different weights.

When a stone was hung at one end, the band stretched 5 cm. What is the force of gravity on the stone (its *weight*) and what is the mass of the stone?
They repeated their investigation using *two* bands instead of one. First they tried with the bands *in parallel*, and then with the bands *in line*. Which arrangement will show the greatest stretch for a 10 N weight – will it be one band, two bands in parallel or two bands in line? Which will show the least stretch?

Out of shape

If forces are applied to flexible objects (such as rubber bands and springs), they can cause the objects to *change shape*. If the object has **elastic** properties, it goes back to its original shape once the forces are removed. This change of shape can be used to measure the forces, since *the larger the distortion, the larger the forces causing it.*

bands in parallel
10N
bands in line
10N

1 Write down five simple machines or tools that work by:
a only pushes
b only pulls
c both pushes and pulls

2 A push of 20 N is needed to get a supermarket trolley moving on the level. If it is pulled instead of being pushed, how big a pull would be needed? It would need a larger push if the trolley is being moved up a slope. Why?

3 Four people push on the four sides of a table towards the middle with forces A (30 N), B (20 N), C (10 N) and D (20 N), in order. In which direction does the table move? If B and D stop pushing will it make any difference to the movement?

4 Sketch the graphs Raschid and Beatrice may have obtained when they stretched the two rubber bands **a** in parallel, **b** in line. Draw the *single* band graph for comparison.

5 Explain why a pencil rubber is distorted if you hold one end in each hand and twist.

YOU CAN READ MORE ABOUT ELASTICITY ON SPREAD 2.2

Balancing forces

reaction (R) balances weight

reaction increases to balance weight

*If the **reaction** can't balance the **weight**, movement results!*

Reaction forces balance . . .

If you sit on a box, your weight acts down towards the centre of the Earth. Because there is no movement, this force must be *balanced* by another equal and opposite force. This **reaction force** is provided by the box, pushing up on you. If a friend sits on the box too, then the total weight acting down on the box will be greater. If there is still no movement, the reaction force must have *increased* to balance your friend's weight as well.

Sir Isaac Newton realised that a force (or action) always gives rise to a reaction force. His *third law of motion* says that

- *to every action, there is an equal and opposite reaction.*

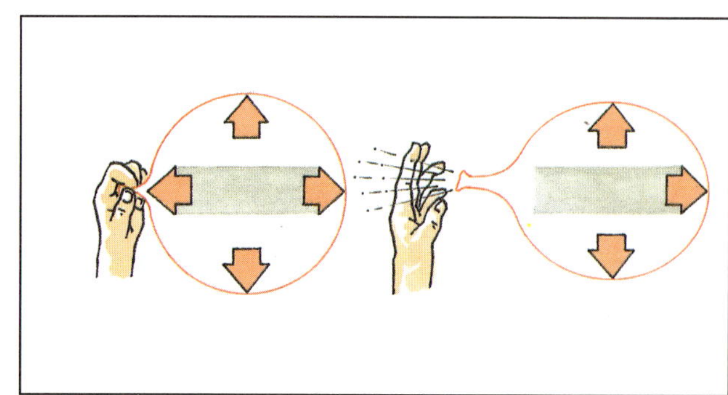

*After release, air escapes – leaving an **unbalanced force** acting on the front of the balloon, pushing it forward.*

. . . if they can

The reaction force provided by the box acts to balance the weight, no matter how many people sit on the box – until the box is no longer strong enough to provide a sufficient reaction force. At that point, the box will break. All the weight is now an unbalanced force, causing you all to move until you reach the ground – which *can* supply a sufficient equal and opposite reaction force to the total weight.

Using equilibrium

When equal and opposite forces act on a body and cancel each other out, they are said to be in **equilibrium**. Structures such as bridges are designed to *maintain* equilibrium, even under heavy loads – to prevent them from collapsing!

Moving objects can be in equilibrium too. A cyclist free-wheeling downhill will reach a constant speed. At this point, the forces on the cyclist are in equilibrium. **Gravity** pulls the cyclist downhill, but is balanced by **friction** and **wind resistance** (which try to slow the bike down).

*Balanced forces can produce a **moving equilibrium** – to change this motion needs an extra force (such as pedalling or braking).*

Keeping your balance

Gravity pulls down on each part of your body, but the total weight of the body always appears to act from a single point – called the **centre of mass**. The centre of mass of your body is a point just below the rib-cage. When you stand upright, your body is in equilibrium because your weight and the reaction force from the ground are exactly equal and opposite. In judo, the idea is to move your opponent's centre of mass so that their weight is no longer over their feet. The weight and the reaction are no longer directly in line, and the pulled person will have to move their foot forward to *restore* equilibrium. If you stop them moving their foot, they cannot restore their balance; they will fall over under their own weight – not because of your strength!

A pull disturbs your opponents balance; stopping her foot from moving means she can't restore her balance – and so falls over.

Stability

If, even after a slight push, the total weight of an object acting from the centre of mass still acts along a line that passes *through* its base, then the object is said to be **stable**. If the weight acts *outside* the base after a slight push, the object is said to be **unstable**. A racing car has a very low body, set between very wide wheels. This combination of a *low* centre of mass and a *wide* base makes the car very stable. A bicycle has a very high centre of mass and a very thin base. Now you know why it is so easy for a bike to fall over!

Floating forces in balance

When an object floats, it is in equilibrium. The reaction force (pushing up to balance the weight) is called the **upthrust** from the liquid. This upthrust is caused by the object sinking slightly below the surface of the liquid. This *displaces* a volume of liquid equal to that volume of the object which has sunk below the surface.

The upthrust actually depends on the **weight** of liquid displaced by the floating object. Look at the diagram; as the weight increases, the boat sinks lower in the water. It displaces more water and this increases the upthrust which acts to balance the weight of the boat. Once an object has displaced liquid equal to its *whole* volume, it can't displace any more. If the upthrust at that time is *not* enough to balance the weight, then the body will **sink**.

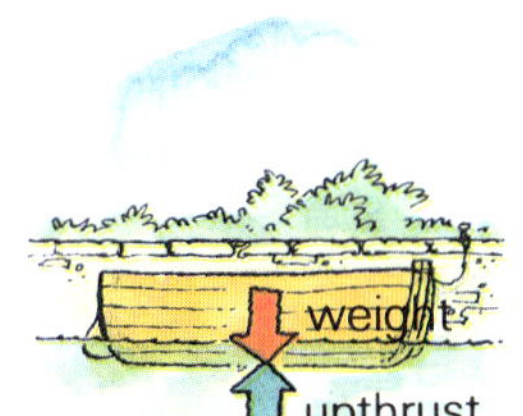

Empty boat – floats high in the water

The boat sinks slightly – more weight, balanced by more upthrust

Any more weight will displace more water – into the boat!

1. Explain how a firework rocket can fly into the sky.

2. Why do you think twin-hulled catamarans are more suited to rough seas than single-hulled boats?

3. People stop themselves being thrown forward, say after a vault in gymnastics, by bending their legs and lowering their body. Why do you think this helps?

4. An empty crate of weight 50 N floats upright. What could happen if you placed a 20 N sack inside the crate?

   If the crate still floats, what weight of water (in Newtons) has been displaced?

5. If a sealed balloon filled with hydrogen is released, it rises up into the air. What do you think causes this?

'Got the energy to do some work?'

Moving forces do work

When you push a trolley in a supermarket, you are providing an **unbalanced force** which *causes motion*. When any unbalanced force acts on a body and moves it, the force does **work**. The amount of work done is measured in **joules** [**J**] and depends on the force used, and the distance moved by the force (while applied to the object).

1 joule of work is done when a force of 1 Newton moves 1 metre

$1\,J = 1\,N \times 1\,m$

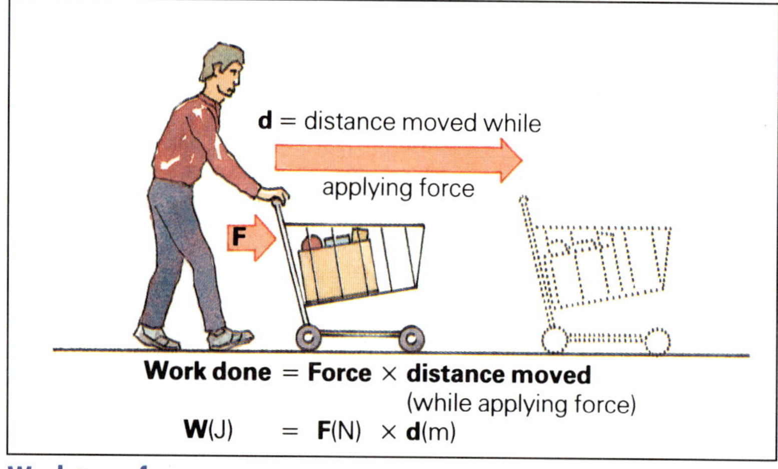

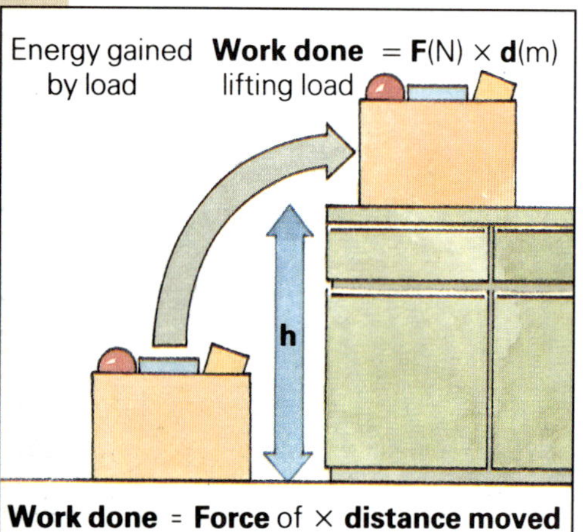

Work transfers energy

A box of shopping sitting on a table has more energy than when it was on the floor. Why should this be so? When work was done in lifting the box, the energy which gave rise to the force was transferred to the box. This extra energy can't be seen, but it can be released to do work if the box falls. This energy is called *position* energy (or **potential energy**). Any object with potential energy is able to do work – because it can release the energy which was used to put it in position. Potential energy is a form of stored energy.

How much energy does work transfer?

To lift a load (such as your shopping), you have to do work to overcome the force of gravity, **mg** [Newtons] *(See 6.2)*.

If *all* the energy used is transferred to the load, then the **work done**, **W**, in raising the load is the *same* as the energy gained by the load.

Energy gained by load = **Work done** lifting load = **Force** × **vertical distance** moved by force

W [J] = **F**[N] × **d** [m]

= **mg** × **h**

Using stored energy

Any stationary object has *some* potential energy. If it falls, its potential energy begins to *change* into moving energy (also known as **kinetic energy**). When this happens, the kinetic energy released can be used to do work. For example, if you had to use your hands to push a nail into a board, it would be very hard work – but if you use a hammer, it's easy! Raising the hammer stores the energy from your lifting force *gradually*. During the *fast* downwards motion of the hammer, this potential energy is released as kinetic energy – which does the work of driving the nail into the wood.

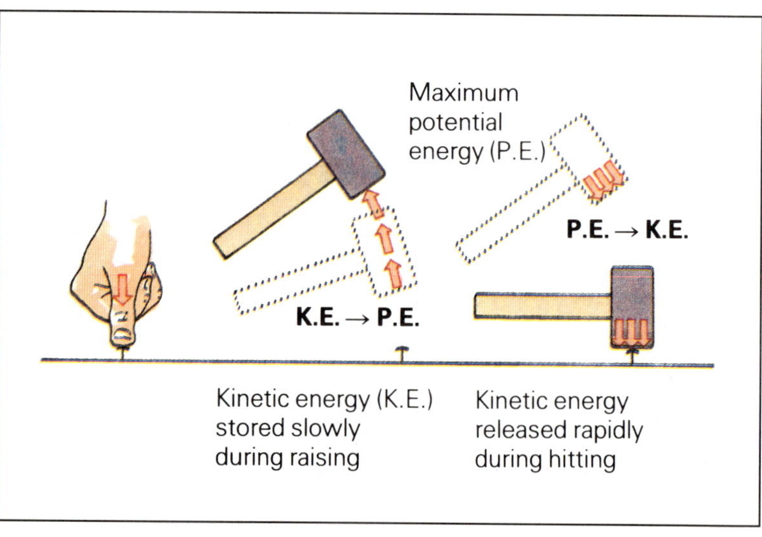

Changing energy, 'losing energy'

When energy changes from one form to another, some of the energy gets 'side-tracked' into other forms of energy. People often say that such energy has been 'lost' – but **energy cannot be created or lost**, it can only be transferred (by releasing or storing). What they really mean is that *not all* the energy has been changed into the form they were expecting!

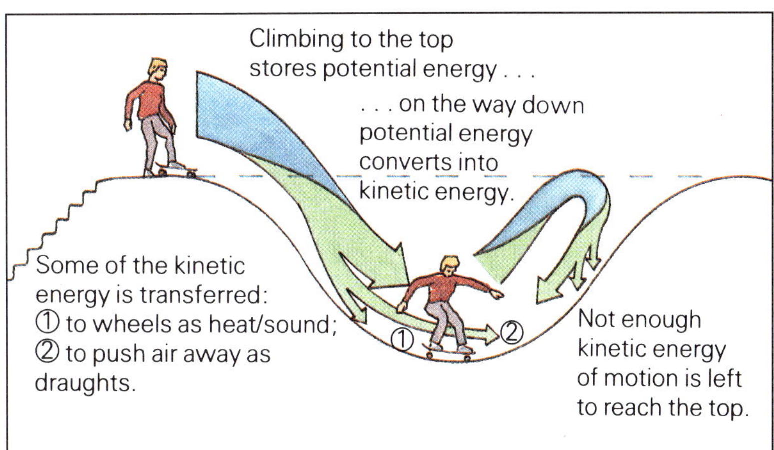

As you can see, some of this skater's energy has got 'side-tracked'.

How can you measure kinetic energy?

Kathy and Sadeep had an idea that measuring the speed of a moving object might help them to work out its kinetic energy. To test their hypothesis, they measured the increases in speed as marbles fell different distances. They knew that

- potential energy released by a falling marble = mgh
  Since the mass m of the marble, and the acceleration due to gravity (g) did not change, they decided that only the difference in heights would change the potential energy.
- any potential energy released changes into kinetic energy
  This meant that any change in the height of the marble's fall would cause a change in the marble's kinetic energy.
- the greater the kinetic energy of an object, the faster it would move
  Any increases in the marble's kinetic energy would also increase its falling speed.

At first they plotted **v** against **h** – and got a steeply curving line. This reminded them of the curve given when plotting numbers against their square roots. So then they tried $\mathbf{v^2}$ against **h** – and got a straight line!

This proved there was a relationship between **h** and $\mathbf{v^2}$. They confirmed their hypothesis by checking in a reference book – which told them that **kinetic energy** = $\frac{1}{2}\mathbf{mv^2}$.

Now they were able to relate the two forms of energy together:

Potential energy (mgh) released during falling = **Kinetic energy** $(\frac{1}{2}\mathbf{mv})^2$ of falling object

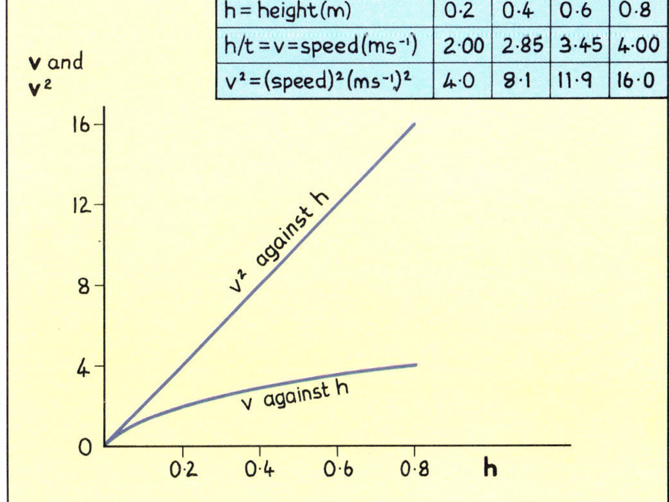

h = height (m)	0·2	0·4	0·6	0·8
h/t = v = speed (ms^{-1})	2·00	2·85	3·45	4·00
v^2 = (speed)^2 (ms^{-1})^2	4·0	8·1	11·9	16·0

1 A pile-driver can drive building supports firmly into the ground. It works by raising a load and dropping it onto a 'pile' which is driven into the earth.

a If the mass of the load is 500 kg and it is raised 20 m, how much potential energy can it release by falling to the ground?

b How much kinetic energy will it have when it hits the 'pile'? At what speed will it hit?

2 On a rollercoaster, all the energy is given to the car by taking it up the first hill.

a Why is no hill higher than the first one?

b Why do the hills get lower as the ride goes on?

c Where would the ride be fastest?

6.5 Machines as force-multipliers . . .

Machines make work easier

When lifting something up, you have only your muscle power to help you. When pulling *down*, you can use the force of your muscles . . . and *your weight* too! A **pulley** can be used to let you *pull down* to lift a heavy weight.

E An effort *E* can lift a load *L*.

L The load *L* will move as far as the effort moves.

E A single fixed pulley changes the direction of the effort.

L Load *L* still only moves as far as effort moves.

*A single **fixed pulley** is a simple machine that changes the direction in which a force acts.*

Machines can multiply forces

Your muscles can provide only a limited force. Some machines can *multiply* the effect of your force. A system of pulleys can do this – provided that some of the pulleys are *'free'* to move up and down. Look what happens when a 'free' pulley is added to a fixed pulley.

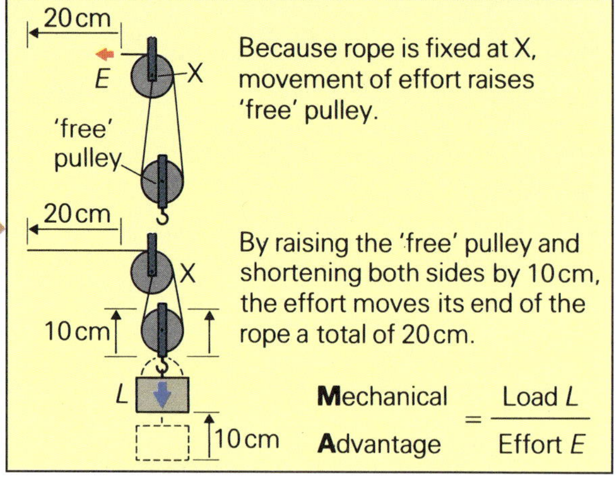

*A system using **'free' pulleys** can do more than just change the direction – it can also **multiply** a force.*

Overall, this shortening (of the connecting lengths of rope) raises the 'free' pulley by *half* the distance moved by the effort. This may seem like a waste – but it is the key to why pulley systems can act as **force-multipliers**. If a load *L* is attached to the 'free' pulley, then as the effort *E* moves 20 cm, the load *L* moves up only 10 cm. The pulley system *can't 'add'* any energy of its own, so to lift the load *L* . . .

Work done moving effort (*E*) = **Work done moving load** (*L*)

Force of effort × **distance** moved by effort = **Force** of load × **distance** moved by load

Example: $E \times 20\,cm = L \times 10\,cm \rightarrow E \times \frac{20}{10} = L$

So a pulley system can multiply the force of an effort (and cause it to move a much larger load) by making the effort *move further* than the load.

The more 'free' pulleys in the system, the more the force of the effort is multiplied. Using a *machine* which multiplies forces gives you an *advantage* over your muscle power (or whatever force is used). The *number* of times that a machine can multiply a force (effort) is called its **mechanical advantage (MA).**

Are all machines force multipliers?

Not all machines are designed and used to multiply forces. Sometimes the purpose of a machine is to change *small* movements into *large* movements – such as the **distance-multiplier** effect of gears (*see 6.6*).

Generally, if the distance moved by the effort is *greater* than the distance moved by the load, then the machine is a force-multiplier (and its **MA** is greater than 1).

*A machine need not have any moving parts – this **ramp** is a very basic machine which helps to lift a load gradually.*

Lever lifting

What do your fingers, hands, arms, toes, feet, legs, neck and jaw have in common with scissors, tweezers, wheelbarrows and spanners? They are all levers!

A **lever** is a simple machine which *turns* (or pivots) about a **fulcrum** (or pivot point) to use the work done by an effort to move a load. There are *three* basic types of lever – each type has a different *arrangement* of effort, load and fulcrum.

To act as a force-multiplier, the effort applied to a lever must move further than the load – which two types of levers are force-multipliers?

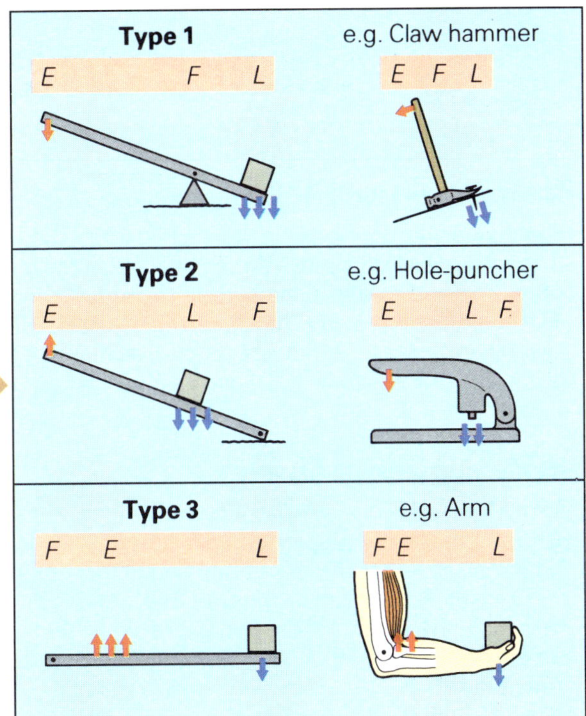

A lever makes the effort E and load L move in circular paths around the fulcrum. If the lever moves through *one-eighth* of a circle . . .

Work done by effort = Work done moving load

Force of effort (E) × distance moved by effort = Force of load (L) × distance moved by load

$$E \times \tfrac{1}{8}(2\pi R) = L \times \tfrac{1}{8}(2\pi r)$$

$$E \times \frac{\tfrac{1}{8}(2\pi R)}{\tfrac{1}{8}(2\pi r)} = L = E \times \frac{R}{r}$$

$$\textbf{Mechanical Advantage} = \frac{L}{E} = \frac{E \times \frac{R}{r}}{E} = \frac{\mathbf{R}}{\mathbf{r}}$$

This means that moving a load *near* to the fulcrum (decreasing **r**) *increases* the MA of the lever – and even *less* effort is needed to move the load. How else could the MA of the lever be increased?

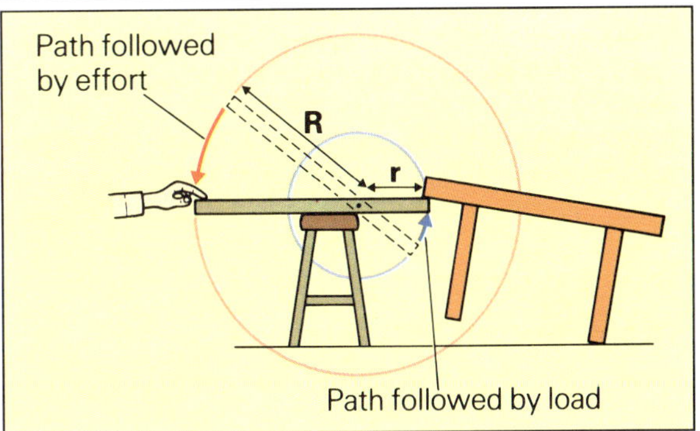

With simple levers, the distances moved by the effort and load depend upon *their distance from the fulcrum* (R and r).

Pedal power

When you pedal a bike, the load placed on the chain is the result of the **pedal-crank** acting as a *force-multiplier.*

Pushing the pedal-crank round half a circle (of circumference $2\pi R$) moves the chain wheel – *and the chain* – round by half a *smaller* circle (of circumference $2\pi r$)

As before,

$$\text{Mechanical Advantage of pedal-crank} = \frac{\mathbf{R}}{\mathbf{r}}$$

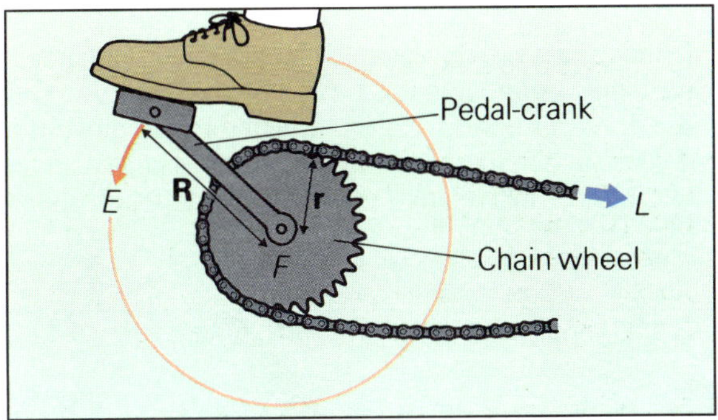

The 'pedal-crank and chain wheel' system – the ***force-multiplier*** *part of a bike.*

1 On a small dinghy, a force of 100 N is needed to raise the sail 1.5 metres up the mast. A four-pulley system allows you to raise the sail with an effort of 25 N. How far will you have to pull the rope from the pulley system to raise the sail?

2 Give two more examples of each type of lever. Label a simple drawing of each to show the effort, load and fulcrum.

3 Why do some shops have ramps at their entrances? Do you think the ramp acts as a force-multiplier? Explain your answer.

. . . and distance-multipliers too!

Machines can multiply 'distance moved'

Some machines can be used to multiply the 'distance moved' by the effort E – making the load L move *much further* than the effort. For example, in some levers, the effort-fulcrum distance is less than the fulcrum-load distance. Such levers are **distance-multipliers.** Your arms, legs and lower jaw are distance-multipliers – a small movement of the muscle connected to your elbow will move your hand a long way.

Multiplying force *or* distance

A simple machine can be *either* a **force**-multiplier *or* a **distance**-multiplier (depending upon how it is used) – but it *can't be both* at the same time! Sometimes, more complex machines combine the two: a bike uses the *force*-multiplying effect of the **pedal-crank** system *along* with the *distance*-multiplying effect of the **rear gear wheel.**

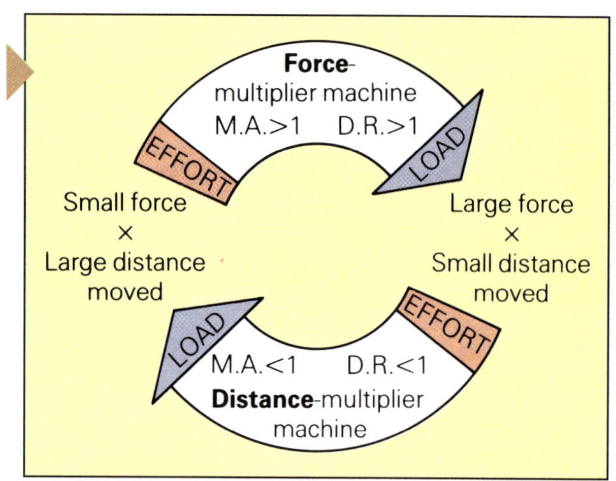

The *ratio* of the distance moved by the effort E and the load L is called the **distance ratio** of the machine:

$$\textbf{D}\text{istance } \textbf{R}\text{atio} = \frac{\text{Distance moved by effort } E}{\text{Distance moved by load } L}.$$

Gear systems

Gears are wheels with 'teeth' (or cogs) cut into the rim. These teeth can **mesh** (fit into) the teeth of other suitably-sized gears. Look at gear wheel A (60 teeth) meshing into gear wheel B (12 teeth). Each tooth can push against only one tooth on the other gear – so when A turns *once* (turning its central axle once), B will turn $60/12 = 5$ *times* (turning the axle on B five times).

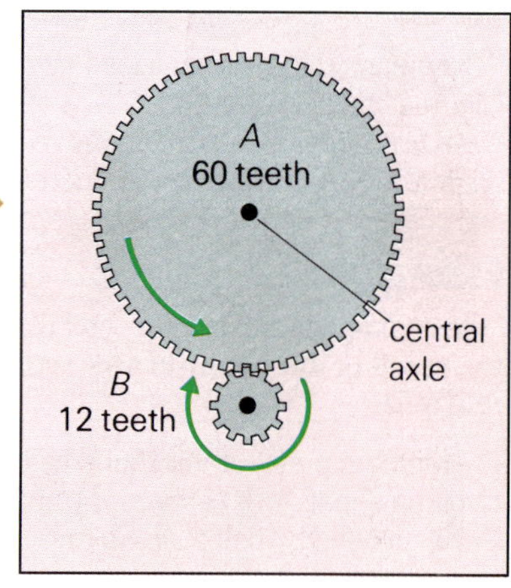

In any gear system, when two gears mesh, one gear will be the **driving** (or input) **gear** – and it is turned by the effort E. The other gear will be the **driven** (or output) **gear** which turns to move the load L. (The gears do not have to mesh *directly* together – a chain can link them). The *rate* at which they turn relative to each other depends upon the number of 'teeth' they have:

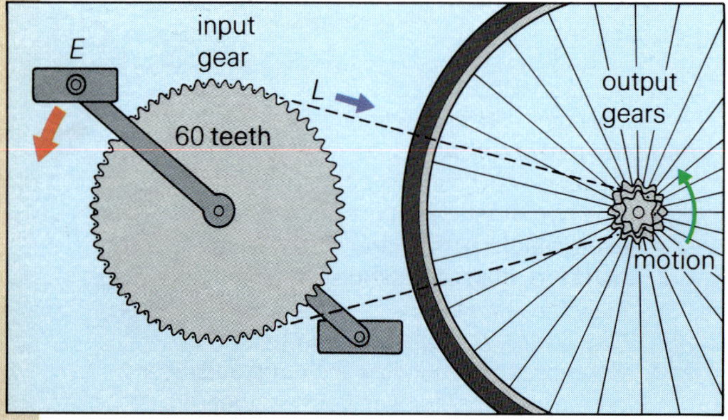

$$\textbf{Gear ratio} = \frac{\text{No of teeth on } \textbf{driving} \text{ (input) gear}}{\text{No of teeth on } \textbf{driven} \text{ (output) gear}}$$

The larger the gear, the *more* teeth it will have – and so it will turn *less* far.

*This bike has three gears on the rear wheel, with 6, 10 and 12 teeth. By selecting different (**output**) **gears** on the rear wheel to mesh with the chain from the crank-wheel (**input**) **gear**, you can vary the gear ratio. Which 3 gear ratios could be obtained here?*

Gear systems act as . . .

. . . **distance-multipliers** when the input (driving) gear is *smaller* (and turns *faster*) than the output (driven) gear.

. . . **force-multipliers** when the input gear is *larger* (and turns *slower*) than the output gear.

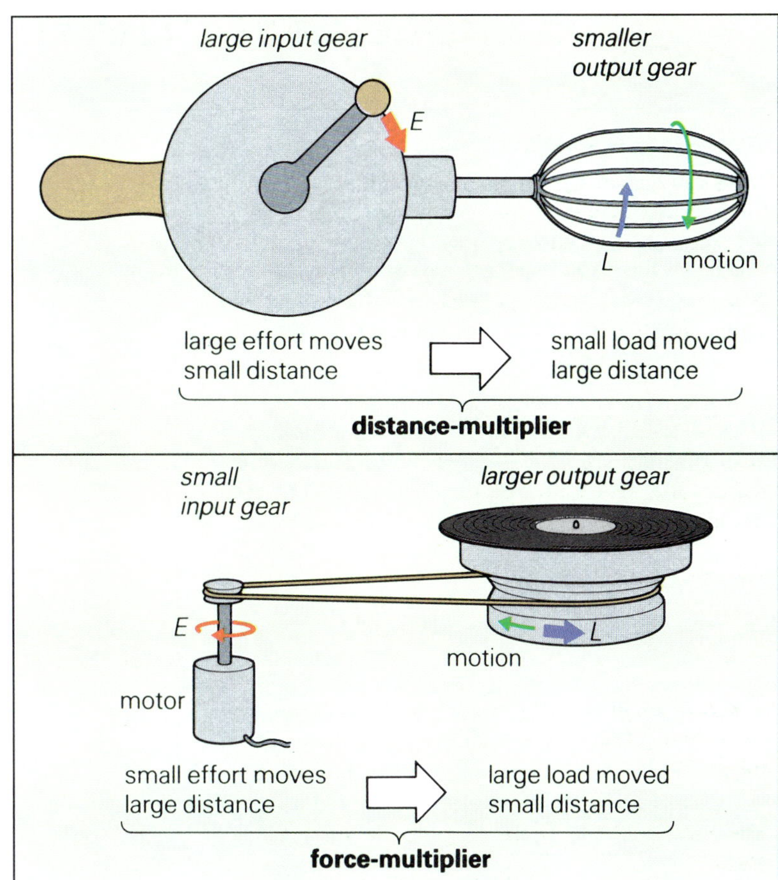

Which way now?

Like pulleys, gears can be used to change the *direction* of a motion – as you can see by studying a rotary food whisk. For hundreds of years gears have been used to manipulate motion.

In the sixteenth century, Leonardo da Vinci designed several machines which convert the circular motion (of a turning handle) into either up and down, or horizontal motion.

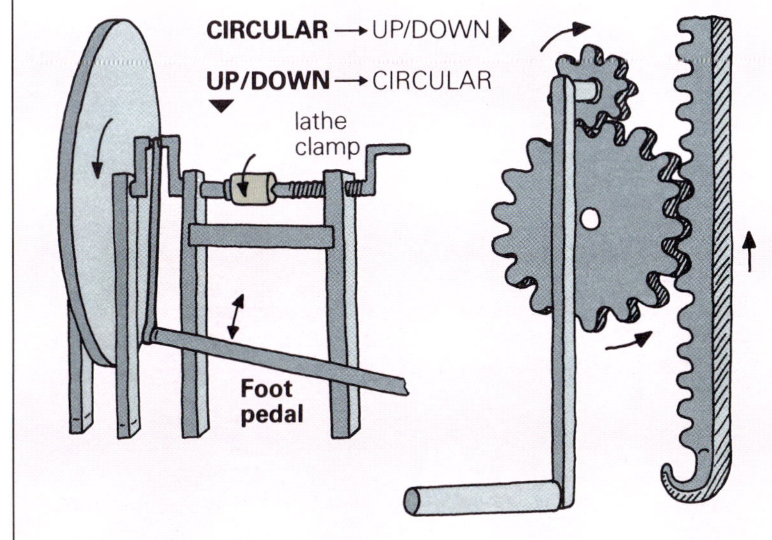

Work and power

Whether a machine is a force- or distancc-multiplicr, it still cannot add 'extra' energy to the system – it can only *transfer* energy. The *rate* at which a machine does work (*transfers energy*) is called its **power**. Power is measured in **watts [W]** – which are a measure of the number of joules of energy transferred every second.

$$\textbf{Power}\text{ (Watts)} = \frac{\textbf{Work done}\text{ (joules)}}{\textbf{Time}\text{ (seconds)}}$$

$$= \frac{\text{Energy transferred}}{\text{Time}}$$

1 **a** Riding up a steep hill, you do more work than riding up a slight slope. Why?
b Which of the three rear gear wheels shown opposite would be most effective at overcoming a large load?
c Which of the gears would you use to ride up a steep hill? Why?
d Which gear would allow you to ride the furthest distance for one turn of the pedal?

2 How much work is done by a 50 W hi-fi system playing a record for 20 minutes?

3 Draw a labelled diagram of da Vinci's machines. Use your labels to explain how the machines transfer energy.

A cause of friction

Friction resists movement

When you pull on the brakes of a bike, it slows down. *Why?* Newton's first law of motion (*see 6.2*) tells us that some unbalanced force must have been used to slow down the bike. The force appears when the brake block is pulled into contact with the rim of the wheel. This is a **friction** force which is caused by an *interaction between the two surfaces.*

No matter how smooth a surface appears, if you looked at it under a microscope you would see that there are small 'hills' and 'valleys' on the surface. The friction force arises because the 'hills' on the brake hit the 'hills' on the rim.

Friction always acts against the direction of movement.

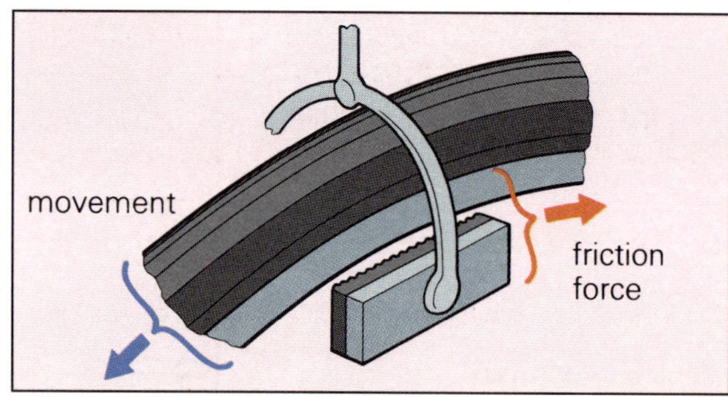

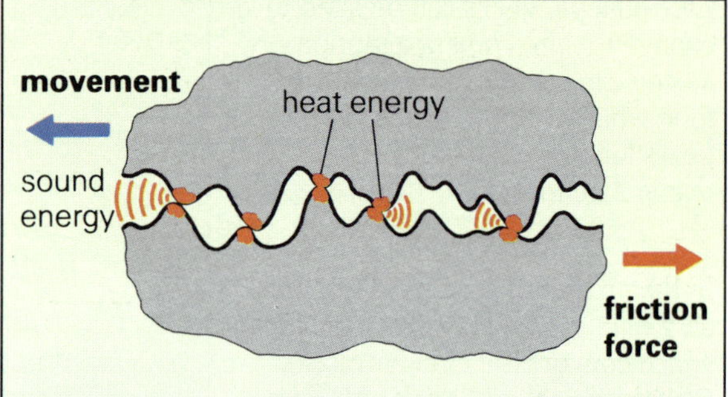

Friction diverts energy

If you use your brakes to slow down, then you might think some of your **kinetic** energy has been 'lost'. But energy *cannot* be created or destroyed, it can only be changed into other forms. Friction causes the kinetic energy to be *changed* into **heat** and **sound** energy. If you brake hard, you can hear the brakes squeal – and if you feel them afterwards, you will find that they are warm!

Friction wastes effort

In a *perfect* machine, the *work put in* would equal the *work that comes out.* However, in most machines there are moving parts – and whenever there is movement, friction acts *against* it. Whenever friction appears, *some* of the energy supplied by the effort does *not* get transferred to act on the load. The purpose of machines is to transfer energy to do work on the load. So the energy transferred by the friction force (and changed into heat and sound) is *wasted.*

A very large friction force is needed to stop a plane – and it releases a lot of heat and sound energy.

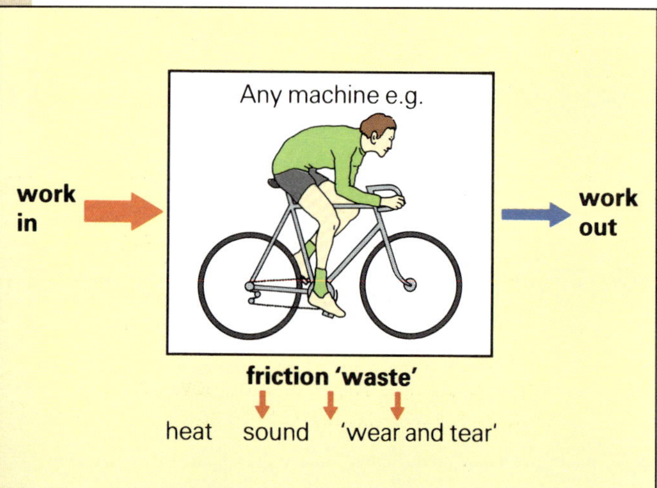

Work in = work out + energy released by friction.

Grinding to a halt . . . inefficient machines

If you pedalled a bike with a rusty chain, you would find it hard work. The *rougher* the surfaces that move together, the *greater* the friction and so the greater the amount of energy 'diverted' into heat, sound and wearing down the surfaces.

The **efficiency** of a machine compares how much of the energy put in is used in the way you want it:

$$\text{Efficiency} = \frac{\text{Work out}}{\text{Work in}} \times 100\%.$$

If the efficiency of a bike is 60%, it means that when you ride the bike only just over half the energy you put in will be used to move you forward, and the rest will be used doing other things.

Oiling the works

Friction is caused by surfaces being in contact with each other. But there must be *some* contact between surfaces, to enable one part of a machine to move another! So, to *reduce* energy waste (but still stay working), a machine needs to reduce *unnecessary* contact between its moving surfaces.

Friction forces stop your feet from sliding – if a lubricant stops these forces from acting, you'll fall over!

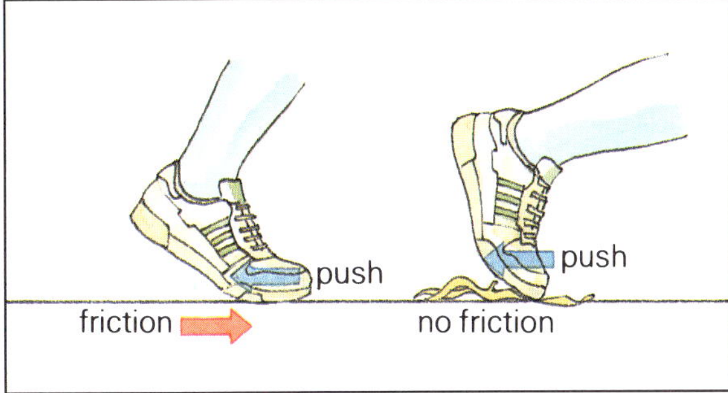

*There are many different **lubricants** – oil, grease, soap, water, ice, graphite, talcum powder . . .*

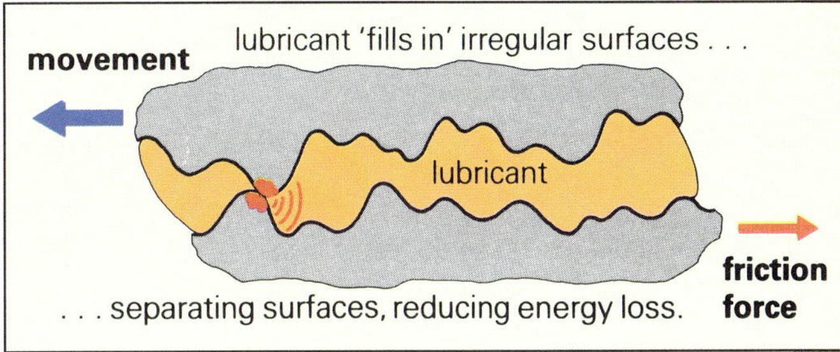

Sometimes friction is useful

When you walk, you push your foot backwards against the ground. Only the friction force stops your foot from slipping right back! If it is wet or icy, then there is a thin layer of water under your foot which acts as a **lubricant**. The friction force is less and you can easily slip over. You can only pick some things up because of the friction between the object and your hand. There is not a lot of friction between your hand and any wet or oily object – and next to none at all if it is wet *and* oily, such as a bar of soap!

Air 'friction'

When you move through the air, you push up against the molecules in the air. To move on, you have to either push them back or to one side. This process of overcoming **air** (or wind) **resistance** wastes some of your kinetic energy – so air resistance is a form of friction!

A Perpetual Motion machine?

If no energy was wasted in a machine – a perfect machine – it could be a **perpetual motion machine**, running forever with *no more energy added* to the system. In the model shown, potential energy at *A* is used to turn a water wheel. This wheel is used to drive a bucket wheel which should then lift up the water and restore its potential energy. This machine should run forever once it has been started – but it doesn't. How many different reasons can you think of to explain why?

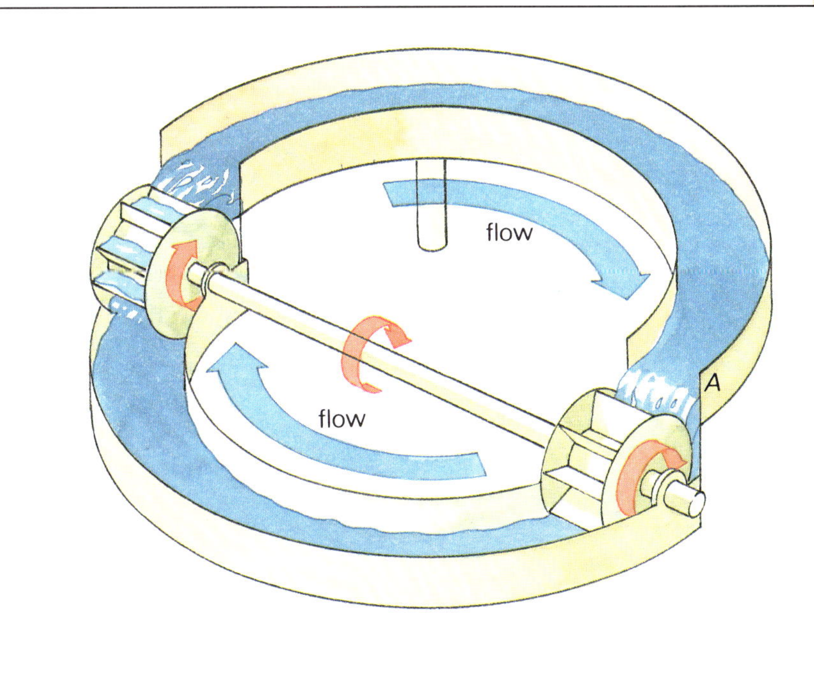

1
- **a** Why are the tyres of a cycle patterned?
- **b** Why do your hands get warm when you rub them?
- **c** Why do jet aircraft have polished wings?

2 In the **water cycle** in nature, water is continually evaporating from the sea, condensing, falling as rain and running back to the sea. Why isn't this an example of a perpetual motion machine?

3 The handle of an egg whisk is turned through a circle of radius 0.1 m with a force of 5 N. It takes 14 turns of the handle to beat an egg.
- **a** What distance does the hand travel in the 14 turns?
- **b** If the machine is 80% efficient, how much work is needed just to beat the egg?

Forces in liquids

Under pressure

When you walk in deep snow, your weight causes your feet to sink. If you had snowshoes, then your feet would not sink in so deeply. Since the force acting downwards (your weight) remains the same, why don't you sink? It is because you have spread your weight over a *larger* area, and so reduced the pressure on the snow.

Pressure is a measure of the force acting on **each unit of area.**

$$\text{Pressure} = \frac{\text{Force}}{\text{Area}}$$

Inuit Indians designed snow-shoes to spread their weight, reducing the pressure *of their feet on soft snow.*

The pressure exerted by a brick depends on which face it stands. Its weight *(a force) is* constant, *but each face has a* ***different area****, creating* ***different pressures****. Pressure is measured in* ***Pascals***

1 Pascal (Pa) = 1 Newton/1 metre^2

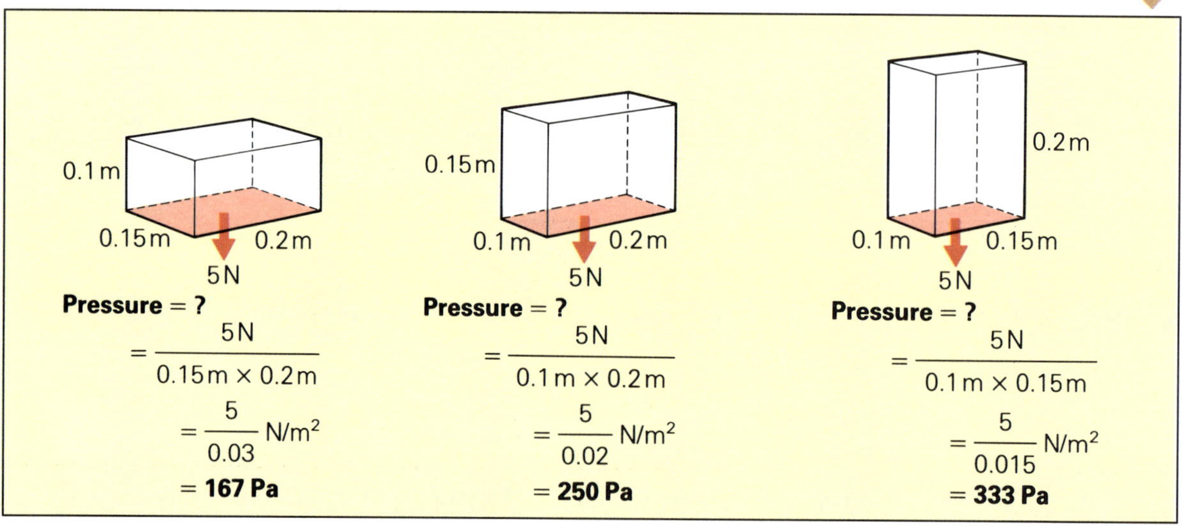

Pressure in liquids

If you swim underwater, you can feel the pressure increase on your body as you go deeper. The pressure at *any* depth depends on the *weight of liquid* above you – because this is the *force* that presses down on you.

Liquids cannot be compressed . . .

Air trapped in a cycle pump can be **compressed** (made smaller) by blocking the outlet, and then pushing down on the handle. This is because air is a **gas**, and so is made up of tiny particles which are quite far apart. If the pump is filled with water, then the handle can *not* be pushed in. Water is a **liquid** and so its particles are already in contact with each other – they can *not* be pushed any closer together. This means that *liquids can not be compressed* by increasing the pressure.

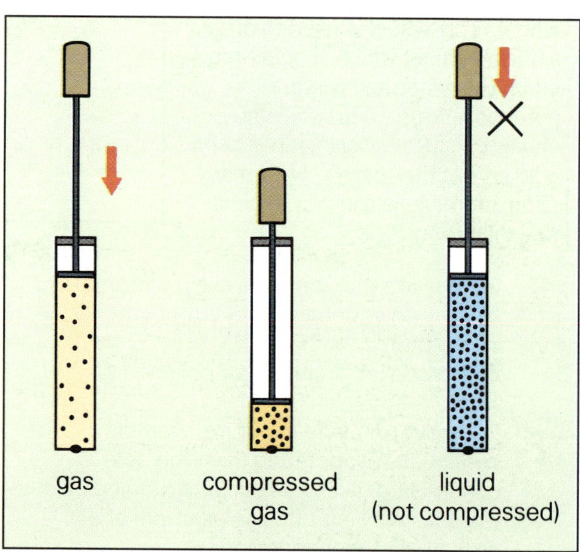

. . . and so transmit pressure

The particles in a liquid are *free to move* in *any* direction. Because of this property, when under pressure from a force, the liquid particles pass the force on in *all* directions. So the pressure can be transmitted *equally* throughout a liquid, regardless of the shape of the container. This **pressure-transmission** effect is used in any machine that has a **hydraulic system** – such as car jacks, hydraulic brakes and hydraulic presses.

Because pressure in a liquid acts equally *in all directions, this fitting sprays water* equally *strongly in all directions.*

Force-multiplying hydraulics

Hydraulic systems can be very effective **force-multipliers**. Look at this example – a small piston in a hydraulic jack raising a car!

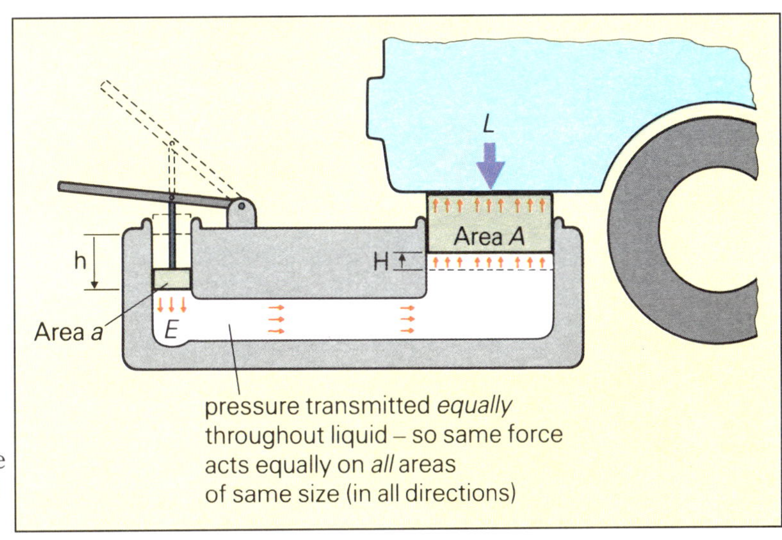

Volume of liquid displaced by small piston (of area a): $V = a \times h$. Since liquids can not be compressed, the same volume V of liquid will displace the large piston (area A): $V = A \times H$.

If the area A of the large piston is, say, 3 times that of the small piston:

$$a \times h = V = A \times H = 3a \times H$$

$$\text{So} \quad \frac{a}{3a} \times h = H = \tfrac{1}{3}h$$

$$\text{Work in} = \text{Work out}$$

$$\text{Effort} \times \text{distance moved} = \text{Load} \times \text{distance moved}$$

$$E \times h = L \times \tfrac{1}{3}h$$

So, the load L raised is three times *greater* than the effort E.

*A **hydraulic brake system** is a force-multiplier machine – a gentle push on the brake pedal is enough to stop a car!*

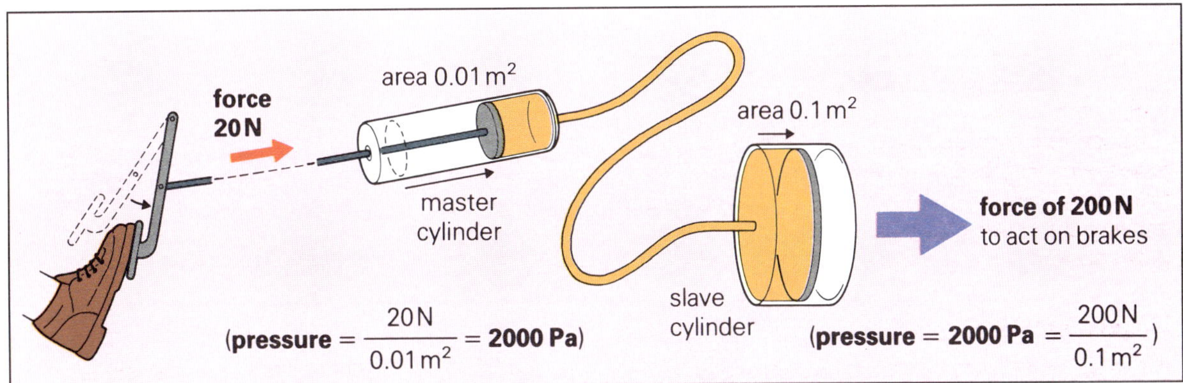

1 Calculate the pressure exerted by:

a a car with a weight 10 200 N acting on 4 tyres, each of which has in contact with the ground an area of $0.12\,m \times 0.05\,m$.

b a girl with a weight of 450 N, when wearing:

i snowshoes of area $0.1\,m^2$;

ii shoes of area $0.006\,m^2$;

iii stiletto heels, area $0.0001\,m^2$.

2 Explain why it is not a good idea to fill your cycle tyres with water.

3 Dams are designed to be thicker at the bottom than at the top, and have a curved shape. Why?

Transferring energy

Using the forces of nature

No matter how strong you are, you can only apply a *limited* force using your muscles. Even using force multipliers, you still couldn't build up enough force to do many tasks. So, over the ages people have *designed* machines that have harnessed the much stronger forces of nature such as wind and water power. However, these machines can only work where their (unreliable) source of energy is found – on hills and by rivers.

Transmitting force wastes energy

The invention of the **steam engine** (*see 6.15*) led to large scale industrial production. At last, a *reliable* energy source (**coal**) could be **transported** to any suitable site. In early factories, such as textile mills, a steam engine was the *only* source of power in a factory – and drove every machine in the place.

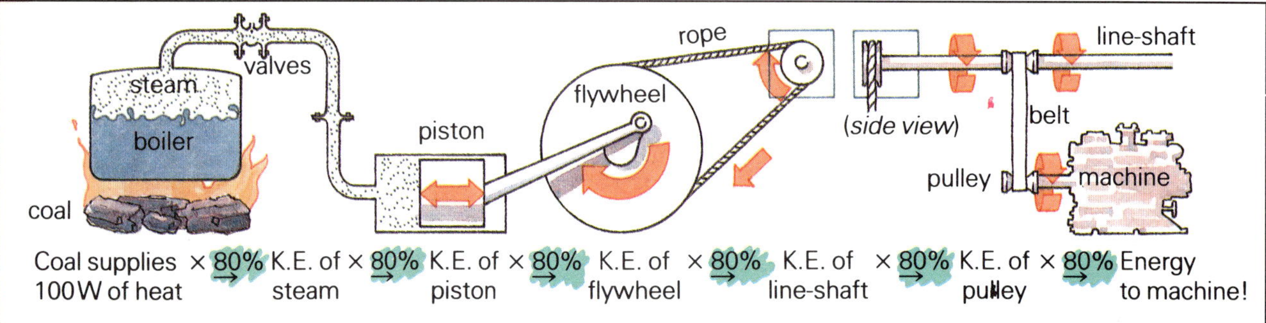

As you can see there is a problem with the **mechanical transfer** of energy. Every time moving parts (such as levers, pulleys and gears) are used as distance or force-multipliers, some energy is *wasted* by **friction**.

If 20% of the energy is wasted at each stage of the energy transfer in the factory system shown above, *how much* of the original energy is available to drive the final machine? If there was *another* linkage, what percentage of the original energy would be available?

*Steam drove large **pistons** which turned a huge **flywheel**. This turned long ropes wrapped around **line-shafts** on different floors of the factory. The individual machines were driven from a line-shaft by a series of **'belt and pulley'** systems.*

Energy transfer made easy

When energy is transferred mechanically, each linkage can cause energy wastage. This restricts the distance over which energy can be transferred. The **electrical transfer** of energy is much more efficient – and quicker. Now we use power stations based close to a source of power. These stations generate electricity, which is transmitted all over the country through the **National Grid.**

How much energy reaches the electrical machine? Which is more efficient – mechanical transmission of energy (above) or this electrical transmission?

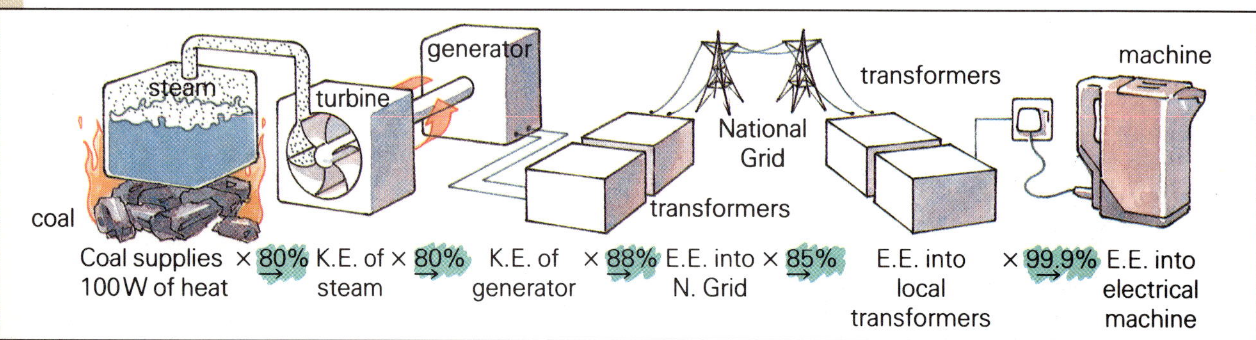

Electricity energy . . . into heat and light

When an electric current passes through a wire, some of its energy is turned into heat. The amount of energy wasted in this way depends on the **resistance** of the wire and the strength of the **current** flowing. A wire is said to have a *high* resistance if *most* of the electrical energy is turned to *heat* when a current flows. If the wire gets hot enough, some of the heat energy will be transferred into *light* energy – just like in an electric light bulb!

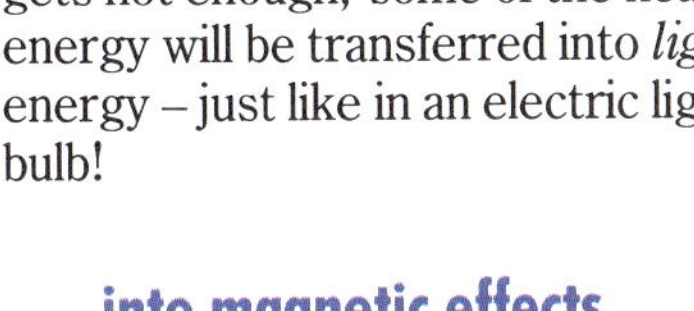

Lights waste a lot of heat energy – but sometimes it is *useful to convert electrical energy into heat energy.*

. . . into magnetic effects

The metal copper is not magnetic, and has no effect on a compass needle. When a current flows through a copper wire, the compass needle *is* affected – so the current itself must have a **magnetic effect**. The area around a magnet where it can affect other magnets is called its **field**. A current-generated field creates a spiralling magnetic pattern around the wire. This magnetic field can be used to generate movement (kinetic energy).

On coiling the wire, the spiral field starts to overlap itself. Such a coiled wire is called an **electromagnet** because when **electr**icity flows, it acts like a **magnet** (*see 6.10*).

The electrical energy supplied to electromagnets can be used to produce *two types of movement*. One is the **'back and forth'** movement used in machines like loudspeakers and doorbells. The other is the **'round and round'** movement used in machines like record players and food mixers.

Electrical energy is used to establish the magnetic field around a wire. An **alternating current**, which flows first in one direction, then reverses and flows back again (and so on), is constantly having to build up a new magnetic field, first in one direction and then in the other. Alternating currents waste a lot of electrical energy *building* and *destroying* these fields.

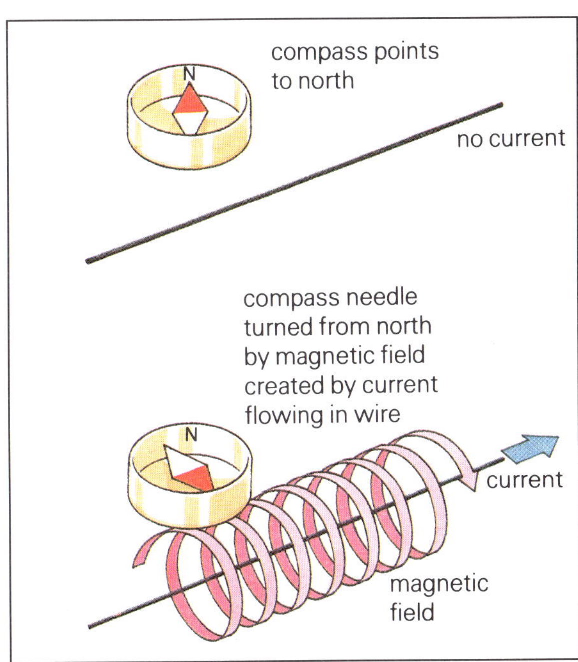

When electrical energy flows through a wire, some of this energy is used to build up a spiralling ***magnetic field*** *around the wire.*

1 A dynamo on a bike is a simple machine that generates electricity to power a lamp from the kinetic energy of the pedals.

- **a** list all the places where friction could occur between the pedals and the moving part of the dynamo;
- **b** if friction reduces the transfer of kinetic energy by 20% at each stage, and resistance in the wire to the lamp reduces electrical energy by 10%, how much of the energy applied to the pedals will reach the bike's lamp?

2 The amount of electrical energy transferred depends on the voltage and the current. Electricity is passed down the National Grid at a high voltage but with a low current. Find out why this is done.

Moving on from electricity

Motors transfer energy

The **electric motor** *changes* electrical energy into kinetic energy – it is the very 'heart' of the many electrical machines we use at home and at work. The key to this energy transfer is **electromagnetism** – the magnetic effect produced when a current flows along a wire.

The more *a current-carrying wire is* ***looped****, the* stronger *the electromagnetic field becomes at the centre.*

Electromagnets – concentrated fields

Looping a current-carrying wire into a **coil** effectively 'concentrates' the spirals of its magnetic field into the centre of the coil. (The *more* loops there are in the coil, the *stronger* the field in the centre of the coil becomes). The magnetic field now spreads out from one side of the coil, and bends back into the centre from the other side. This means one side acts like a **north pole** of a magnet, and the other side like a

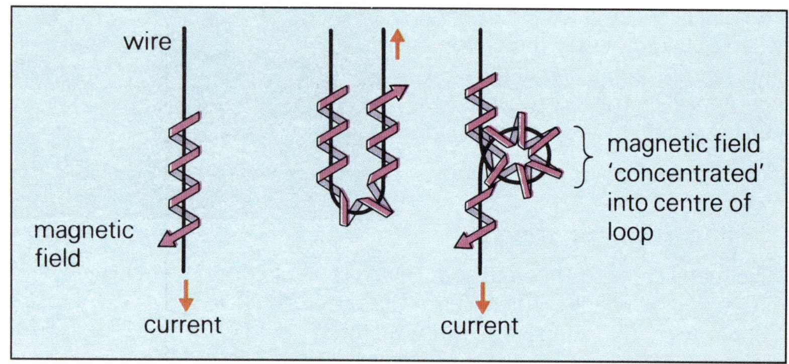

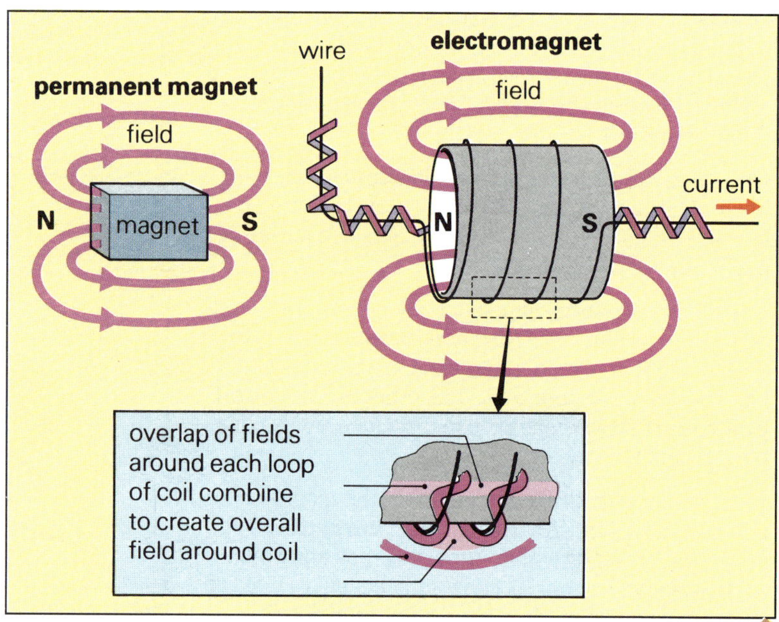

The overall field acts from *one end (the north pole) of an electromagnetic coil* to *the other end (the south pole). This field is just like the magnetic field around an ordinary magnet.*

Magnetic attraction

'Opposite' poles on a magnet attract each other, 'like' poles repel each other. If a current flows through a coil (an electromagnet), which is free to spin, the *north* pole of the coil will be *repelled* by any other magnetic *north* pole. Similarly, the south pole of the coil will be repelled by a magnetic south pole. However, the poles of the coil will be *attracted* by their '*opposite*' poles.

Which end of a coil is which pole? Work out the ***direction of current flow****:*
clockwise = south pole; anti-clockwise = ?

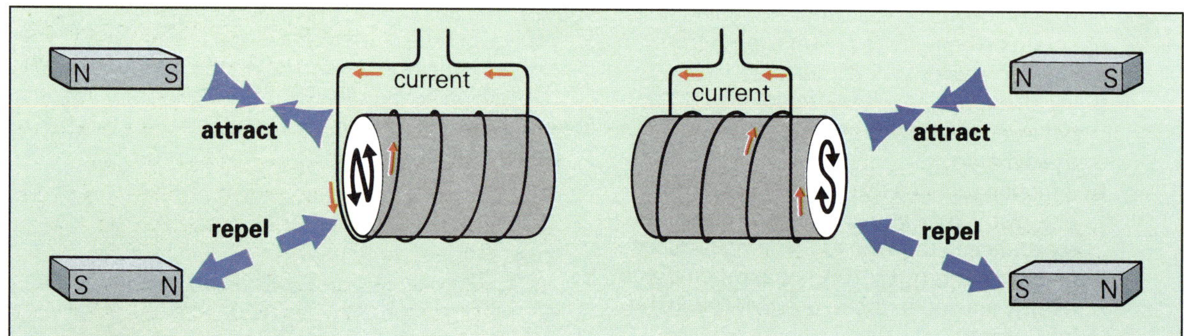

Making moves with electricity

Imagine a coil, that is free to turn, placed between the poles of a pair of **permanent magnets**. When a current is passed through the coil, it becomes an electromagnet. If the north pole of the coil is facing the north pole of a permanent magnet, then the coil is *repelled* and it turns *away* from the magnet. It will keep turning until the south pole of the coil faces the north pole of the magnet. Normally, the attraction between these poles would hold the coil 'at rest' in that position.

If the current through the coil is *reversed* just when the coil reaches the 'rest' position, then the coil's south pole is changed into a north pole and this is again repelled, causing the coil to turn again. A device called a **split-ring commutator** *changes the direction of the current in the coil* every time the south comes close to the magnet's north, causing the coil to keep spinning. In this way, an electromagnet, a permanent magnet and a split-ring commutator act as an **electric motor** – transferring electrical energy into kinetic energy.

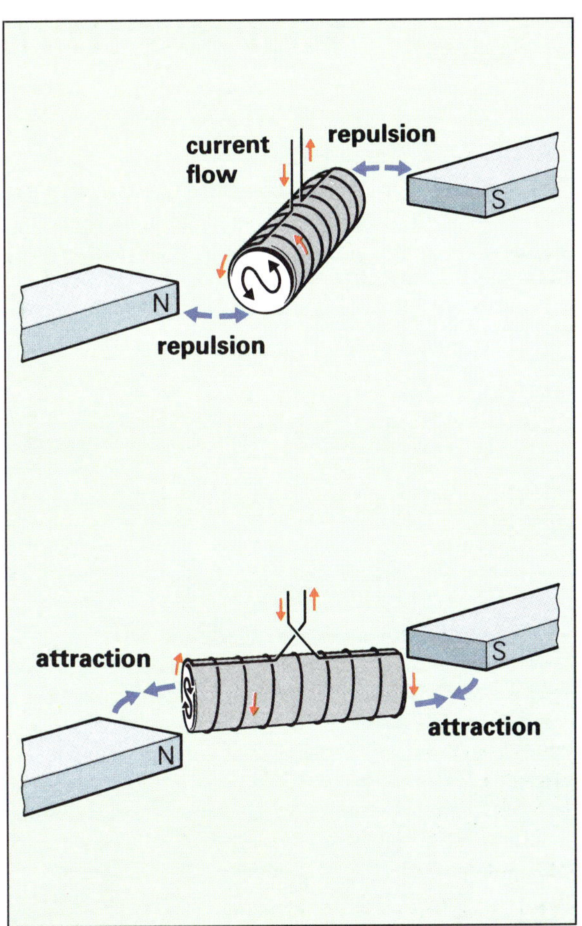

An electromagnetic coil which is free to turn will rotate to align its poles with the opposite poles of nearby magnets.

*A **split-ring commutator** makes a free-turning electromagnetic coil into an **electric motor** – by changing the direction of current flow every half-turn. Attraction is replaced by repulsion, making the coil spin again . . . and again . . .*

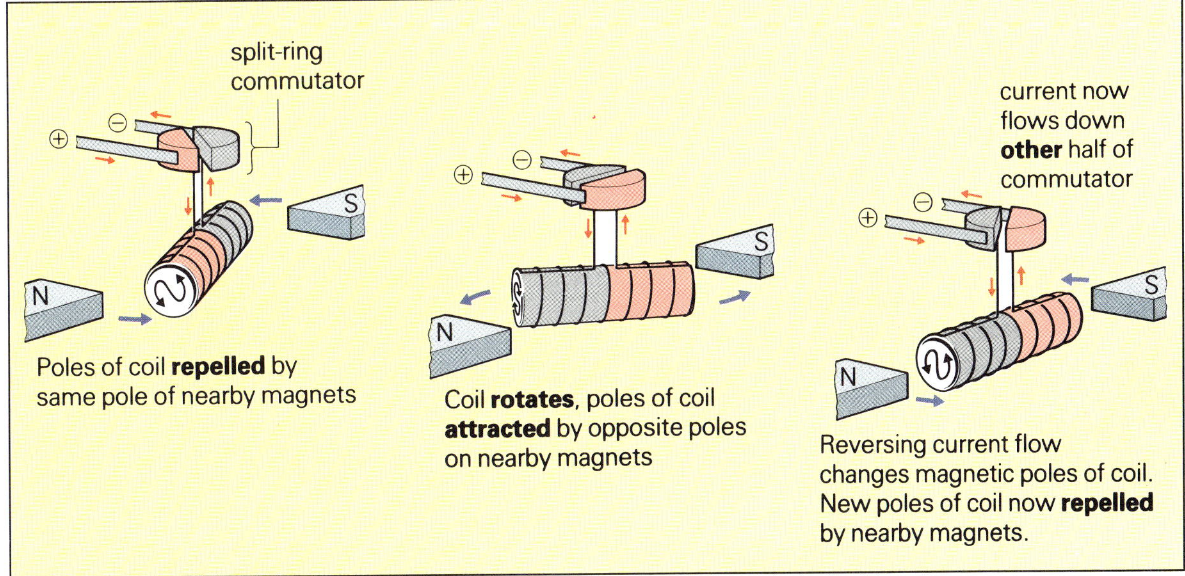

1 List all the machines in your home that use electric motors. Which ones could be replaced by machines which do not use electricity? Suggest examples of non-electrical alternatives.

2 Emergency lighting in public buildings is usually battery-powered. It switches itself on when the mains electricity supply fails – this allows people to find their way out in emergencies. Describe how a simple electromagnet could be used by such lighting to switch itself on.

6.11 How is movement measured?

How fast are you going?

The speedometer in a car shows the speed at which a car is travelling at any one instant. A reading of '30 km an hour' tells you that you would travel 30 km in one hour (if you kept at the *same* speed!) But you don't need a speedometer to work out your speed – you can easily work out your average speed of, say, walking. Just measure how far you go and the time it takes!

A ***speedometer*** *tells you your speed at any one instant – but it can't tell you your average speed.*

$$\textit{Average } \textbf{speed} = \frac{\textit{Distance covered}}{\textit{Time taken}}$$

Where are you going?

On a road, your direction of travel *changes* at every bend. To describe all your movements accurately, you would have to record your **speed** *and* the **direction** in which you travel. Speed *in a given direction* is called **velocity**.

$$\textbf{Velocity} = \frac{\textit{Distance covered in a specific direction}}{\textit{Time taken}}$$

Velocity is a relative thing

In a train travelling at 30 m/s, all the seated passengers have the *same* velocity – they do not move relative to each other! If one walks at 2 m/s towards the front of the train, she has a velocity of 2 m/s relative to the other passengers (who are already moving at 30 m/s). What would be her velocity relative to a person beside the track? Because she is walking in line with the train's movement, we can easily calculate her velocity by adding her 'two' velocities together, and then subtracting the velocity of the stationary bystander.

If the train overtakes a cyclist (riding at 5 m/s in the same direction as the train), what would the train's velocity be relative to the cyclist?

You can simply add (or subtract) velocities *only* when they act **in line** (either in the same, or opposite, directions).

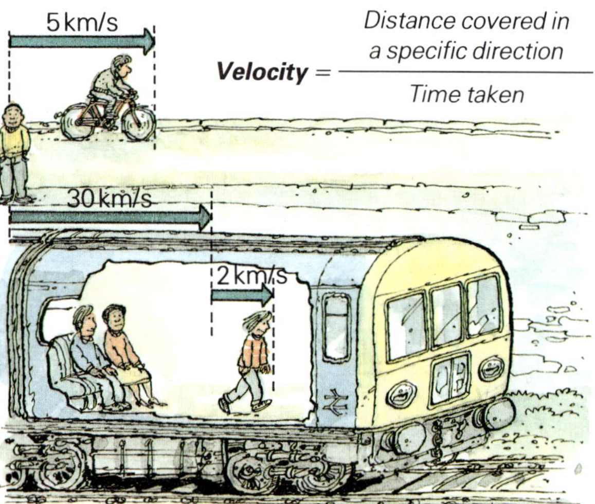

Velocities which act along the same line can be added together.

Adding velocities . . . life and death!

Imagine: you're on holiday, about to land at an airport . . . but a strong wind is blowing from one side. How can you be sure the plane will land on the runway – and not be blown off course?

Nowadays, pilots use **computers** to calculate the necessary course and speed. The calculation involves combining the velocity of the plane (v_p) with the velocity of the wind (v_w). But, because the velocities do *not* act along the same line, you *can't* just add them together!

The combined effect of *non-aligned* velocities is called the **resultant velocity** (v_r). It can be calculated by drawing a **scale diagram** of the size (speed) and direction of the velocities. The *diagonal of a parallelogram* based on this drawing indicates the size and direction of the resultant velocity (v_r).

To work out the resultant velocity of non-aligned velocities, you have to draw up a ***velocity parallelogram****.*

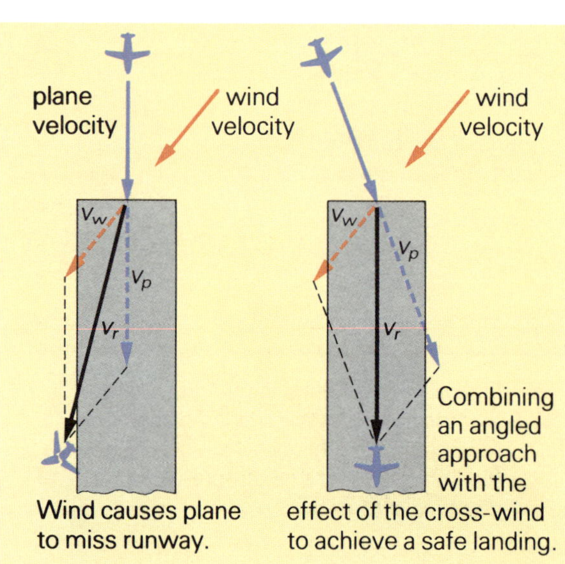

Momentum can be deadly!

Watch out for bullets and buses – they can both be deadly! A bus (mass 8000 kg) with a velocity of 25 m/s can kill you – so can a bullet (0.2 kg), but *only* if it is moving at a velocity of at least 500 m/s. The danger represented by these two moving objects depends on *both* their mass and their velocity. **Momentum** is the name given to this property of a moving object which depends on both its *mass* and *velocity*.

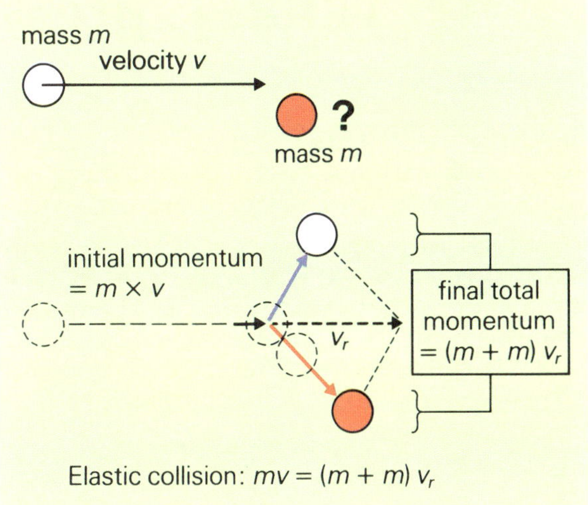

Drawing a velocity parallelogram confirms that momentum is conserved after an elastic collision.

Conserving momentum in elastic collisions

Elastic collisions are ones in which *no kinetic energy is changed* into other forms of energy. An elastic collision is an 'ideal' situation – usually friction, heat and sound waste some of the kinetic energy transferred in the collision.

However, the collision of two snooker (or pool) balls is pretty close to an ideal elastic collision. In the collision, the momentum of each object will change, but the **total momentum** (of the balls' motion) remains the same *after* the impact. If Stephen Hendry wasn't so talented, he could use momentum calculations to plan his shots!

Because **inelastic collisions** are the norm, momentum is *rarely* completely conserved in most collisions. When you bounce a ball, it won't bounce back to the same height. The collision between the ball and the ground is inelastic – during the collision *some of the kinetic energy is changed* into other forms of energy . . . sound, energy to deform the ball and the ground, heat released after deformation, and so on.

*Modern cars have **crumple zones** – these are designed to make severe collisions very inelastic. Much energy is transferred into crumpling the front of the car – so momentum is not conserved, and there is less chance of you hitting the screen.*

Belt up!

So what happens when momentum is (more or less) conserved? If you bump into an object either it will move – or you will bounce off it! One dangerous aspect of conserving momentum occurs in car crashes. On collision, any objects in the car that are free to carry on moving, will *continue moving* in order to conserve momentum. This could include you – unless you are 'strapped in' with seat belts stopping you from smashing into the windscreen (or back of seats).

1 Some friends cycled to the coast 60 km away. They travelled 20 km in 72 mins then rested for 20 mins. They completed the journey in 148 mins, including another rest of 40 mins. What was their average speed:

a while they were cycling?
b over the whole journey?

2 Explain why it takes so long to pass a cyclist cycling at 5 m/s, if you are cycling at 6 m/s.

3 An aircraft is flying at 160 km/hr due West across a wind. The wind is itself moving with a current of 40 km/hr towards the North. Find the **resultant velocity** of the aircraft. What would be the resultant velocity if the wind came instead from due West?

What is acceleration?

Acceleration changes velocity

You are cycling slowly along at 3 m/s and suddenly pedal hard for 10 seconds. What happens? You would go faster – but how much faster?

You would have provided an unbalanced force by pedalling hard – this force will have made you **accelerate** (*see 6.13*). Any *change in velocity* is called an acceleration. **Acceleration is a measure of the rate of change of velocity.** If your initial velocity (v) was 3 m/s, and 10 seconds later your final velocity was 13 m/s, the change in your velocity was simply (13−3)m/s = 10 m/s. But how quickly did that change occur?

$$\text{Acceleration} = \frac{\text{Change in velocity (m/s)}}{\text{Time taken for change (s)}}$$

$$\text{In this case, acceleration} = \frac{13-3\ \text{(m/s)}}{10\ \ \text{(s)}} = 1\,\text{m/s}^2$$

This means that after every second of hard pedalling, you would be travelling 1 m/s faster than before.

Acceleration does not always make things go faster; things *slow down* because of a negative acceleration (**deceleration**) since this will act to *decrease* the velocity.

Cyclists can often accelerate away faster than cars. Why do cars catch them up and soon leave them behind?

Recording velocity . . . and acceleration

Driving when tired can be very dangerous, so (by law) drivers of coaches and lorries are only allowed to drive for a certain time and distance in between rests. Their vehicles have to be fitted with **tachometers** which record (on tachographs) the vehicle's speed at all times throughout the journey. The tachograph is one example of a **velocity-time graph.**

To draw a velocity-time graph, you obviously need data on the velocities at different times; but drawing one highlights the changes in velocity over time – i.e. any periods of acceleration.

*The **tachograph** cannot lie – breaking the speed-limit or driving without a break are recorded for all to see. This driver had to slam on the brakes to do an emergency stop at one point. At what time did this occur? Why do you think much of the graph is a horizontal line at 50 km per hour?*

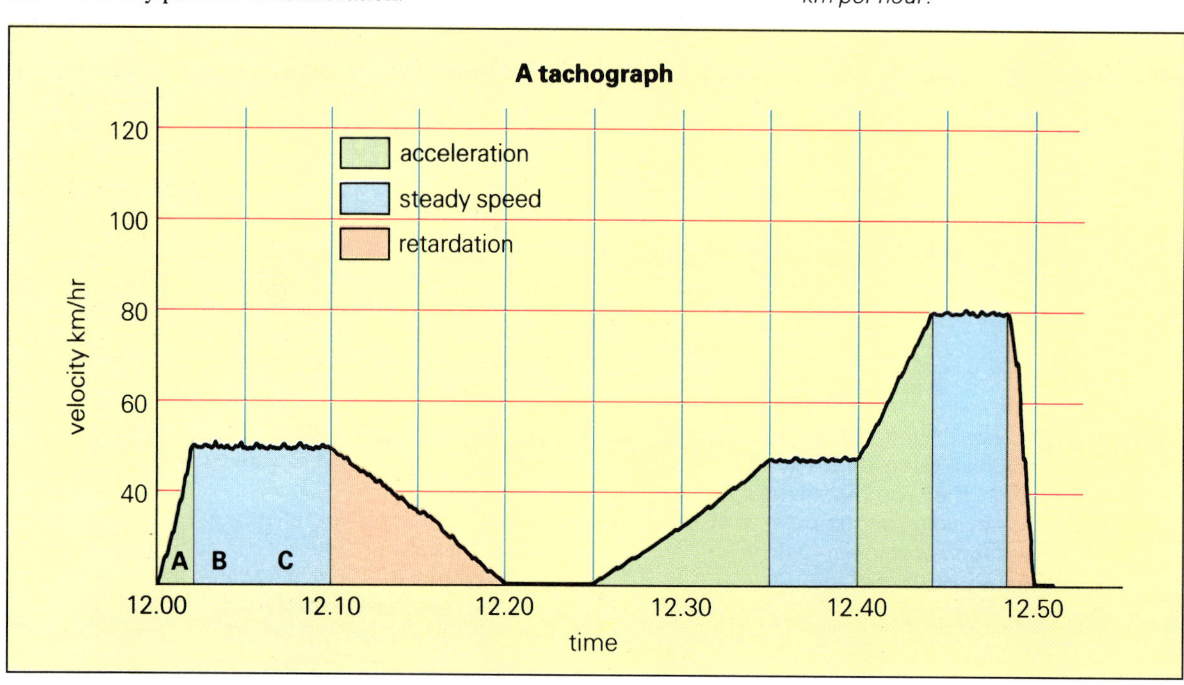

How far?

Most speedometers keep a record of the total distance travelled. The 'distance travelled' by a moving object can also be found from its velocity-time graph.

$$\text{Since velocity} = \frac{\text{distance travelled (in one direction)}}{\text{time taken}} \quad (\textit{see 6.11})$$

$$\text{then velocity} \times \begin{matrix}\text{time}\\ \text{taken}\end{matrix} = \begin{matrix}\text{distance travelled}\\ \text{(in one direction)}\end{matrix}$$

The **area under a velocity-time graph** represents *velocity × time*, and so it also **represents the distance travelled.**

Acceleration due to gravity

You know that before something falls, it is not moving – but once it falls, it moves quickly. There must have been an *acceleration* to cause this change in velocity. But what causes the acceleration? When falling, do heavy things accelerate faster than light things?

About 2300 years ago, a Greek philosopher called Aristotle suggested that heavy things had gravity, and light things had levity. He thought that heavy things with a lot of gravity fell faster than light things. Nobody came up with a clear alternative for a long time. Then in the sixteenth century, an Italian scientist called Galileo carried out an experiment which proved that light objects fall just as fast as heavy ones: he dropped cannon balls of the same size but different weights off the top of the leaning tower of Pisa!

Time after release	Velocity	Distance fallen each second
0 sec	0 m/s	0 m
1 sec	10 m/s	5 m
2 sec	20 m/s	15 m
3 sec	30 m/s	25 m

= constant acceleration due to gravity (approximately 10 m/s^2)

The longer an object falls, the faster and faster it falls – because it undergoes a ***constant acceleration due to gravity (g).***

Velocity *(height of graph),* ***acceleration*** *(slope) and* ***distance travelled*** *(area under graph) – all are revealed by a velocity–time graph.*

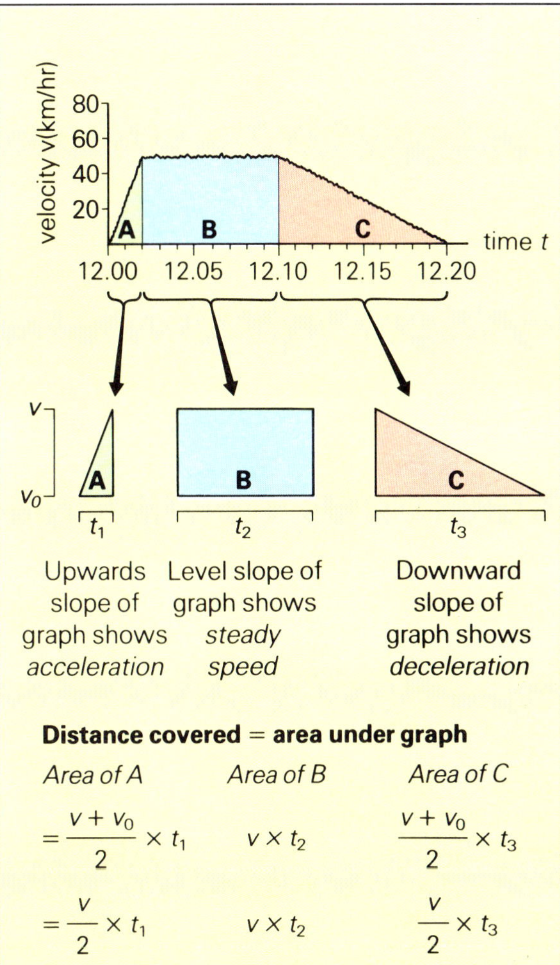

Thanks to Galileo challenging the old ideas, other scientists began to investigate gravity more fully. Nowadays, we know that any object falling freely is accelerated by gravity at a rate of **9.8 m/s^2**. The symbol g is used to represent this **acceleration due to gravity**, and it arises due to the force of attraction which exists between any object and the Earth.

1 A bus accelerated for 10 seconds until it reached a speed of 20 m/s. It carried on at that speed for 5 minutes – but braked suddenly, stopping in just 2 seconds.

- **a** plot a velocity-time graph for this journey
- **b** what was the acceleration:
  - **i** at the start?
  - **ii** at the end?
- **c** how far did the bus travel?

2 Find out more about Galileo. What other scientific achievements was he responsible for? Why was he placed under 'house-arrest' in later life?

6.13 Forcing a change

Force and acceleration

An unbalanced force makes things move by accelerating them in the direction of the force. The **rate of acceleration** depends upon the *force applied* and the *mass of the object* being moved.

Force (N) = mass (kg) × acceleration (m/s^2)

$$\frac{\text{Force}}{\text{mass}} = \text{acceleration}$$

You can pedal a bike faster than you can push a car along. The force you apply to each is more or less the same, but your force creates a *greater* acceleration when acting on the *lighter* mass.

Which one will give the greatest acceleration?

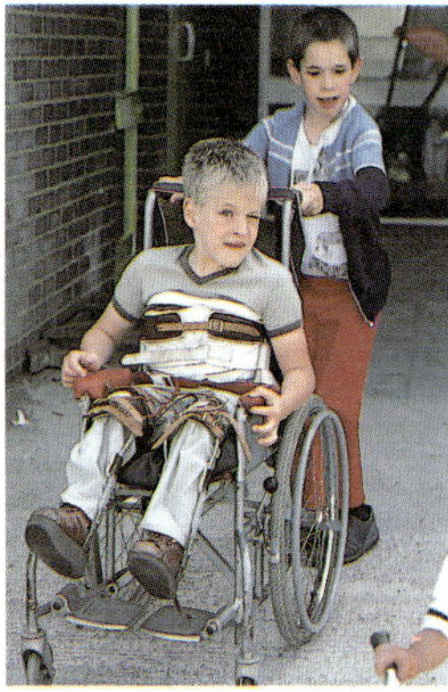

Force and deceleration

All vehicles have a **braking system** to stop them moving. But the brakes can only exert a limited force to stop the wheels turning. This force will create a negative acceleration (deceleration), slowing the car. Because the car's *maximum* braking force cannot be increased, although it will decelerate a *small* mass fairly *quickly*, it will only decelerate a *large* mass *slowly*. Drivers need to remember that the mass of their vehicle will affect the rate at which they can stop moving!

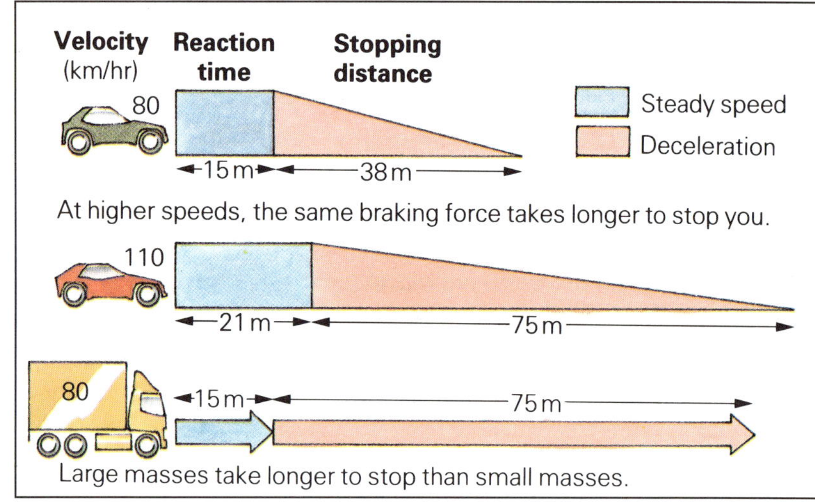

Stopping distances

Speed also affects **stopping distances**. The *faster* a car is travelling, the *greater* the change in velocity needed to stop the car. The maximum braking force will only stop the car at a certain rate. This means that, when travelling fast, it will take more time to stop. In this longer 'stopping' time, the car will travel further before stopping than would a slower car.

At high speeds "only a fool breaks the 2-second rule". Keep a gap of 2 seconds travelling time behind the vehicle in front . . . and you have more chance of stopping in an emergency!

If there were no resistance forces, your first few pushes would keep you going forever!

Conflicting forces

Many forces act against objects which are accelerating – frictional forces, including air resistance. Depending on their size, the combined **'resistance' forces (R)** can *reduce* the acceleration of the object, or cancel it entirely – or even *decelerate* the object, stopping it completely!

The effect of resistance forces explains why you do not keep accelerating when you keep providing a force to the pedals of a bike. The 'resistance forces' build up as you go faster, and eventually they cancel out the force you apply to the pedals. Then you stop accelerating, and so your 'top' speed remains *constant*. If you apply less force to the pedals, the 'resistance forces' will even cause you to slow down!

Terminal velocity

Gravity causes 'free-fall' parachutists to accelerate towards the ground. As they fall faster, their resistance force (due to air resistance) increases rapidly. Once their deceleration (due to air resistance) *equals* their acceleration due to gravity, their falling speed remains constant. Unfortunately this **terminal velocity** is about 190 km per hour – so they could still hit the ground with deadly momentum! To prevent this mishap, they *increase* their air resistance even further by opening their parachutes. The extra deceleration (caused by the large air resistance of the parachute) slows them to *'only'* 25 km per hour (about 7 m/s). This *new* terminal velocity means they hit the ground at a fast running pace – not comfortable, but survivable.

Free-fall parachuting isn't dangerous or painful – it's only hitting the ground that is!

Movement under gravity

Gallileo showed that the *acceleration due to gravity is constant for all masses.* This holds true even when an object is moving sideways as it falls. Once, say, a stone is thrown from the hand, there is no longer a sideways force to create any further horizontal acceleration. So the only direction in which there is any acceleration is downwards – due to gravity.

At whatever angle you throw an object, it will follow a **parabolic path** as first the acceleration due to gravity causes a deceleration in any upward movement and then causes a familiar downward movement.

Because the acceleration due to gravity is constant, a sideways-thrown object falls at the same rate *as any other object.*

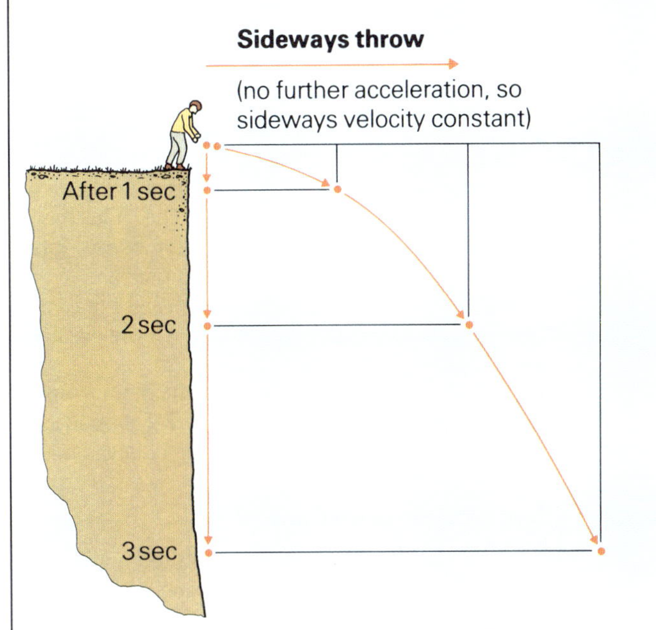

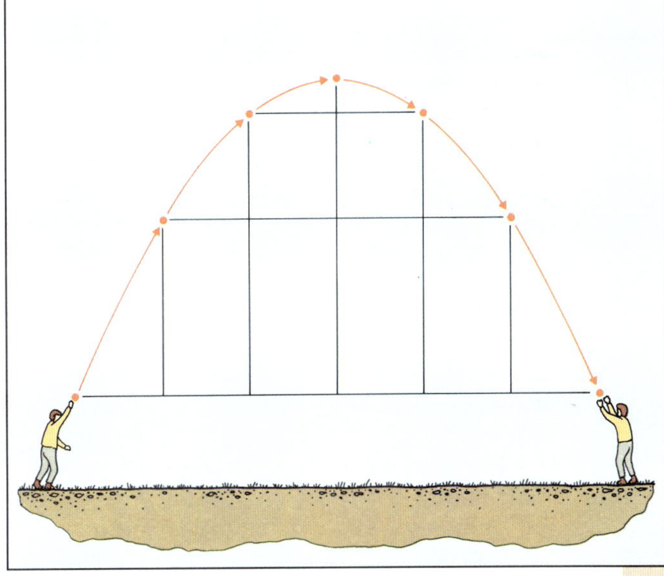

A ball thrown in the air follows a parabolic path. *The curve is the same for any sideways-moving object.*

1 If a cyclist with a mass of 120 kg pedals with a force of 480 N, calculate the initial acceleration. What would the cyclist's acceleration be at a time when the air resistance is:
a 300 N?
b 480 N?

2 Explain why it is advisable for drivers to keep a 2 second gap from the car in front, irrespective of the speed.

3 Streamlining vehicles reduces the amount of air resistance that they create. How can this help to make the vehicles have a faster 'top' speed?

4 **a** How would the graph of the stone's flight from the top of the cliff change if the stone was first thrown with a greater velocity
b How would that change the time of flight?

Motion in a circle

What causes it?

According to Newton's laws of motion, we know that a moving object will continue to move in a straight line *unless* it is acted upon by an unbalanced force (*see Spread 6.2*). If you try swinging round a small ball of plasticine from the end of a piece of string, when you let go, the ball will fly off in a straight line. This means that, before you let go, there must have been a force (provided by the *tension* in the string) which prevented the ball from moving in a straight line. Such a force is called a **centripetal force** – it always acts *towards the centre* of any circular motion.

Try slowly swinging round any small object from a piece of short string. What can you *feel* happen as you swing the object round faster and faster?

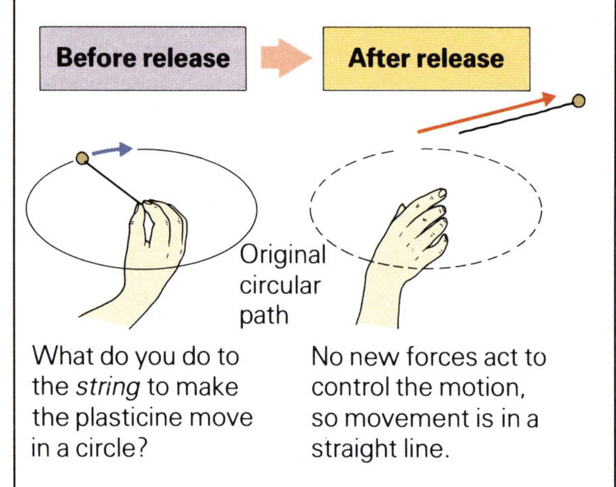

Before release
After release
Original circular path
What do you do to the *string* to make the plasticine move in a circle?
No new forces act to control the motion, so movement is in a straight line.

Effect of centripetal force

There are no other new significant forces now acting on such a swinging object, so the centripetal force must be an *unbalanced* force. This unbalanced force acting towards the centre must be continually accelerating the object towards the centre. Although this acceleration is not obvious, it becomes clearer if you imagine '*what if*. . .':

What would happen if the ball was free to move at *A*? It would move in a straight line to *B*!

The tension in the string provides a centripetal force which pulls the ball round to *C*. Like any acceleration, the acceleration due to a centripetal force causes a *change in the velocity* of an object – but centripetal acceleration does this by changing the *direction* of the velocity of an object. The end result is that the centripetal acceleration has moved the ball from *A* to *C* – in effect accelerating the ball in *towards the centre* from the path (*A* to *B*) which it would otherwise have followed.

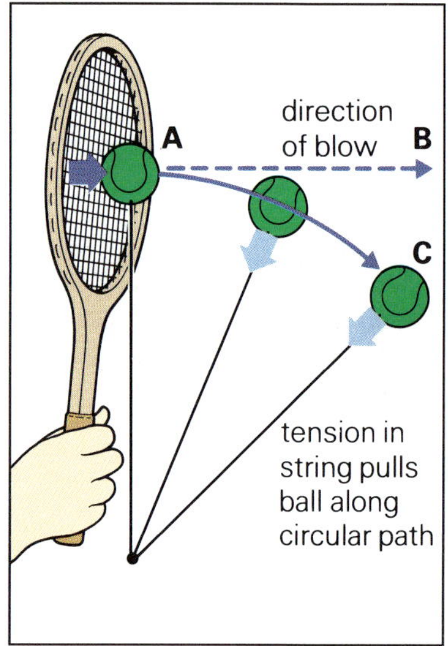

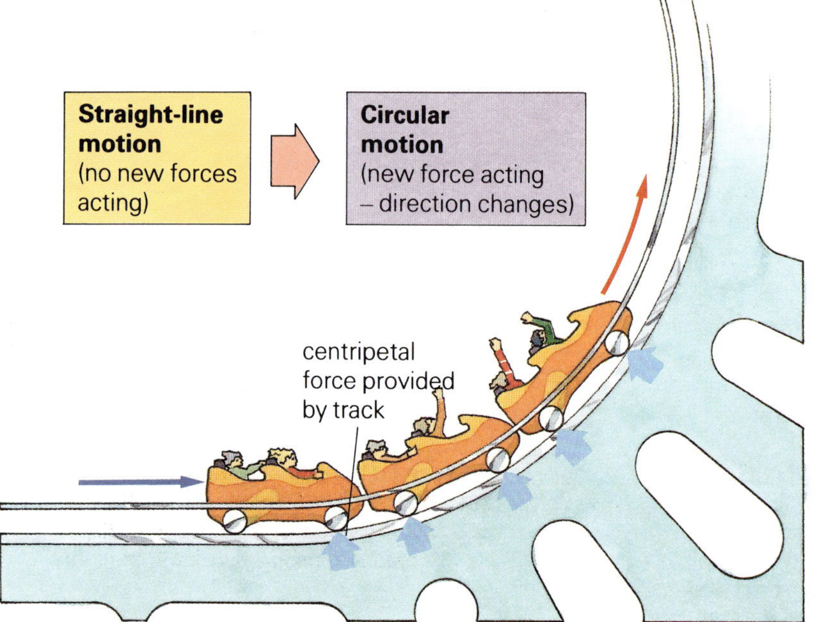

Going round the bend

A 'loop the loop' fairground ride is one example of how straight-line motion can be turned into a circular motion. The 'car' is free-wheeling – it has no power of its own to generate a force to move it along. As the car moves into the loop, the track forces the car to move round in a circle. This force is the centripetal force that sets up the circular motion around the loop.

You can feel this centripetal force in the way that the seat presses into you, firmly holding you in place and pushing on you in the direction of the centre of the loop.

Gravity makes the planets go round

When a satellite orbits the Earth, **gravity** provides the centripetal force that keeps the satellite moving around a circular orbit. When objects with immensely large masses are involved, gravity can act over very large distances. Gravity causes the Moon to keep orbiting the Earth. Gravitational attraction between the Sun and the Earth keeps the Earth orbiting around the Sun.

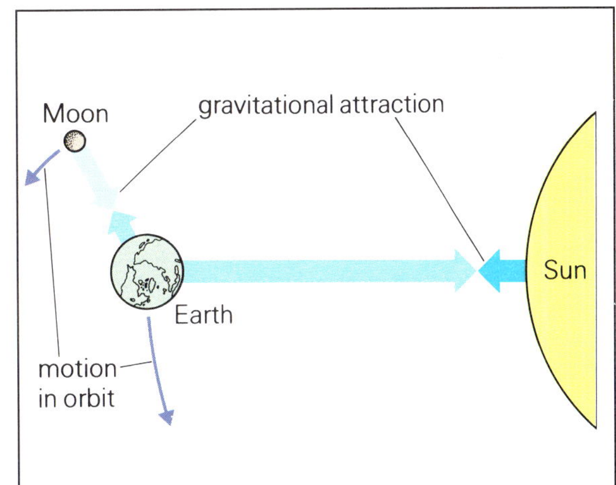

Getting away

It is possible to *overcome* the effects of gravity *provided that an object moves fast enough*. There are two options:

① provide a constant **acceleration** upwards (away from the centre of the Earth) that is greater than the downwards acceleration due to gravity;

or ② give an object a very large sideways **velocity**. Gravity will act as a centripetal force, changing the object's straight-line motion. However, if the velocity is very large, the change in the object's motion caused by the centripetal force will not be enough to make the object return all the way to Earth.

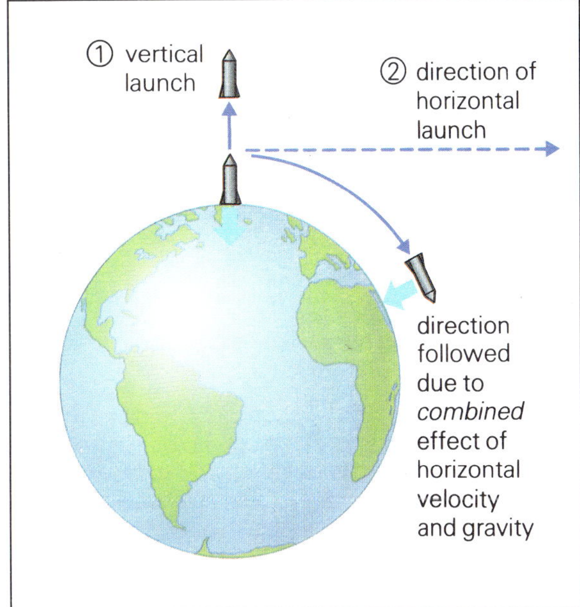

Option ① requires a rocket to provide an acceleration greater than gravity itself. Option ② only requires a suitable acceleration to create the large sideways velocity – gravity is not being directly opposed as in option ①.

The velocity needed to escape the gravity of a planet in this way is called the **escape velocity**. It depends on the square root of both the *mass* and the *radius* of the planet.

	Compared to Earth				Escape velocity (km/s)
	Gravity	Radius (R)	Mass (M)	$\sqrt{\frac{M}{R}}$	
Earth	1	1	1	1	**11.2**
Moon	0.17	0.27	0.01	0.2	**2.2**
Mars	0.38	0.53	0.11	0.5	**5.6**
Saturn	1.00	9.06	95.2	3.2	**35.8**
Jupiter	2.60	10.78	318.4	5.4	?

1 **a** Write down five examples of straight-line motion changing to circular motion.
b Try to suggest what provides the centripetal force in each example.

2 **a** Write down five examples of circular motion changing to straight-line motion.
b Try to suggest what provides the centripetal force in each example.

3 On a 'loop-the-loop' ride, if the car keeps moving do you think you need straps to keep you in place? Why?

4 Draw a graph of √(M/R) against escape velocity for the planets in the table above. What is the escape velocity on Jupiter?

6.15 Controlling the machine

In control?

Even very simple machines need to have some kind of **control** – to control their speed; to stop them overheating, breaking up etc. If you use a hammer to hit a nail, *you* are the control centre: you can change the direction of each hit or stop hitting, as necessary. On your bicycle, you pedal faster or brake as necessary. In semi- or fully-automatic machines, the control processes have to be *part* of the machine. The more complex the machine, the more parts have to be controlled and kept in step with each other.

*Watt's steam engine used **control rods** and **valves** to control the direction in which steam moved the piston.*

Keeping in step

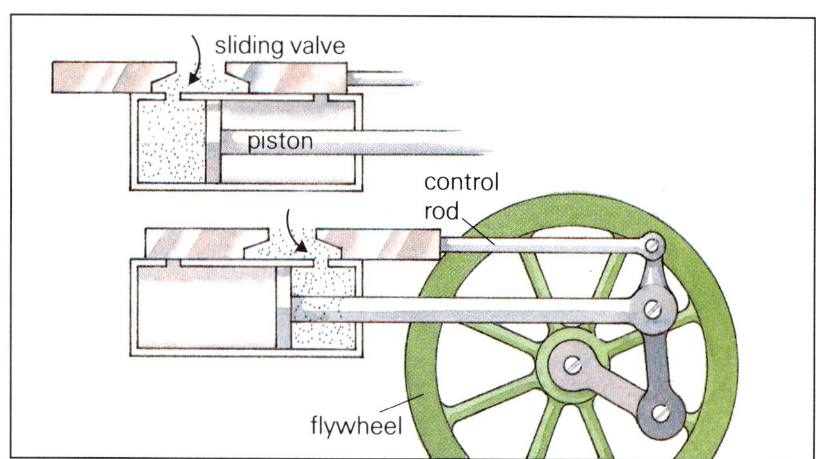

James Watt designed an early **steam engine** which used the backward and forward motion of a piston under pressure to turn a driving wheel by means of a crank. In this machine **steam** is pushed through a sliding valve into each end of the cylinder containing the **piston**. But movement of the sliding valve always has to be *in step* with the piston movement, no matter how fast it goes. As the piston is pushed to one end of the cylinder, the valve has to move to that end to let in the steam to push the piston back again.

The faster the piston goes backwards and forwards, the faster the wheel is turned. So, to keep the valve in step with the piston, another **crank** on the wheel is used to move a **control rod** backwards and forwards, which moves the sliding valve. In this way the faster the pistons go, the faster the wheel is turned, the faster the valve is moved, and so on.

Feedback and control: mechanically . . .

It is also necessary to **regulate** (control) the *speed* of a machine like the steam engine. Otherwise, it could go faster and faster and then overheat and break up. Regulating can be done by a person constantly controlling the amount of energy available – in the steam engine, this would be the amount of coal (**fuel**) shovelled in – or it can be done automatically. In factories, it is better to have the machine's speed controlled automatically. Automatic systems need some sort of **sensor**, from which a signal can be used to **feed back** the information to a controlling system.

Much of the complexity of large machines comes from the control systems regulating the machine, and linking all the moving parts together. The sort of control system often used on a steam engine is called a **governor**. A governor has two or more heavy masses which rotate as the engine turns. As the engine goes faster the spin on the governor causes the masses to swing out in a larger circle. As they do so they lift up the valve, which then closes off the steam to prevent the engine from going faster.

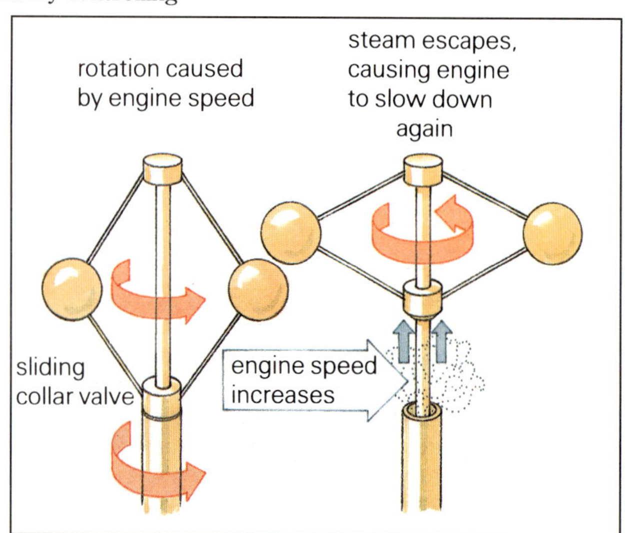

. . . and electrically

Many machines used today are powered by **electrical energy** and so an electrical system of feedback and control is used. These systems often use some form of **logic gate** in which an electrical **input signal** from a sensor causes the gate to produce an **output signal**. This output signal is used to control the machine. The **sensor** provides the signal from the 'real' world and this feeds back data about how the system is operating. This data is used to control the original operation within its set limits. A complicated computerised machine can operate with many different sensors and feedback systems at once.

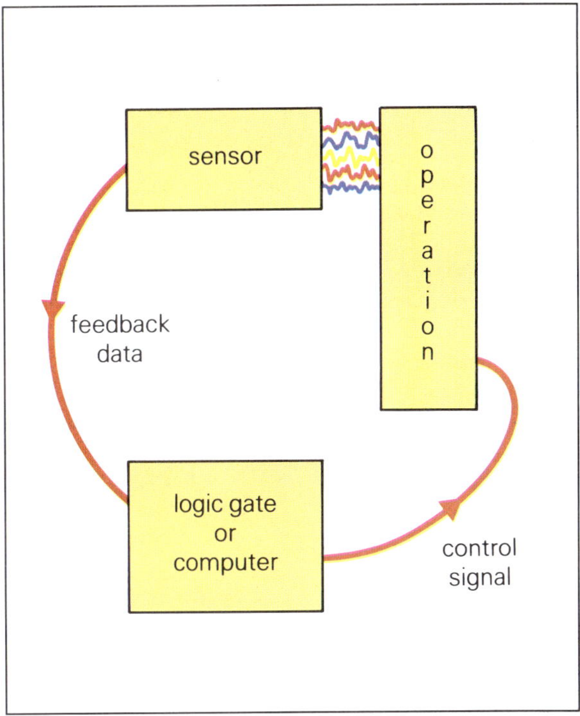

Paper thin

In the final stages of industrial paper making, a pulp (of fibres and water) is squeezed between two rollers. The *more pulp* that is released by a hopper valve in the machine, *the thicker the paper* formed by the rollers. Fifty years ago the thickness of the paper being made by machines was tested by cutting off sheets and weighing them. (Paper is still graded by its weight). This had to be done manually – by hand – regularly, to ensure that the right weight of paper was being made.

Nowadays, the whole process is controlled automatically using the **radioactive properties** of a material. When **beta rays** pass through a material, some are absorbed. The *thicker* the material, the more the rays are absorbed and so the electrical signal they generate is *weaker*.

If the paper being made is thicker than required, then it will absorb more of the rays, so giving a weaker signal. The computer will detect the difference and will send a signal to close the hopper valve, so less pulp will be released. How would the system work if the paper is too thin?

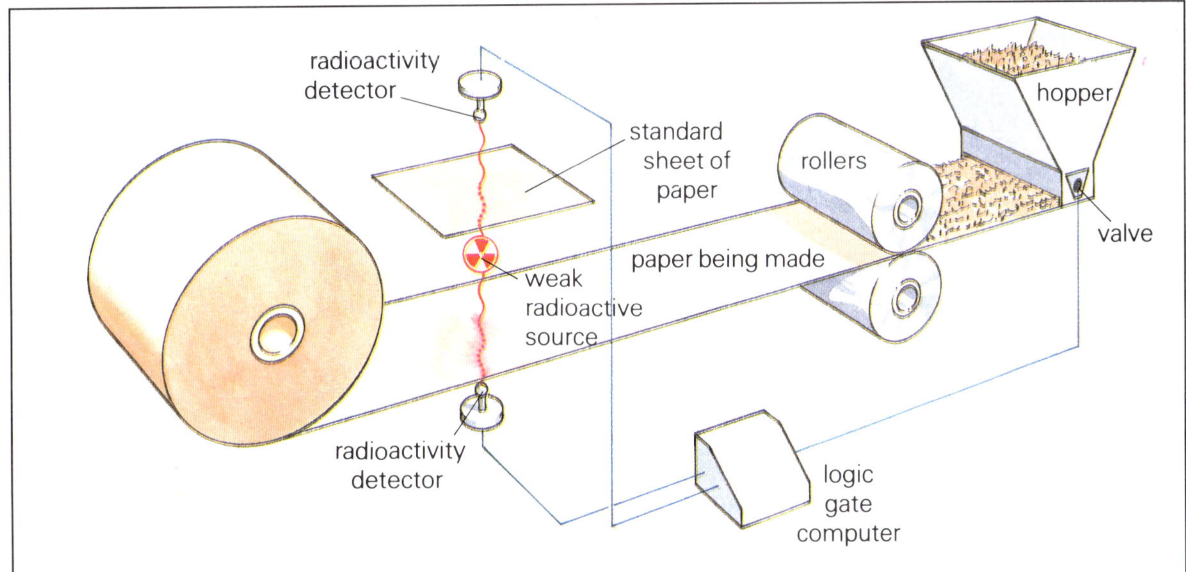

1 Do some research to find out how the valves in a car engine are kept in step with the pistons.

2 An electric cooker has to be kept at a set temperature. Explain how the signal from a heat sensor might be used to control the cooker.

3 As packets of soap powder are filled they pass down a conveyor belt where they are checked to ensure that they are full up to a certain level. Devise an automatic system that can detect partly filled packets and remove them.

Index

For additional information, see the following modules:

1 Energy
11 Nuclear Power and Electricity

Photo acknowledgements

These refer to spread number and, where appropriate, the photo order:

B. & C. Alexander *6.8/1;* Aviation Picture Library (J.A. Brown) *6.7;* GeoScientific Features *6.1/1;* Sally & Richard Greenhill *6.3, 6.5, 6.9, 6.12, 6.13/1, 6.13/2, 6.13/3;* Trevor Hill *6.8/2;* MIRA *6.11/2;* Quadrant Picture Library *6.11/1;* Science Photo Library *6.1/2;* Sporting Pics *6.13/4.*

Picture Researcher: Jennifer Johnson

7 WAVES, ENERGY AND COMMUNICATION

Waves of many different kinds carry energy and information from one place to another. Light and sound waves, for example, bring information about the world around us to our eyes and ears. These and many other waves are used to transfer information in modern communication systems. This module looks at the properties of the different waves, how we use these waves today, and how they affect our lives.

Relevant National Curriculum Attainment Target: (11), 12, (13), 14, 15

7.1 Waves and energy

Energy on the move

These pictures show different types of **waves**. They are all carrying energy on the move. We can use the energy carried by waves to do all sorts of jobs – communicate, generate electricity, move mechanical parts. You can sometimes see waves, like water waves. Other forms of wave motion (such as radio and sound waves) are invisible. But *every wave form carries energy* of some sort from one place to another.

How many different types of waves can you think of?

Water waves are fun – but they carry a huge amount of energy.

In a microwave oven you can cook food in minutes using the energy carried in the waves.

Sound waves carry 'the sound of music' from instruments and voices to your ears.

Using waves

Waves have certain properties. They behave in a characteristic way. The fact that waves are **reflected** is used in fibre optics to enable you to see inside a person's body. **Light waves** are first guided down glass fibres in a tube. If the tube is then placed inside a person's body the light can be reflected back up along *another* optical fibre so you can see inside – from outside!

Radio waves keep us in touch with each other.

Microwaves are waves that are easily reflected by solid or metal objects, but are *absorbed* by water to produce heat energy. In a microwave **oven** when the microwaves hit the food, the water in it becomes hot. This in turn heats up the rest of the food matter very quickly. Microwaves are also used in **radar** systems to detect other aircraft. The waves are beamed out from a source, hit the other aircraft, are reflected back, and are received back at the source – almost immediately!

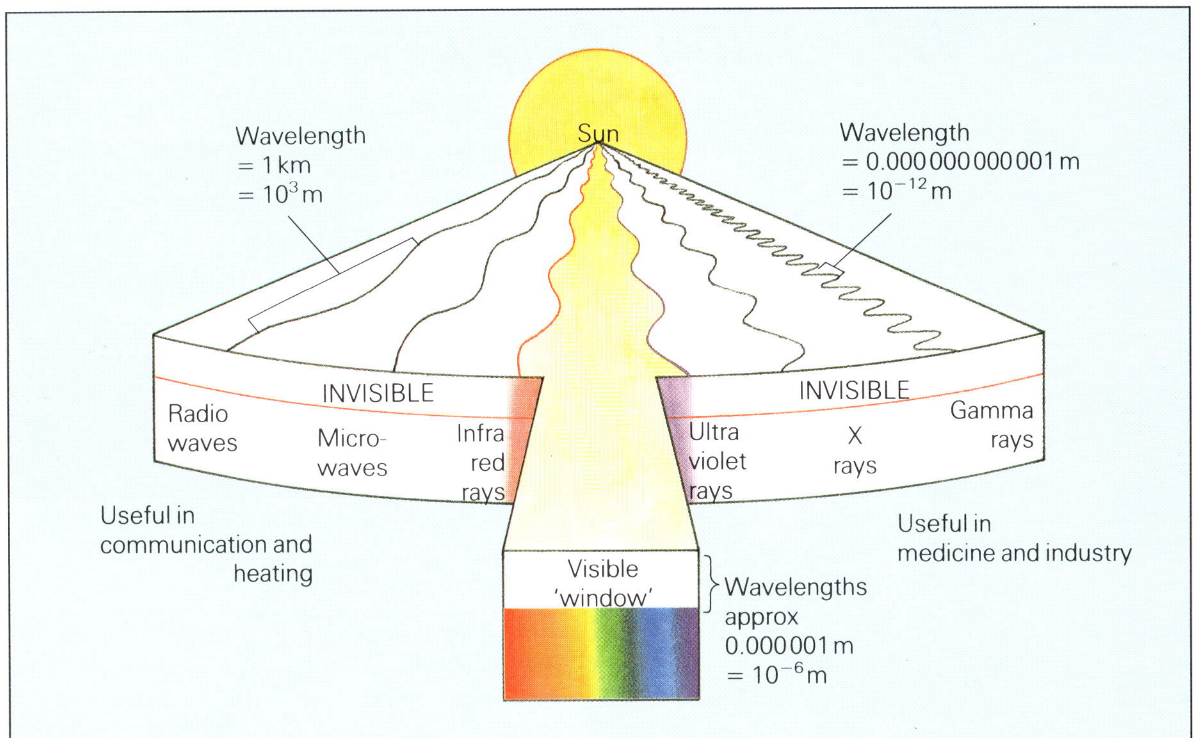

The electromagnetic spectrum – a family of waves all with different wavelengths.

Energy to live

We need a constant supply of energy to live. All of this energy is supplied by the sun and most of it is carried by a group of waves. Although *all* these waves travel at the same speed of 300 000 000 metres per second (**the speed of light**), there are different types of wave within the group. Waves of a particular type have a similar **wavelength** – a similar distance between each set of peaks (or crests) of a wave. Waves of different types have different wavelengths. The different types in the group make up the **electromagnetic spectrum**. When these waves reach the Earth, we notice their effects even though we cannot see them.

A spectrum of difference

The invisible **infra red** energy part of the electromagnetic spectrum provides us with heat energy that not only keeps us warm, but also powers the weather systems of the whole planet. The energy heats the oceans and land, and consequently winds are produced due to the movement of hot air rising from these heated areas (*see 7.2*). We can also collect some of this energy directly using solar panels or even solar cells to heat our homes.

Visible light is part of the electromagnetic spectrum. Light energy from the sun bounces off objects – allowing you to *see* the world around you. Plants use light energy in **photosynthesis** to make food – so light from the sun is the ultimate source of energy for *all* living things.

The solar panels on this roof absorb infra-red light waves. The energy from these waves heats water for the house – reducing the need for electricity from the nuclear power station in the background.

1 Gamma rays are a very penetrating wave form. They can pass through several metres of concrete. Yet microwaves cannot pass through even thin layers of metal or solid materials. What property of each of the wave types in the electromagnetic spectrum is different and causes this variation? Can you explain why this might be?

YOU CAN READ MORE ABOUT PHOTOSYNTHESIS ON SPREADS 1.2, 4.6, 4.7.

Earth, wind and waves

The Earth's power house

The energy you need to do anything originally comes from the sun. On average, *every square metre* of the surface of the Earth receives 2 500 000 joules of energy *every second* from the sun, transmitted as various electromagnetic waves. That is enough energy, received by each square metre, to throw about 5 of you 1 kilometre in the air . . . every second! Some of this energy is trapped by plants to produce food through **photosynthesis.** Some of it is used directly to keep you, and other living creatures, warm. But much of the energy is used to heat the land and water, producing movement of warm air called **convection currents**. Heat energy is transferred in gases and liquids through convection. You notice the effect of these convection currents in air as **wind**. Wind is the movement of air from areas of large air masses (high pressure) to areas of smaller air masses (low pressure).

The energy in high winds and huge waves can be very destructive.

Wind energy

Water in oceans and seas covers about 2/3 of the Earth's surface. As winds pass over the surface of all this water a lot of the energy is transferred to the water. When this happens the water begins to move *up and down*. This energy and motion is passed on to surrounding areas of water across the surface of the water. The up and down movement of a single wave is transmitted across the water. (Think of sending a single up and down flick along a rope fixed at one end).

This kind of wave motion is called a **transverse wave motion** – the movement of the **particle vibration** (*up and down*) is at right angles to the overall direction of the **wave** (*across*).

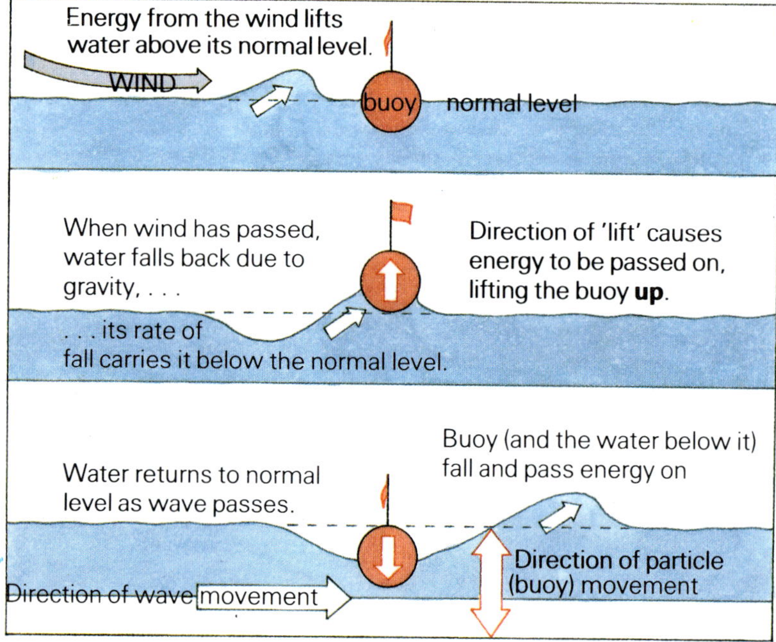

Spreading waves

Water is made of small particles which are held together by weak forces of attraction. Waves move across the surface of the water because of the way these particles are held together. As the wind causes some of the particles near the surface to move, they push and pull *other* particles nearby. *Some* of the energy from the wave is used up as the particles move, but *most* of it is passed on to other nearby particles as the wave moves on.

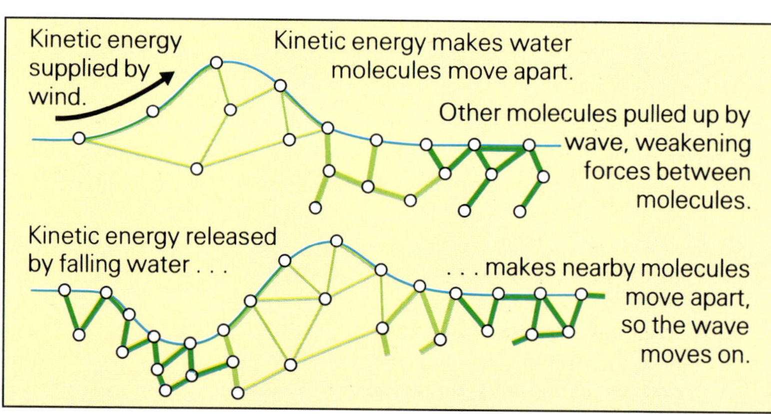

The individual particles move up and down, but the energy is passed along with the wave. 

YOU CAN READ MORE ABOUT CONVECTION ON SPREAD 1.13.

Controlling the power in waves

The rate at which energy hits the Earth's surface can be up to 2500 kilowatts (2 500 000 joules per second) per square metre. (This is equivalent to the power released when 250 sledgehammers hit the floor together.)

Large waves contain a lot of energy from this source and can be very powerful and damaging – able to demolish cliffs and reshape coastlines. Harbours have to be protected by solid walls built up from the seabed. But even these structures can be damaged by the constant pounding of water waves.

Sand and shingle beaches can absorb much of this potentially damaging energy. The energy in the wave moves the pebbles and grinds rocks together into smaller and smaller pieces while some of it is reflected back as waves heading out to sea or is converted into sound energy. If all the energy of a wave is channelled in these ways, then little damage will be done.

The land is protected from the energy of the water waves by rocks, pebbles and sand, all of which absorb the energy gradually.

Using wave energy

The energy in a water wave can be changed into useful forms such as mechanical or electrical energy. To generate electricty from water waves, the up and down motion of the water is used to turn an **electric generator**. There is probably enough energy in the waves around Britain to generate *half* our present consumption of electricity. The problem is to extract this energy efficiently and convert it into a usable form. Engineers have come up with several ideas – like the '**nodding duck**' system – to tap this energy source.

Different devices – like this 'nodding duck' mechanism – can be used to turn the rapid up-and-down motion of water waves into circular motion to turn a generator.

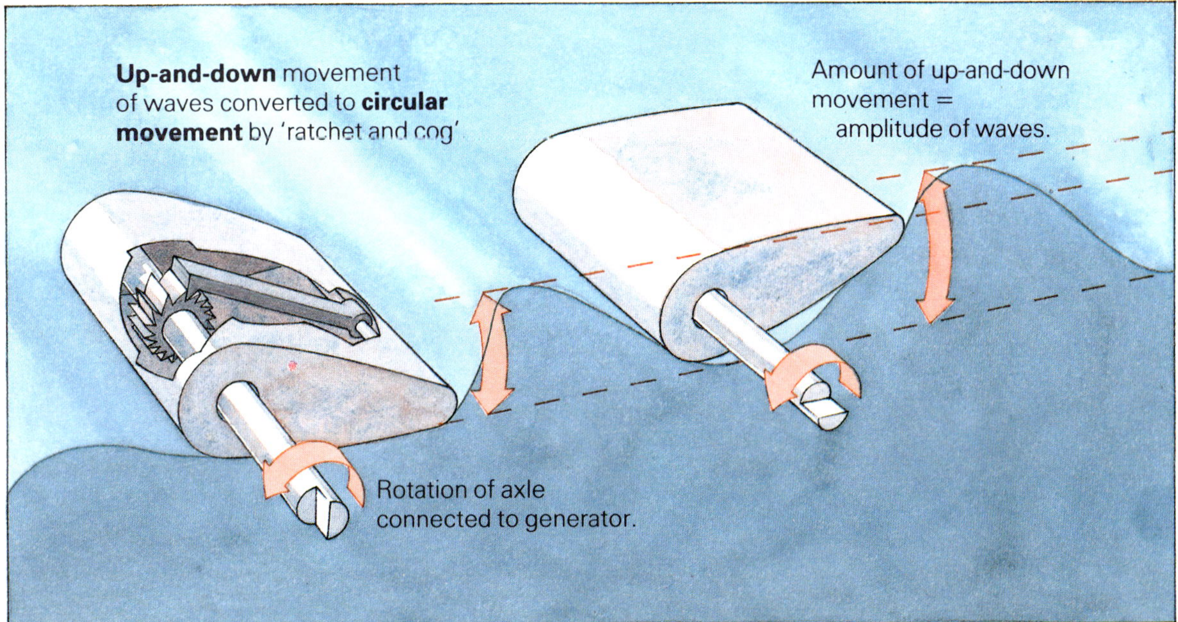

1 a How much energy from the sun hits the top of your head every second if you are out in the bright sun?
b What happens to this energy?

2 Water waves of up to 10 metres can be seen in the Atlantic Ocean. Where does the energy in water waves come from?

3 Explain how the beach in the picture above protects the town from damage by heavy seas and high waves.

4 The sea moves in two ways – by waves and by tides. **Tides** slowly raise and lower the 'normal level' of the water over a day. Design a way of changing this slow rise and fall into a rotary motion to generate electricity.

Producing and receiving sound

Good vibrations

Most sounds you hear, like speech or music, are a continuous flow of **sound energy**. Sounds are produced by **vibrations** which travel through a material or **medium** (like the air). You can feel the vibrations in the air produced by a guitar string if you get close enough (and if the sound is loud enough!). Waves of sound energy are generated by a vibrating object, like the guitar string. They spread out in all directions, carrying information about the kind of vibration that set them up. A *low* **pitch** sound produced by, say the skin of a bass drum vibrating, will have a *low* **frequency**. A *high* pitch sound wave, say produced by a whistle, will have a *high* frequency.

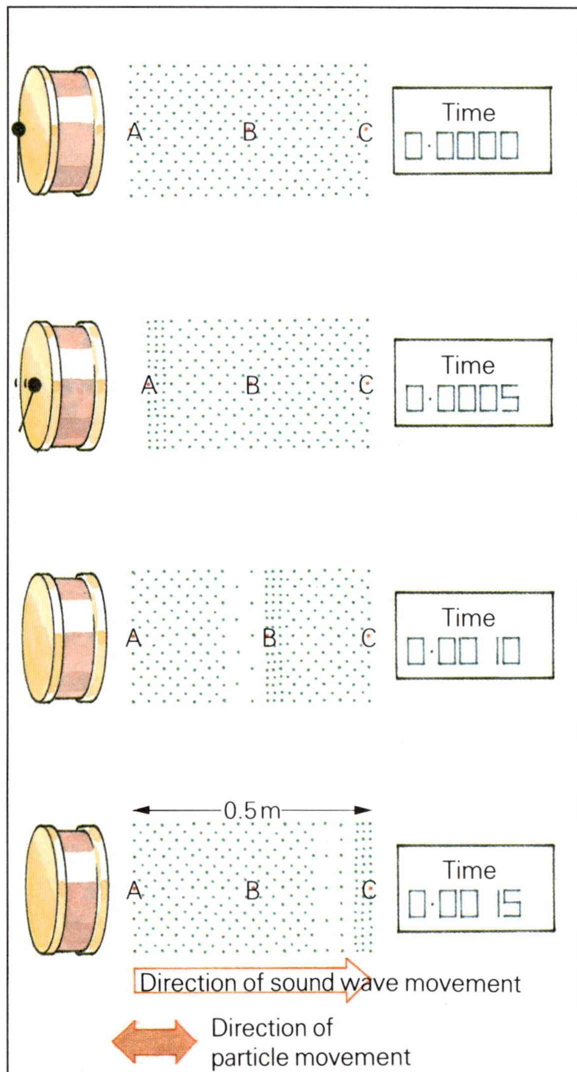

Can you see the longitudinal motion of the sound wave? What is happening to individual molecules like A, B and C?

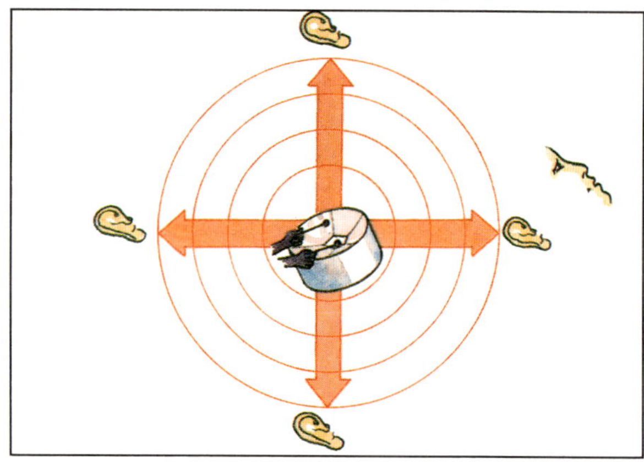

You can hear the noise from the drum beat wherever you stand. The waves of sound energy travel out in all directions.

Energy in the air

A sound wave is a series of pressure changes (caused by a vibrating source) which travel through a material. When any sound wave is produced, for example, by a loud bang on a drum, waves of energy travel in all directions away from the bang. The energy in the bang causes the particles (molecules) of air to move outwards and away. The energy is passed on to more and more molecules in the air. When each molecule moves outwards, it collides with others and passes on energy. It then moves back to its original position. This happens to all the molecules nearby as the energy from the bang is passed on. The molecules move forward and backwards regularly *along* the transmission of the path of energy in the wave. This motion of the molecules *along the same direction* in which the sound wave is travelling is called **longitudinal motion.**

If there are no molecules to pass on the energy then sound cannot be carried. In other words, sound needs a medium in which to travel.

The speed of sound

The speed of any sound wave in air can be found by working out how far the wave travels in one second, since

$$\text{speed} = \frac{\text{distance (metres)}}{\text{time (seconds)}}.$$

Using the information from the diagram,

$$\text{speed} = \frac{0.5}{0.0015} = 333.3\,\text{m/s}.$$

The speed of sound in air is usually taken to be about 330 m/s.

Your ear as an amplifier

The energy from a sound source spreads out in all directions. Although the total amount of energy making up the sound is always the same, it is spread out over a large area. So only a small amount of this energy will 'hit' your ear. This energy causes a thin layer of skin – **the outer ear drum** – to vibrate backwards and forwards. This skin vibrates at a certain rate (frequency) – the same frequency as the original vibrating source of the sound. Inside the ear this vibration is **amplified** by three connecting bones (**hammer**, **anvil**, **stirrup**) which act like very delicate and very sensitive levers.

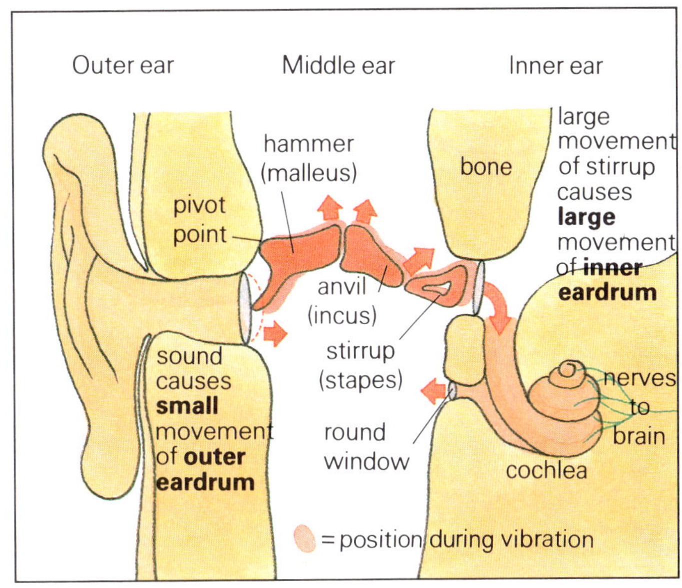

*The bones in the middle ear act as **levers** – turning the small movement at the outer ear drum into a larger movement. Tiny muscles on the stirrup can stiffen, reducing its movement – protecting the inner ear from destructive loud noise.*

Your ear as a detector

Once in the middle ear region, the vibration is then passed on to another layer of skin – the **inner ear drum**. The movement is passed along in fluid inside a coiled tube called the **cochlea.** Fluid in the outer tube ① of the cochlea is compressed as the inner ear drum (**oval window**) moves inwards due to pressure from the stirrup. This distortion is transmitted to the inner tube ② and then out to another part of the outer tube ③ causing the **round window** to bulge out. In the inner tube, the passing distortion moves small hairs which are attached to nerve cells. These send messages to your brain – carrying information about all the sound waves that have entered your ear.

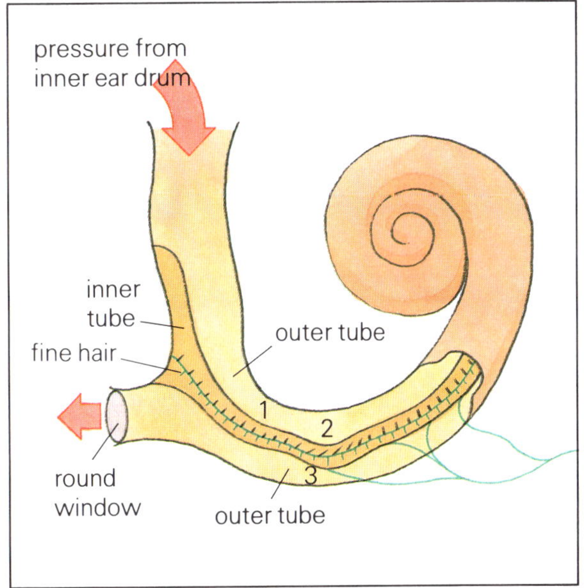

This drawing of a partly uncurled cochlea shows how it responds to sound waves by distorting as the pressure changes are transmitted along the fluid in its tubes.

A sensitive detector

Your ear is able to send messages to your brain that describe not only whether the sound waves have a lot of energy and movement (**loudness**) but also whether the sound has a high or low pitch (high or low frequency). A low pitch causes the tubes of the cochlea to distort near the start, while a high pitch causes distortion right in the middle of the cochlea spiral. If the amount of energy/movement is large, then a lot of cells will send a lot of messages – so the brain will register that the sound is loud. In this way your cochlea sorts out the different sounds and then sends the correct message to your brain.

1 Describe the passage of a sound wave from the vibration of a guitar string to receiving it in your ear.

2 Why is it difficult to hear a guitar being played if it is a long way off?

3 What do you think is vibrating in a whistle?

4 How does your ear help you to hear the sound of a pin dropping but also protect you against damage from very loud sounds?

5 Your brain must learn the difference between loud and quiet sounds and sounds with a high or low pitch. How does your ear help your brain to 'know' these differences?

Communicating sound

Passing sound messages

You can't usually hear someone whisper unless you are very close to them. But in St. Paul's Cathedral in London, there is a room called the '*Whispering Gallery*'. There you can hear a person whisper from the other side of the room! Sound waves from the person whispering can bounce or be **reflected** all the way round someone over the other side because of the shape of the room. When a sound wave hits something – like a wall – the particles of air (that carry the energy) are reflected carrying the energy in a new direction. This new direction can be *predicted* from the angle at which the sound wave first hit the surface.

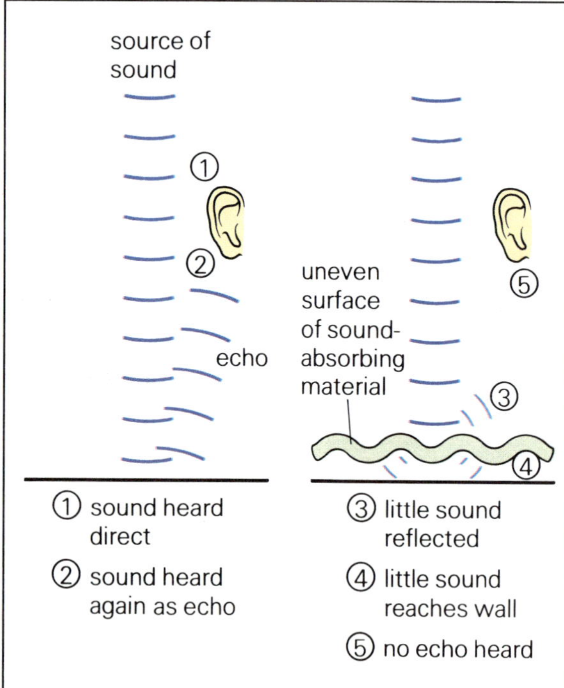

Curtains and other absorbent materials – like egg boxes – can be used to 'sound proof' a room.

Storing sound information

Through recording you can collect the sound produced by a group or singer and store it on a tape, record or compact disc. In this way sound messages are stored for use at any time. In the early days of recording sound, the sound energy was collected and stored by scratching a series of marks on a wax or plastic cylinder. The size and depth of the grooves made depended on the loudness of the original sound being recorded. With a loud sound, the size or **amplitude** of the sound wave is increased and so a greater amount of energy cuts a deeper groove in the plastic record cylinder.

Only sound waves travelling in certain directions can be heard by someone on the other side of the Whispering Gallery. The sound waves follow a series of reflections.

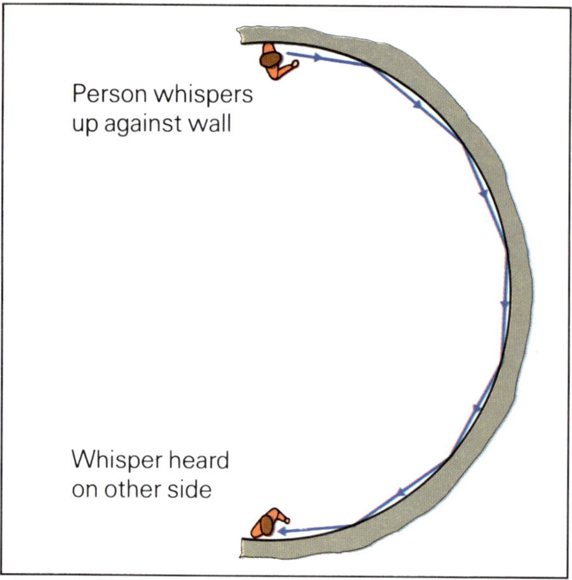

Trapping sound

Reflected sound may reach a listener *after* the sound has been heard. This repeat of a sound is called an **echo**. Sometimes echoes are a nuisance. In concert halls and recording studios, for example, the reflections interfere with the other sounds reaching the audience direct from the stage. The walls of rooms can be draped with cloth to reduce reflected sound waves. The cloth allows most of the sound energy to pass between its woven fibres – which move slightly, absorbing the sound energy as they do so. Once 'behind' the cloth, the small amount of sound that has passed right through is trapped between the cloth and the wall. In modern halls and recording studios the walls and ceilings are made of particular materials which absorb sound in a similar way to cloth.

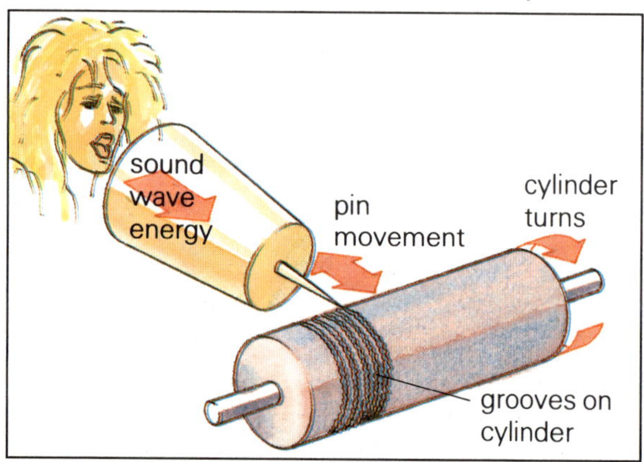

The energy from the singer's voice is being used to cut a pattern out on to a record cylinder.

Modern sound-storage systems

Nowadays when recording, **microphones** are used to change the sound energy from a voice or instrument into electrical energy. The movement of the particles of air carrying the energy is used to produce a small electrical current inside the microphone. This changing current passes along wires to be stored on, say, a tape. The changing electrical current produces a changing magnetic field which is stored as a **magnetic pattern** on the tape. For example, a loud sound will produce a larger electrical signal from the microphone. The larger the electrical signal, the stronger the magnetic pattern stored on the tape. When you play back the tape you get an exact copy of all the original sounds.

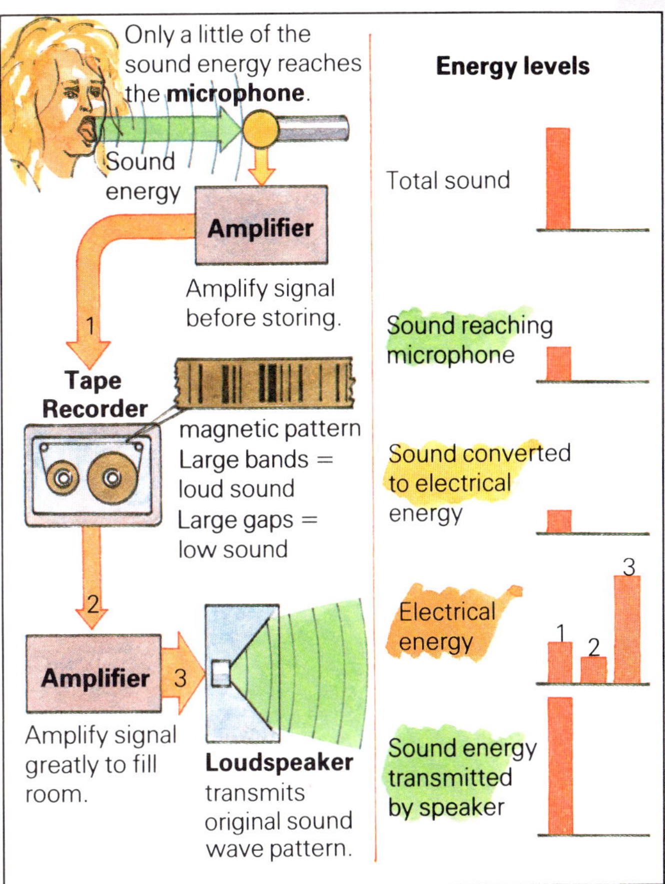

Sending out the sound

You may have a *hi-fi* system at home. It will be made up of an amplifier, speakers (loudspeakers) and a deck – tape or record. All this equipment is used to convert the stored original music on a tape or record back to sound energy which you can hear. The **amplifier** is used to increase the size or amplitude of the changing electrical signal generated from the magnetic pattern of the tape or the grooves of the record. The **loudspeakers** then change these electrical signals back into the original sound waves. When you play a tape you instantly hear the recorded music though, as you can see, this has gone through many processes before it reaches your ears.

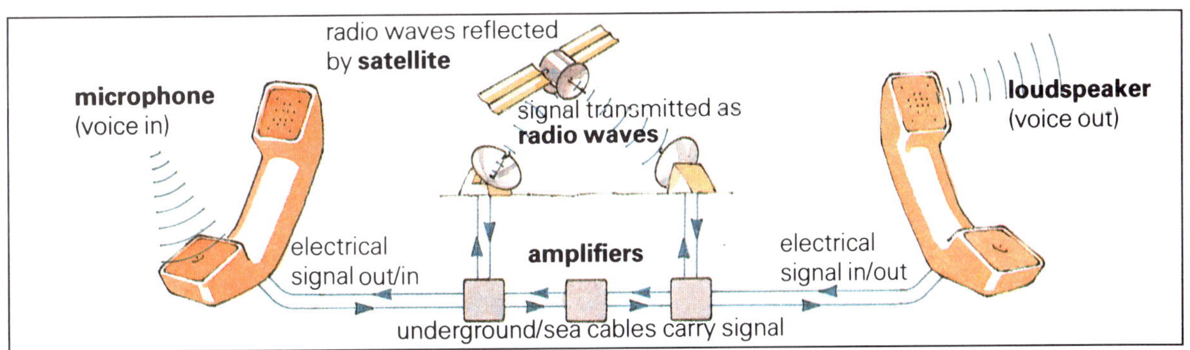

Messages carried by radio waves, transmitted by satellite, travel much faster than sound waves carried in electrical signals in the underground cables of the telephone system.

Sound communication

If you shouted loud enough could you talk to someone on the other side of the world? Even if you could produce enough energy the sound waves would hit a good many obstacles, and be reflected and dispersed. before getting very far. It would also take the sound of your voice 18 hours to travel through air across the world! But by using the telephone you can talk to nearly anyone, anywhere almost instantly – assuming they have a 'phone!

In the telephone system, the sound of your voice is changed into electrical signals by a microphone. These signals are sent along wires and sometimes also as radio waves. When they reach their destination, the signals are amplified and then changed back into sound waves (using a loud speaker) so that your voice is then heard.

1 What is an echo and how is it produced?

2 Sound information can be recorded in many ways for many uses. Explain one method of storing information carried in sound waves.

3 Why do you think it is expensive to telephone countries on the other side of the world?

Uses and abuses of sound

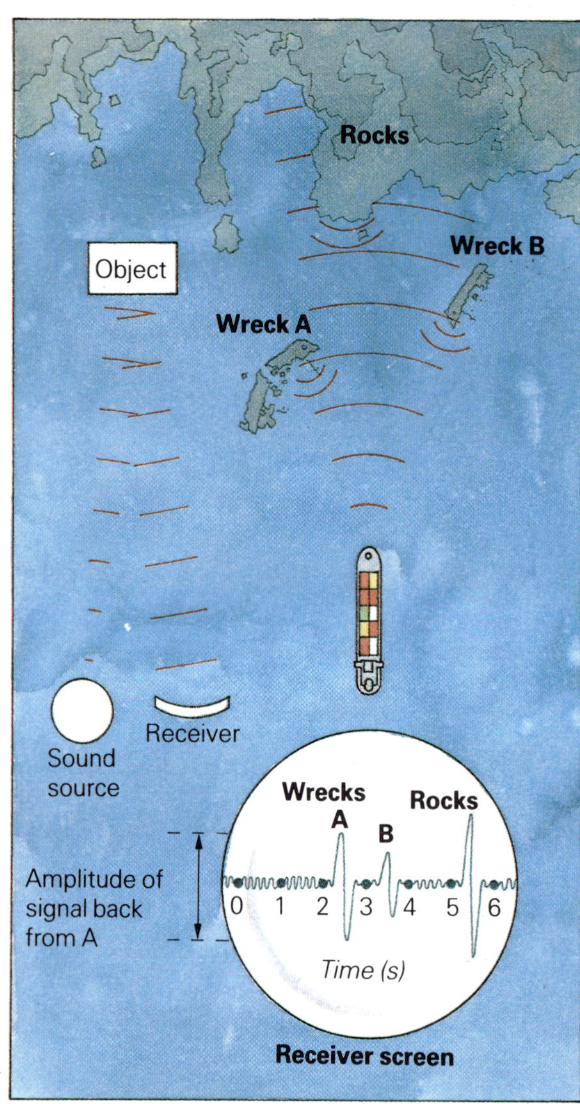

The sound wave is sent out and an echo is received back. The echoed wave produces a signal or movement along the oscilloscope. The position of the signal depends on how far away the object is. The size (amplitude) of the signal depends on how far away or how big the object is.

Water temperature (°C)	0	20	40	60	80
Speed of sound in water (m/s)	1596	1590	1580	1570	1556

Temperature (°C)	0	20	40	60	80
Density (g/cm^3)	0.99987	0.99823	0.99224	0.98324	0.97183

Look at the table of water temperature and density. Do you think their hypothesis is correct? Why?

Using echoes

Sound waves are used by submarines to help locate objects in the water, like rocks or mines, and find out how far away they are . . . pretty important if you can't see where you are going!

Beams of sound waves are 'fired' out into the water, and are reflected by objects in the path of the wave. These reflections (**echoes**) form pulses that can be received inside the submarine. The time between firing the beam and receiving the echo depends on the *speed* of the sound wave in water, and the *distance* of the object from the submarine. These pulses of sound energy can be picked up and shown on a screen (oscilloscope). The screen shows a bright dot moving across it. As it moves, the dot rises and falls for each pulse of reflected sound waves received. Measuring the distance of objects by receiving echoes is known as **echo-sounding**.

Sound waves travel at 1500 m/s in water. If the time taken (t) for an echo from an object to be received back is 2 seconds then since

$$\text{speed} = \frac{d}{t}$$, where d is the distance travelled,

$d = 1500 \times 2 = 3000$ metres.

The sound waves had to travel *to* the object and *back*. So the distance to the object from the submarine is

$3000/2 = 1500$ metres

Problems in the arctic

Echo-sounding is not a very accurate way of measuring distance. Scientists found that it appeared to take longer for a pulse to be received back in warm tropical waters than in cold waters. In an attempt to find out what was causing this difference, they did a number of experiments to find the speed of sound in cold, warm and hot water. The results of their investigations are shown in this table.

From the results they made the *hypothesis* that the temperature of the water caused the distances between the molecules of water to change. The separation between molecules of water, when the water is warm, is larger and so the energy in a sound wave is not passed on as quickly . . . so the sound wave travels more slowly in water as the temperature increases. If there are *no* molecules, such as in a **vacuum**, then *no* sound can travel at all!

YOU CAN READ MORE ABOUT SPEED, TIME AND DISTANCE ON SPREAD 6.12.

Sound scans

Sound waves and echoes can be used to 'see' inside your body. Just like in the submarine, a doctor can fire sound waves into a human body and use the reflections to produce an image of the internal organs. Sound scans use high frequency (short wavelength) **'ultrasonic'** sound waves. Flesh, bone and muscle absorb sound energy of normal frequencies (about 10 000 Hz) but higher energy sound waves (frequencies of 30 000–50 000 Hz) can pass through flesh. Any reflections are collected by electrical **transducers** that *change* sound energy into electrical energy. These electrical messages are used by computers to create images of the bones, muscle and flesh that reflected the sound.

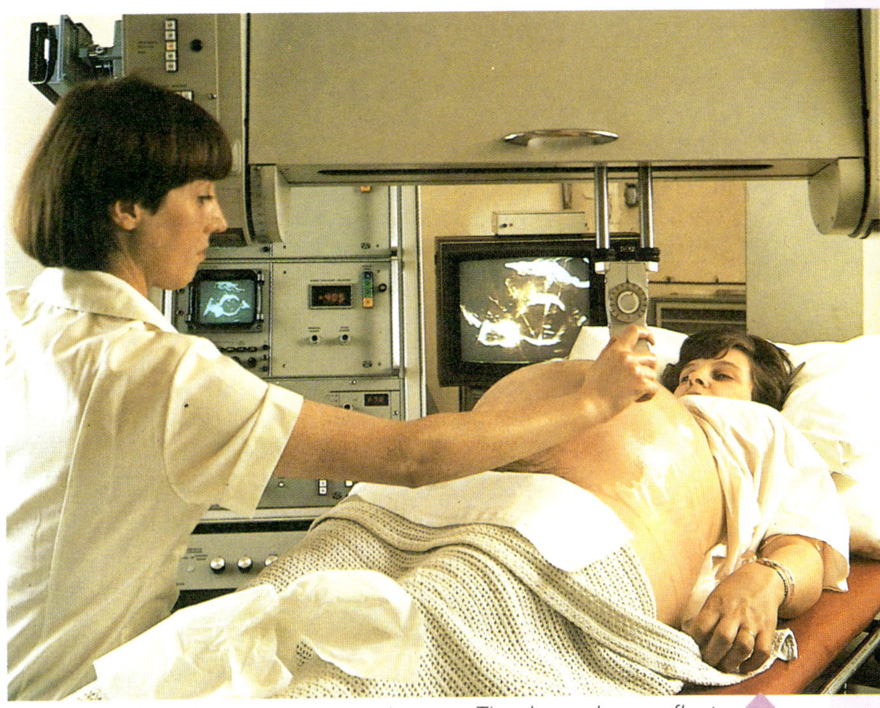

Bone, muscle and flesh reflect sound waves. The denser bone reflects more sound and produces a clearer image. You can see the baby quite clearly on the screen.

Noisy travelling

Sound energy can also be annoying or even dangerous. The inside of cars can become very noisy when different items inside begin to vibrate as the engine moves at different speeds. Some of the energy from the engine is passed through the different parts of a car in the form of mechanical **vibration**. Some of these parts are not always fixed, and can move a little; these parts will vibrate more easily at certain frequencies – they will **resonate**. If the vibration produced by the car engine matches this natural (**resonant**) frequency of a part, then it will begin to vibrate as well. The frequency at which each car part vibrates naturally (resonates) depends on the shape of the part and the material it is made from. Car parts are carefully designed and tested to make sure that they do not vibrate at frequencies that are annoying to passengers or drivers!

Car part	Resonant frequency (Hz– revs/second)
Short gear stick	200
Long gear stick	50
Window lever	300
door lock – If steel lever	75
door lock – If plastic lever	400

A car engine usually runs at about 3000 revs per minute. Which of these parts do you think will vibrate in resonance at normal speed?

1 **a** Use the time/sound trace on the opposite page to find the distance of the submarine from the wreck B.
b Why are the amplitudes of the three pulses different?

2 Use the information in the table opposite to estimate the speed of sound in arctic waters. You will need to explain how you have used the information.

3 Use the information in the table above to help explain why long gear sticks are not used much in modern cars.

4 Car manufacturers can alter the resonant frequency of the parts they use to make cars. Explain what you could do to alter the resonant frequency of a car part so that it did not vibrate at a certain frequency.

Energy from the sun

The Sun . . . centre of life

All the energy that we need to live is released by the Sun. Electromagnetic energy, produced in uncontrolled nuclear reactions in the Sun, passes across the vacuum of space to our planet. Unlike sound waves *all* the family of electromagnetic waves, including light, can pass across empty space. The speed of all of these waves is 300 000 000 m/s – they take about 8 minutes to reach us from the Sun. A part of the electromagnetic spectrum which is clearly important to all of us is visible light. **Light energy** – is detected by your eyes so that you can see the world about you.

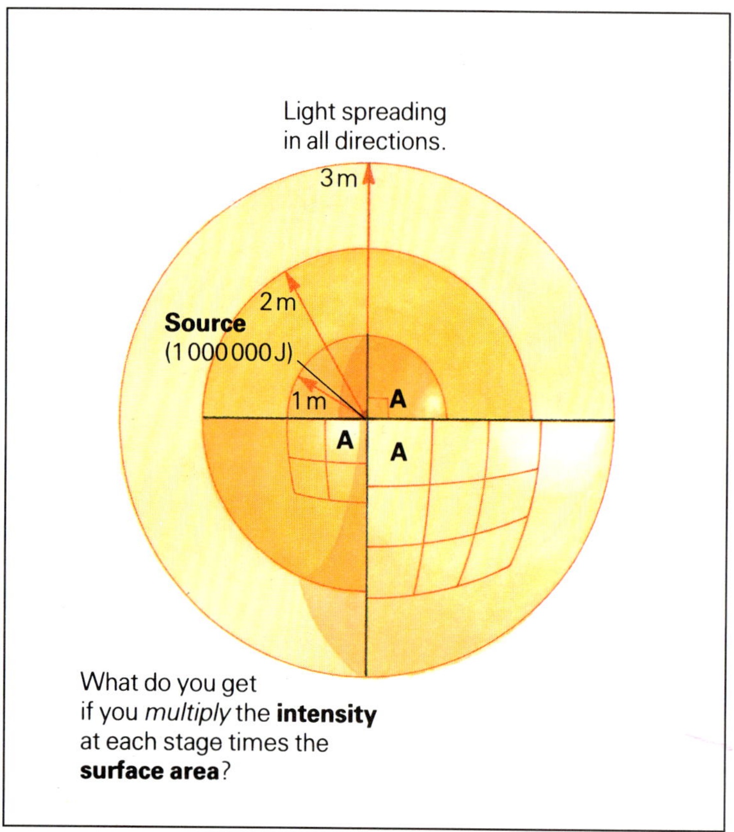

What do you think will happen to the intensity of the energy at a distance of 4 m from the light source?

Spreading energy

Like sound waves, light waves will spread out in all directions from a source. As the light wave spreads out, the total amount of energy carried in any one wave remains the same. As the wave spreads over an increasing area, the **intensity** of the energy – the amount of energy *per square metre of the wave surface* – decreases. In the same way, energy waves from the Sun spread out as they travel to the planets in the Solar System. Planets that are a long distance from the Sun receive little energy per square metre of their surface area.

On Pluto, the outermost planet of the Solar System, the energy received from the Sun is very small – not even enough to stop any atmospheric gases (like nitrogen) from solidifying!

Light cannot pass through an opaque object. The nature and position of shadows so formed is evidence that light travels in straight lines – why?

Making a shadow from light

Light waves naturally spread outward from their source. If light waves hit a solid object they are often stopped or absorbed. This produces a **shadow** on the other side of the object. Light waves always travel directly away from their source in perfectly straight lines. This means that the size of the shadow depends upon the size of the *object* and the size of the *light source*.

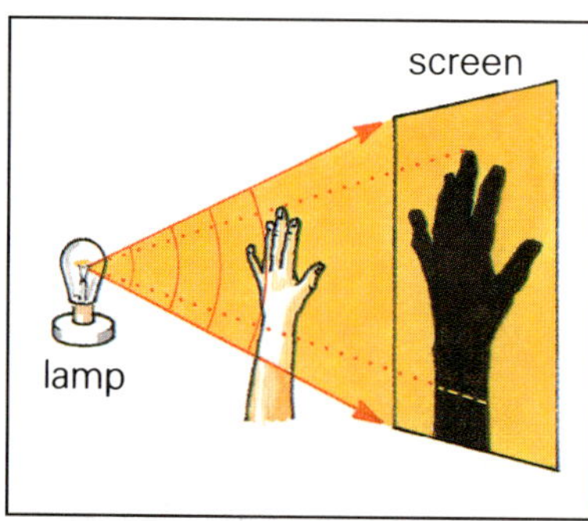

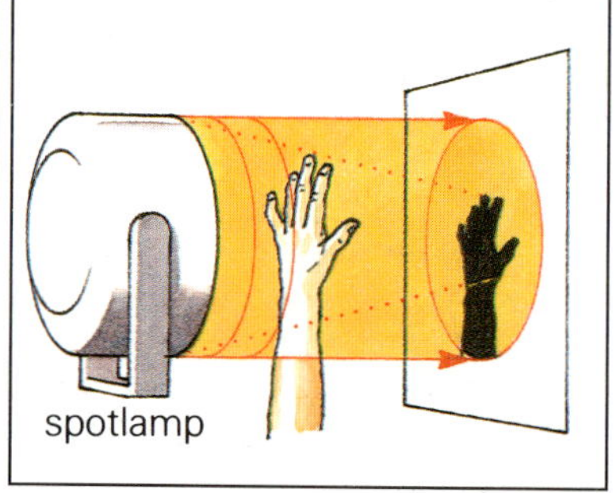

What would happen to the size of the shadow if the hands moved closer to the light, in each case?

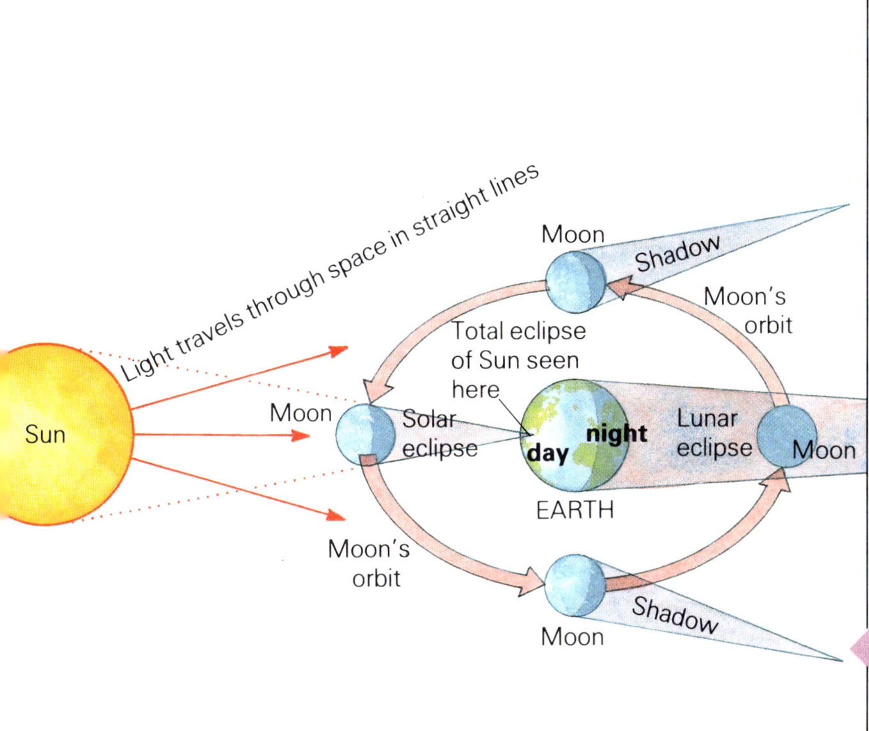

Shadows from the Moon

The Moon orbits Earth every 28 days and so it sometimes comes between Earth and the Sun. The Moon creates a shadow because it stops some of the sunlight from reaching the Earth. If the Moon is in the right place, the shadow is long enough (about 800 000 km) to block out all the Sun's light energy from reaching Earth – resulting in a total **eclipse** of the Sun. This means that the Sun cannot be seen at all for a short time at a particular position on Earth. However this happens very rarely because the orbits of the Earth and Moon are not in the same plane – they do not very often get in the same straight line with the Sun.

The size of the Sun is much greater than that of the Earth or Moon, so their shadows decrease in size.

Reflection and absorption of light allow you to see everything around you . . . . and read this book!

Light from the Moon

Light energy that strikes the surface of the Moon is not totally absorbed, some is **reflected** back into outer space. This reflected light enables you to see the Moon. Other planets also reflect light from the Sun. **Venus** has a thick cloud layer which reflects much of the Sun's light, making it the brightest planet in the night sky. You can only see objects around you because they too reflect the light of the Sun. Some objects, like planets and moons, are good at reflecting light while others are poor. Some objects reflect light in many directions at once – like the paper of this book!

Light waves from the sun

Some materials absorb the energy from visible light waves

Some materials reflect light waves. Light reflects in all directions from the irregular surface of the paper

1 What are the differences between sound waves and visible light waves?

2 Explain fully why the outermost planet of our Solar System receives very little energy from the Sun.

3 Explain **a)** how the Moon can produce an eclipse of the Sun.
b) how the Earth can produce an eclipse of the Moon.

4 The planet Jupiter also has a thick cloud layer. Explain why Venus appears so much brighter than Jupiter.

7.7 Looking at light

Reflecting light

Some materials can easily reflect the path of the energy of a light wave. Smooth surfaces of *polished metal* or glass *mirrors* are **good reflecting surfaces** – reflecting light waves in one direction. However, even such surfaces do not reflect all the energy of the light wave – some of the energy is still lost. When light passes through the glass of a mirror, a small amount of energy is absorbed. Constant reflection of a light wave will eventually result in all of the energy of the light wave being converted into other forms of energy (e.g. heat). When reflectors are made, they need to reflect as much of the energy of a light wave as possible. For example, the glass of a good mirror is made as thin as possible and the back surface is silvered. Other reflectors are made of highly polished metal.

Rays from each point on the flower are reflected at the mirror. When the reflected rays enter your eye they appear to come from a corresponding point on the image.

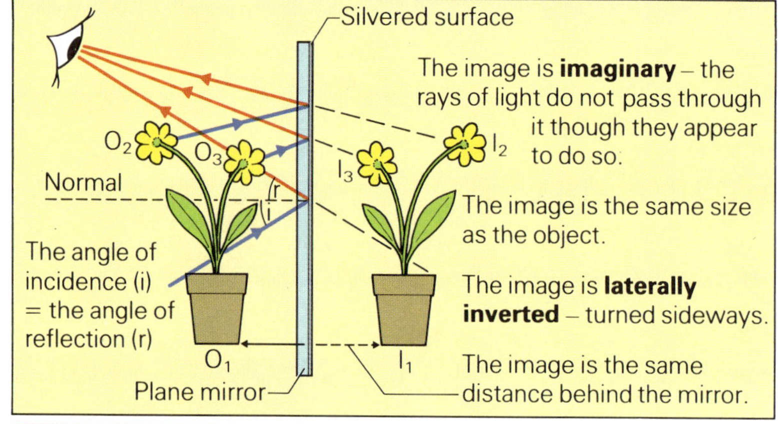

The right mirror for the job

You can use different kinds of mirrors designed specially for a particular purpose. Mirrors used by dentists are *designed* so they can see the back of a patient's teeth. You have to consider the shape of the patient's mouth, the position of the dentist's eyes and how the dentist holds the mirror when producing the best mirror for this job. The one thing that can't be altered is the fact that the light waves are **reflected** at certain angles from a mirror's surface. When checking the direction of light waves all measurements are made from a **normal** line drawn at right angles to the mirror where the reflection is taking place.

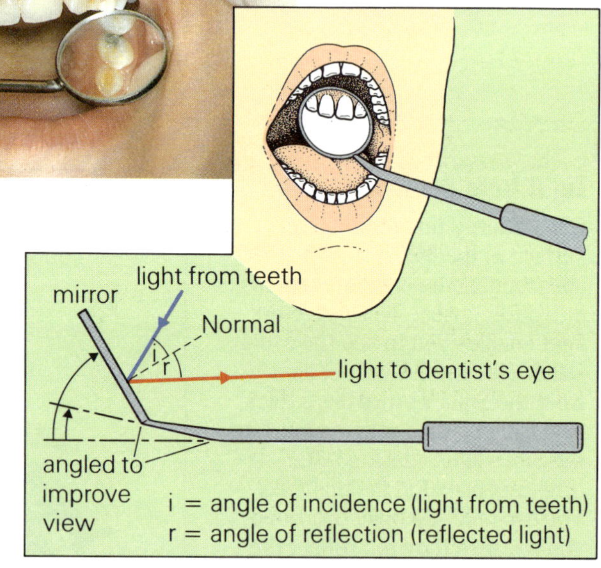

Looking over the top!

You can use a pair of **plane** (flat) **mirrors**, angled at 45° in a tube, to make a simple periscope. The angle *and* position of the mirrors are important, otherwise the information carried in the light waves produces an image that is unclear.

Look at the periscopes here and decide which one has been correctly fitted.

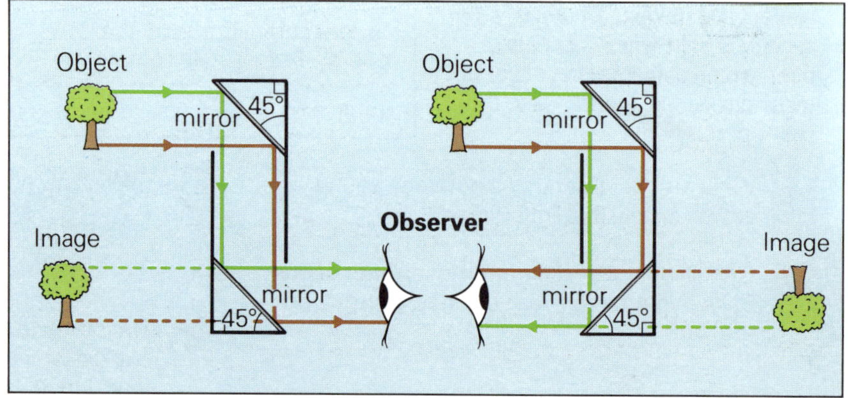

Directing the energy in light

Solar energy (in the form of sunlight) is a very important, renewable source of energy – it is a significant alternative to fossil fuels, nuclear power etc. But it has to be collected or concentrated so that the enormous energy it carries can be used. In France, a solar furnace has been made. Large mirrors are positioned very precisely so that the energy in waves of light over a large area can be **focused** (directed) at a central furnace. The heat energy collected and concentrated can produce temperatures high enough to melt metals placed at the **focal point** – the point where all the energy is directed. Replacing the furnace by pipes containing running water can allow water to be heated for use in homes or factories.

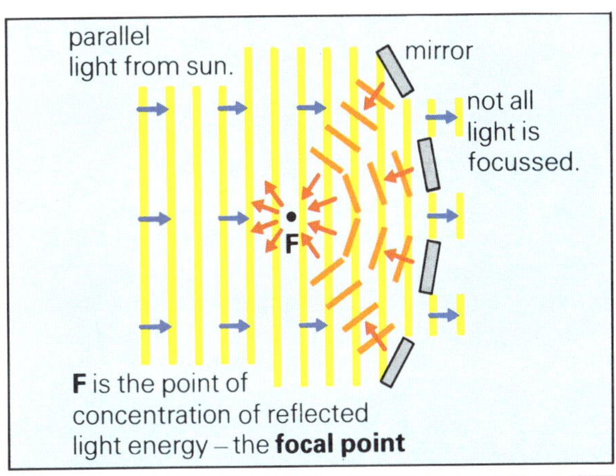

A combination of plane mirrors, angled correctly, will concentrate the energy, but not as efficiently.

A curved (concave) mirror collects most of the energy in the light and focuses it at F.

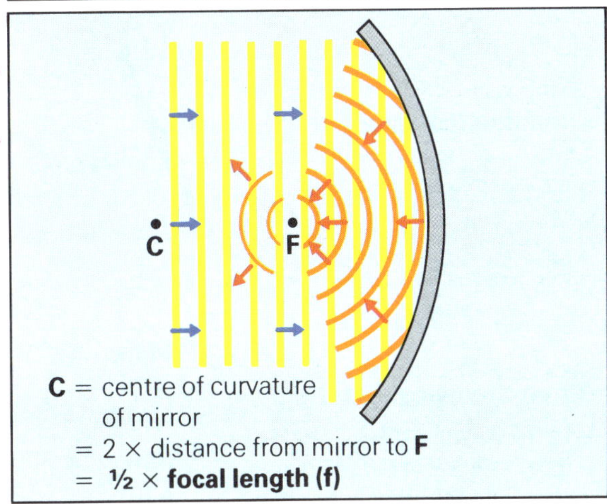

Curved is better

Using plane (flat) mirrors to focus light can be troublesome – they each have to be carefully positioned. A **concave** ('curved in') **mirror** acts like thousands of carefully angled small plane mirrors and is much easier to use. The **curvature** (amount of curve) of the mirror determines the position of its focal point.

Directing the image carried by light

Light waves from the Sun can also be used to produce an image of the Sun itself. The image can be focused, just like the energy, using a concave mirror. The image can be found by placing a card at the focal point of the mirror. If you use a powerful reflecting mirror it can focus a lot of light energy over its surface and produce a very bright image. If you do this yourself you need to take care, on a bright day there may be enough energy to burn the card!

It is dangerous to look directly at the Sun or to use any device such as a telescope to look directly at the Sun.

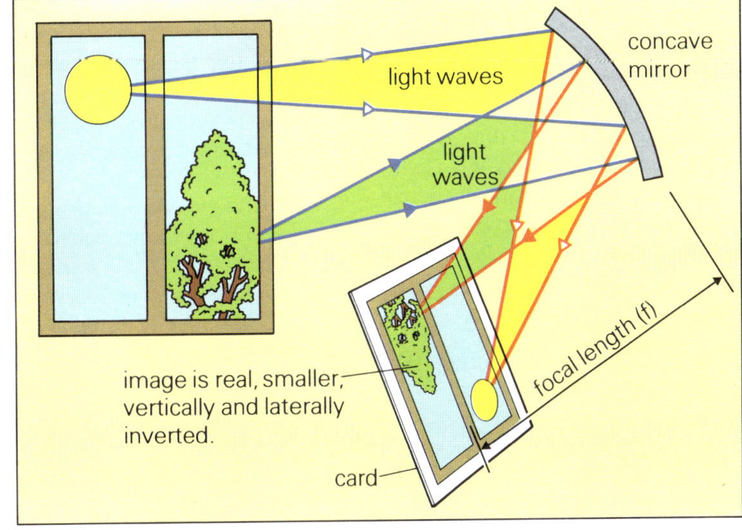

1 Why are some modern mirrors made from highly polished metal?

2 When you look at a reflection of yourself in a mirror, you don't 'see' yourself as other people do. Explain why.

3 How are mirrors used in cars? Describe all the different mirrors you can think of and the images they form.

4 How could you use solar energy efficiently to heat water in your home?

5 Why is a curved reflecting telescope useful for viewing the stars but not as useful for viewing objects on Earth?

YOU CAN READ MORE ABOUT SOLAR ENERGY ON SPREADS 1.12 AND 1.14.

The changing face of light

Changing the path of light waves

Light travels in straight lines, *provided* that it continues to travel in the same material. But what happens when light travelling in air enters a transparent material, like water? Most of it passes *through* the water – it is *not* reflected away at the surface – but the *direction of its path* is often changed. If the light wave hits the material surface at an angle to the **normal**, then the path of the light wave coming through the material is **refracted**. This change in direction depends not only on the material, but on the angle at which the wave hits the material surface.

If 'incident' ray follows path along normal:

normal

air

water

. . . ray passes straight down into water.

If 'incident' ray follows path at an angle to the normal:

normal

air

water

. . . ray refracts, bending towards normal line.

*If a light wave hits a new transparent material at an angle to the normal then the direction of its path will be changed – **refracted**.*

Changing the speed of light waves

Light normally travels at a speed of 300 000 000 metres per second in outer space (i.e. a vacuum), but slows down when travelling through materials like glass or water. This change in speed is one way of explaining why a light wave is refracted. In materials where light travels most slowly, the amount of refraction is greatest. These materials are called **optically dense.**

Material	Vacuum (air)	Water	Glass	Perspex	Diamond
Symbol	C_a	C_w	C_g	C_p	C_d
Speed of light (m/s)	300 000 000 3×10^8	225 000 000 2.25×10^8	200 000 000 2.0×10^8	201 335 500 2.0×10^8	125 000 000 1.25×10^8

Wave theory explanation

When a wave hits the surface of an optically dense material at an angle, the part of the wave that enters the material first is 'slowed down'. The part of the wave *not yet* in the material moves at the original speed. For the whole wave to stay together, the wavefront has to move in a new direction *towards* the normal. When a light wave enters a *less* optically dense material, the wave moves *away from* the normal.

For practical purposes we can assume that the speed of light in air is approximately equal to its speed in a vacuum (space). In contrast, diamond is an optically dense material.

The change in direction of light crossing a boundary between two materials affects the way we see objects. If you look at your legs underwater they will appear short and distorted.

Measuring the change

If a light wave passes through the boundary of the same two materials – say air and glass – the degree of refraction is always the same. This relationship is constant and depends on the change in speed of the light wave in the two materials. When light travels from air to glass, then the **refractive index** of glass (its ability to change the path of light waves from air to glass) μ_g can be found by comparing the velocities in the two materials, thus:

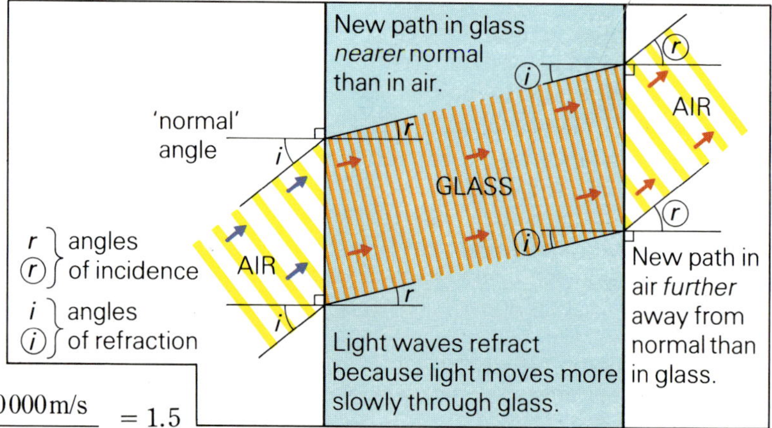
New path in glass *nearer* normal than in air.
'normal' angle
i
r
GLASS
AIR
AIR
r } angles (r) } of incidence
i } angles (i) } of refraction
Light waves refract because light moves more slowly through glass.
New path in air *further* away from normal than in glass.

$$\text{refractive index, } \mu_g = \frac{c_a}{c_g} = \frac{300\,000\,000\,\text{m/s}}{200\,000\,000\,\text{m/s}} = 1.5$$

The shape of waves to come

Knowing exactly how a wave will change direction (once it enters such materials as glass) is essential in designing and producing **lenses**. A **convex** (converging) lens, for example, is shaped to be thicker in the centre. If a plane light wave (parallel light rays forming a flat wavefront) passes through a glass convex lens the wave shape and direction are changed. The waves coming out of the lens are curved, coming together at a point called the **principal focus**.

Waves that are not plane can also be focused to produce a clear image although the image is not produced at the principal focus.

Plane waves (parallel rays) are brought to a point because of the curved, fat shape of the converging lens.

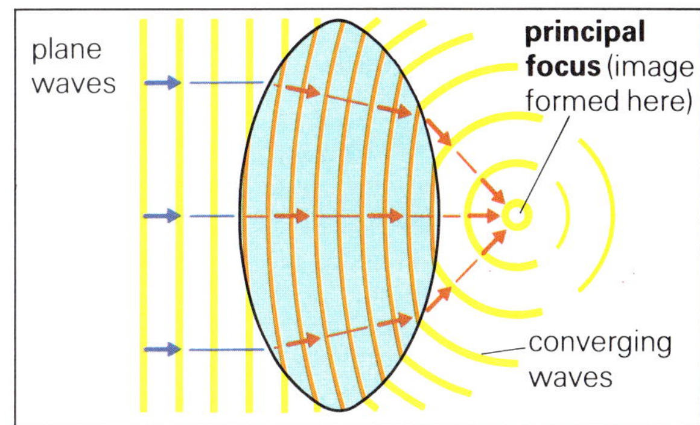

The accommodating eye

The lens inside your eye cannot be moved in the way that the camera lens can. Instead you can adjust the *shape* of your eye lens to get a clear image. The lens in your eye is surrounded by a set of **muscles** (called the iris) which can change its shape. If an object is *close*, then the lens can be made *thicker* to bring the waves in to produce a clear image on the retina. This process of adjustment is called **accommodation**.

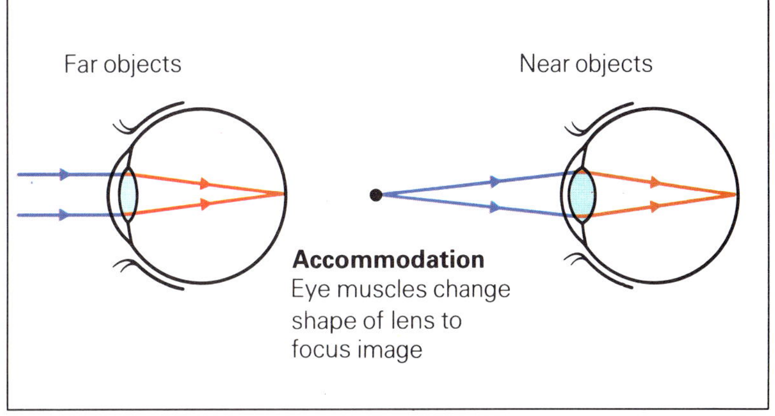

A camera lens can be moved to cope with a moving object – but your eye lens is fixed in position. How close up to your eye can you still see an object clearly?

The eye and the camera

Both the eye and camera contain convex lenses and both producc images. They focus an image on to light-sensitive materials (your retina or the film) placed at the focal point. Light from objects that are close to the lens produces waves that are curved, *not* plane. In order to produce a clear image of objects that are so close, the lens of the camera can be moved backwards or forwards. This is not possible with your eye – objects which are quite close up to your eyes will appear blurred (if you have normal vision).

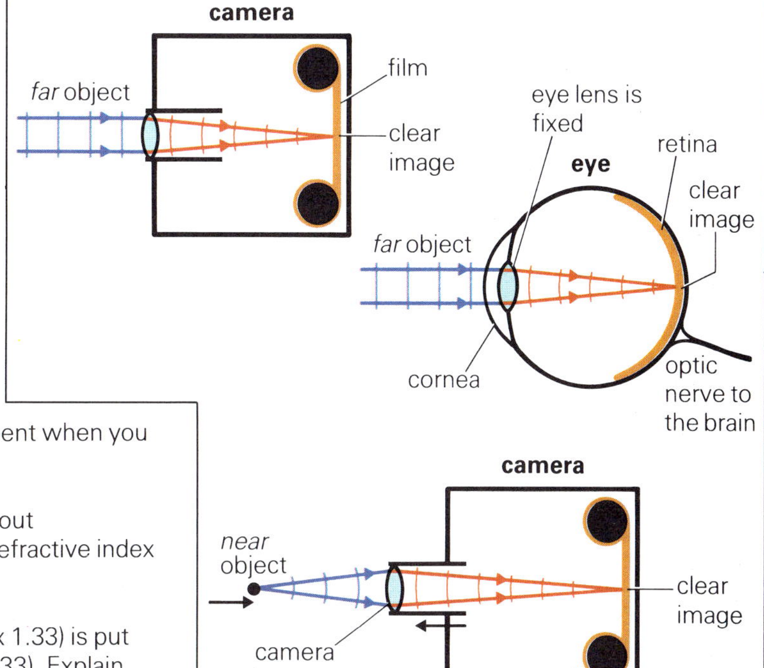

1 Why do you think a stick looks bent when you put half of it in water?

2 The speed of light in water is about 230 000 000 m/s. Calculate the refractive index of water.

3 A glass block (of refractive index 1.33) is put into water (of refractive index 1.33). Explain what happens to a light ray passing through the water at an angle into the block.

7.9 Using light

Extending our eyesight

We can help our eyes by using different arrangements of lenses and mirrors in all sorts of **optical instruments.** If you want to look at anything very small or examine something closely, you can use a magnifying glass or microscope. If you want to see distant objects, you can use binoculars or a telescope.

Image making

The size and position of the image formed by a lens depends on the *shape* of the lens and *how far the object is* from the lens.

A **convex** lens will refract light from a ***distant*** object to form a ***small, upside-down*** image at the **focal point** of the lens.

If the object is brought ***closer*** to the lens, the image formed will be ***further away*** from the lens and ***larger***. This is used in a simple projector to form large images of bright objects, such as slides or films.

If the object is brought so close that it lies *within* the focal length of the lens, it will produce a ***large, right-way-up*** image. This is how a magnifying glass works.

Many optical instruments use more than one lens to produce the required image.

A microscope uses two convex lenses to make very near objects seem very large – such as these fibres in nylon tights.

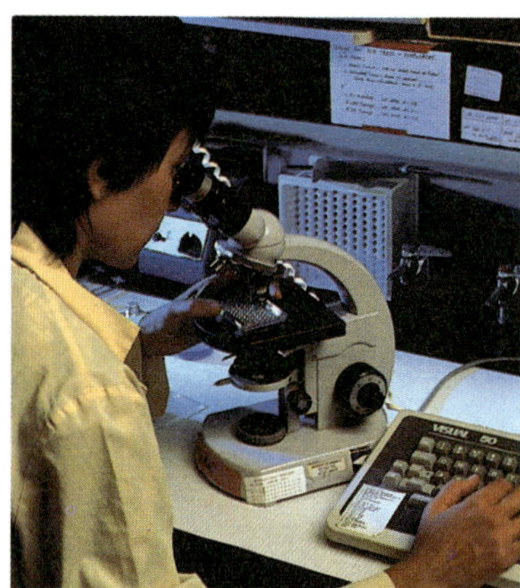

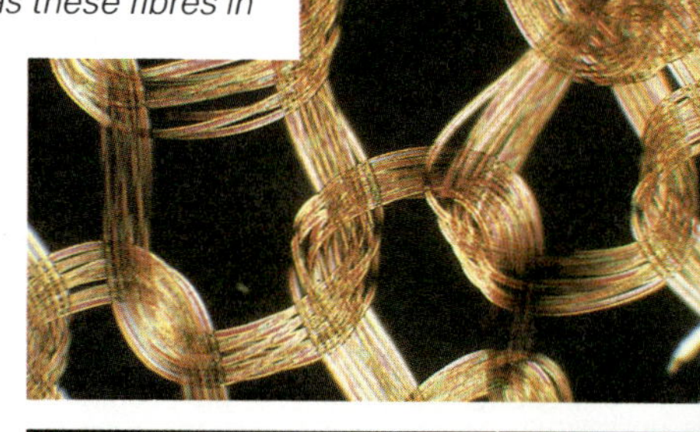

A telescope uses two convex lenses in a different way to make distant objects seem very close. Large lenses are used to view stars; such telescopes are kept in observatories like these, with long moveable slots in the roof that let only starlight in.

refracted ray

r

i

glass air

If i is larger . . .

. . . ray refracted more, moving nearer surface of glass

r

i

glass air

When i is very large, the ray is **totally internally reflected**.

i

glass air

Calculating from the 'right' angle

When light moves from *glass to air* (or from any optically dense material to a lesser one), refraction may 'give way' to a special type of reflection. This **total internal reflection** occurs at a **critical angle** of incidence i_c. How can you find this critical angle? There are two ways – either by experimenting or by calculation.

The light ray shown is moving from glass-to-air – so you need to use the refractive index for glass-to-air:

$$\mu_{(glass\text{-}to\text{-}air)} = 0.67 = 1/\mu_{(air\text{-}to\text{-}glass)} = 1/1.33.$$

In the first example,

$$\mu_{(glass\text{-}to\text{-}air)} = 0.67 = \frac{\sin i}{\sin r} = \frac{0.44}{0.66}.$$

Next, i increases to i_c and the ray is refracted directly along the glass surface ($r = 90°$).

$$\mu = 0.67 = \frac{\sin i_c}{\sin 90°} = \frac{\sin i_c}{1} = \sin i_c$$

This means the **critical angle** i_c (for glass-to-air) is **about 42°.**

As i increases further, the wave is reflected back into the glass – it does *not* pass into the new material (air), so it is *not* refracted.

Optical fibres

We can use the effect of total internal reflection to get to see into quite surprising places! If a bulb (or bright object) is joined to one end of a long **fibre** of glass, then the light from it will be seen at the other end of the fibre. The light travels in straight lines through the fibre, but strikes the sides of the fibre (*from within*) wherever the glass fibre *bends*. There are a series of glancing blows, all at angles *greater than* the critical angle – so the light rays repeatedly undergo **total internal reflection**, until they emerge at the other end!

Doctors can illuminate areas inside your body by using two bundles of optical fibres – *one* carries the light inside your body to light up your insides, and the *other* carries this light (shining back off your insides) out again.

Optical fibres use total internal reflection to direct light waves. A good way to see round corners!

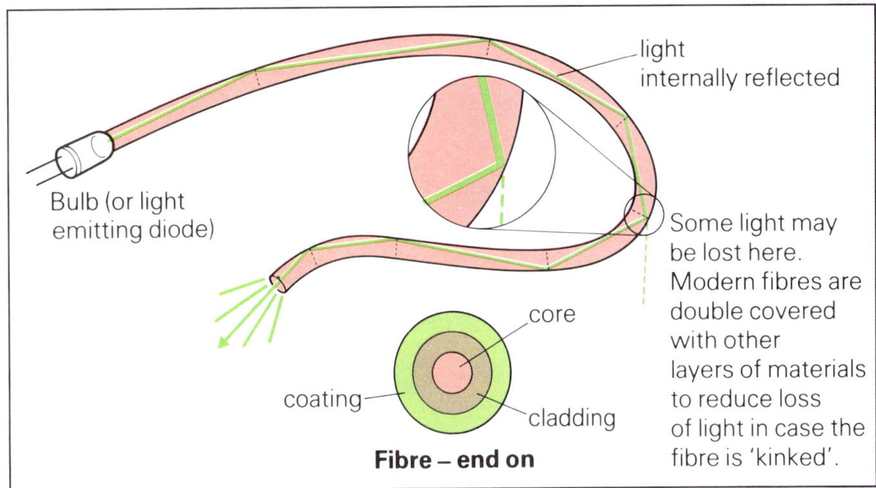

Thinner and better!

Optical fibres of glass are very, very thin – even several thousand bundled together are only as thick as *one* telephone wire. Although the fibres are carefully made, slight **impurities** in the glass may *absorb* some of the light energy. Over many miles, this *reduces* the brightness (intensity) of the light carried by the fibres and it will need to be regularly **boosted**. Boosting signals in this way always used to **distort** the information in the signal. Each time the signal was boosted, **background noise** was boosted too! By 'pulsing' or **digitising** information, this problem can be solved.

Information from the bank money dispenser

Message (electrical)

High energy light beam

(Brightness of light) **Signal**

'Flashing' light carrying message

Signal after travelling along the fibre

Signal amplified

Boosted signal

About *2 000 000* bits of information can be produced every second.

Detector

The signal is converted back into its original form

Optical fibre

Bank computer system

Information is carried by fibre optics almost immediately – at the speed of light.

Digitising information is like using a *code*. The messages carried by optical fibres are coded in an unmistakeable way – so they can always be decoded clearly, no matter how bad the distortion caused by background noise.

A few years ago, before the development of fibre optics, a doctor would have had to operate to see this part of your body.

1 A prism is a block of glass with angles that can 'turn' light through 180°. Explain what happens at A, B, C and D.

A B D C

2 Which material is the best to use in optical fibres? Give reasons for your answer.

Fibre type	$\mu_{air\text{-}to\text{-}.}$	*Cost*	*Purity*	*Flexibility*
Diamond	*2.5*	*High*	*High*	*Low*
Glass	*1.53*	*Low*	*Low*	*High*

Visible light and the em spectrum

What is colour?

For thousands of years scientists have studied the nature and properties of light. In the seventeenth century the observations of Isaac Newton and other scientists led him to suggest that **colour** was *not* a property of an object – grass has no colour *in itself*. He put forward the *hypothesis* that light itself contained different colours and that objects simply reflected some, all or none of these colours. This hypothesis had to be tested to see if light could be split into the colours that scientists had observed in natural phenomena like rainbows. Newton used a **prism** to reveal that there were a number of identifiable colours – a **spectrum** – to be found in the visible light from the Sun. Each colour within the spectrum has a different **wavelength** and **frequency**. When these different waves enter a material, some waves slow down *more* than others.

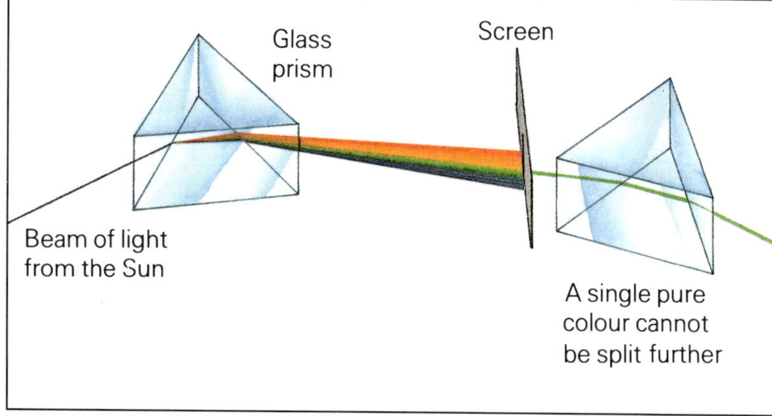

Visible light can be split into a number of different colours.

How do you think Newton may have 'double-checked' his hypothesis, once he had split light into its spectrum?

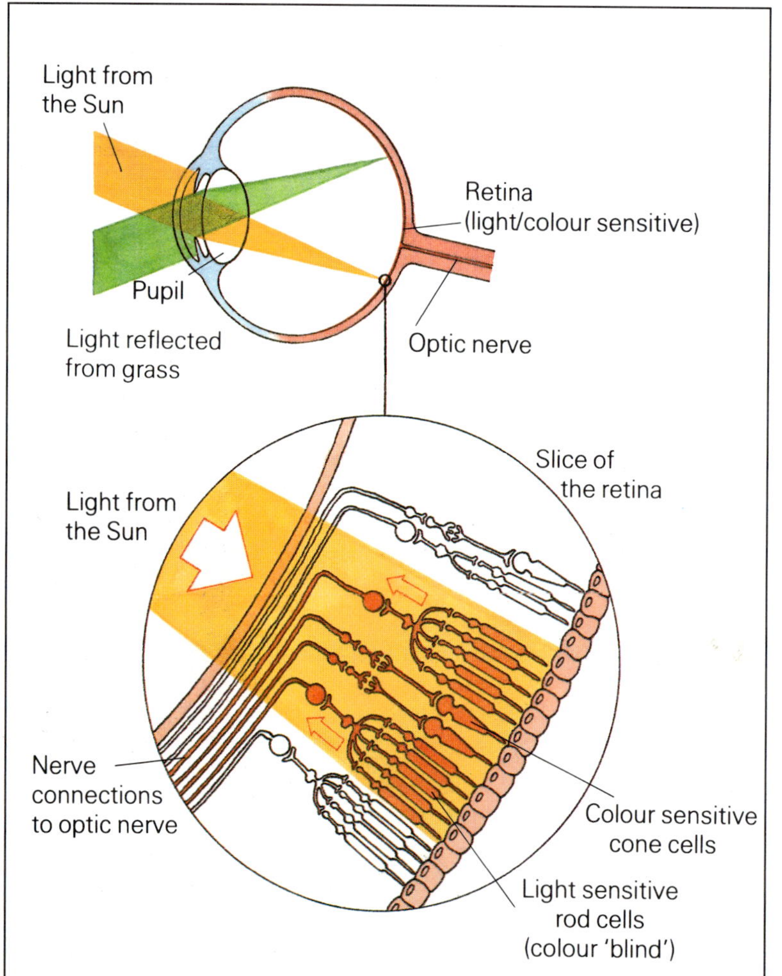

Colouring in

Your eye enables you to take in light from all around you. Your eye contains an area, called the retina, made up of different cells that are sensitive to light. When light waves hit the light-sensitive **retina** at the back of the eye, some cells are stimulated. These cells send electrical messages to parts of your brain. Your brain can make sense of these messages. Some cells in the retina are sensitive only to the *amount* of light – these cells are called **rod cells** and, though very sensitive, only respond to shades of light and dark.

Each of the different colours of light has a different frequency. Other cells in the centre of your retina are called **cones** and respond to the *type* of light waves – those which have a certain frequency (and hence colour). These cells do not function until there is enough light energy to make them active. This explains why it is difficult to see colours clearly in dim light, since *only* your *rod cells* can operate in dim light.

The whole spectrum

The visible light spectrum is only a small part of the whole **electromagnetic (em) spectrum**. There are many other electromagnetic waves that have very similar properties to light waves. But these different forms of wave energy do also have different properties – and so different uses – because of their *different wavelengths and frequencies*.

While reading this section, refer back to the diagram of the electromagnetic spectrum on 7.1.

This guided microwave radio transmitter is cheaper and easier to use than a radio wave transmitter.

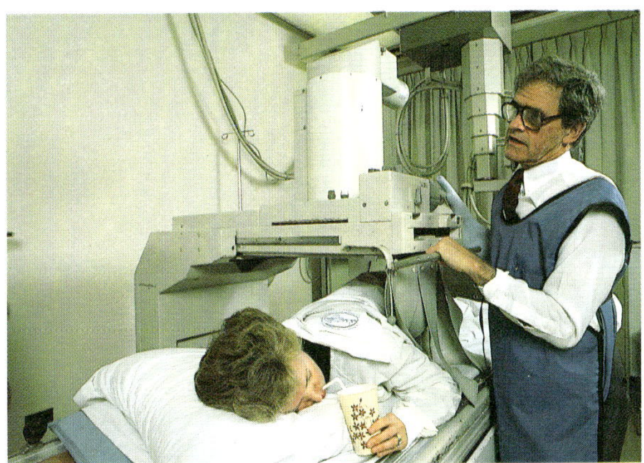

X ray technology has its problems – those using the equipment have to be careful they are not over exposed to the radiation.

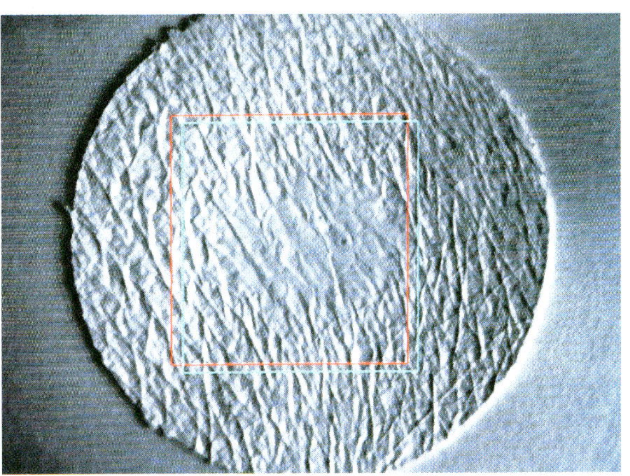

The area of skin in the centre has been damaged by UV light. You suffer this kind of damage every time you get sunburn. So cover up or use sun block creams when out in strong sun for long.

Radio waves have very *long* wavelengths (low frequencies). They can pass through solid materials such as walls – which is why your radio can pick up Radio 1 indoors! However, some types of radio waves cannot pass through a special layer of the atmosphere called the **ionosphere**. These radio waves are reflected back and can be bounced around the world using the ionosphere. Because of their long wavelengths, radio waves are difficult to direct, they spread out in all directions.

Microwaves have shorter wavelengths than radio waves, and so are easier to direct. They can be *reflected* and *directed* – particularly by metal surfaces, which can focus all the microwave energy at a single point. This is why you should *never* put any metal objects in a microwave oven (*see 7.1*).

Like radio waves and microwaves, **ultraviolet** (UV) waves are invisible to the human eye. The energy carried by UV waves can cause chemical reactions to occur – such as those in your skin which cause skin cancer (melanoma). Up to now, most of the UV that comes from the Sun has been effectively blocked by gases in the Earth's atmosphere – particularly ozone. However changes in the ozone layer are occurring and more dangerous UV is thought to be passing through the atmosphere.

X ray waves are invisible, high energy electromagnetic (em) waves, discovered in the nineteenth century. X rays have enough energy to pass through solid materials and (like many other *em* waves) *large amounts* of X rays can cause dangerous, chemical and biological reactions.

1 What features do all the waves in the electromagnetic spectrum have in common

2 Explain why you cannot see colours when walking along a country road in moonlight.

7.11 What is light?

Is it particles?

Light is very important to us. Its behaviour and nature have been the subject of observation, experimentation and debate amongst scientists for centuries. During the seventeenth century, Isaac Newton spent many years studying the nature of light. He observed the **reflection** of light, the formation of **shadows**, the passage of light in **straight lines**, and **refraction**. Newton came up with a hypothesis that light was made up of tiny particles called **corpuscles** which were emitted by bright objects. This theory explained most of the properties of light. Newton's hypothesis was based on his experiments on light, but it was also linked to his other studies on mechanics – forces and movement of objects.

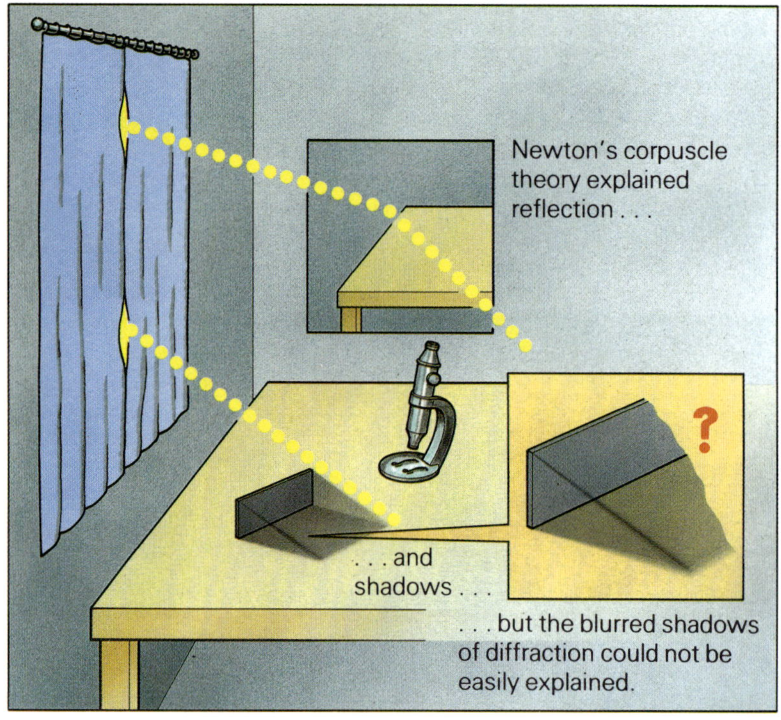

Newton explained the nature of light using a mechanical model of corpuscles.

Another interesting property of light: Newton also discovered that when light hit a very sharp edge (or passed through a narrow gap), the shadows formed were diffused and blurred as if the light had been bent. This bending of light is called **diffraction**.

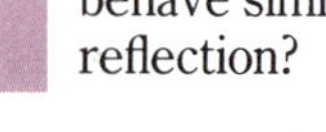

On a larger scale, what sort of object (moving towards a wall) would behave similarly to the way corpuscles of light behave during reflection?

. . . or is it a wave?

Newton was a member of a group called the Royal Society which was made up of many famous scientists (and continues to meet to this day!). A fellow member, Robert Hooke, criticised Newton at the time. Hooke believed that light was a wave. He was supported by Huygens, a Dutch scientist, who put forward a hypothesis that light passed as **waves**, moving through **'aether'** – a substance that filled the Universe. Huygens claimed that the particles of aether transmitted light as pulses of wave energy. This hypothesis also explained all the properties of light – its movement in straight lines, reflection, refraction and, in particular, diffraction.

What a dilemma! Which hypothesis would you have agreed with – corpuscle theory or wave theory? Or do you have a better idea than Newton, Hooke and Huygens?

Light energy is carried by 'aether' in Huygen's view of the wave theory of light. It explained the same properties of light as Newton's theory – plus diffraction.

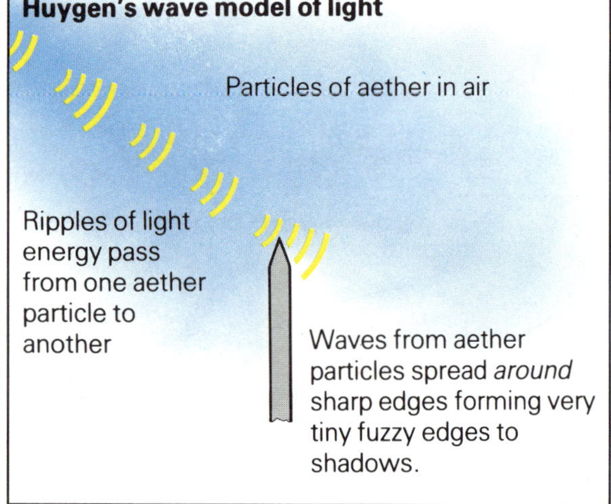

The photo-electric effect

Early this century, scientists observed that when light hit a specially prepared metal surface, electrons were ejected from the surface of the metal. Light waves with a high frequency produced fast-moving (high energy) electrons. An experiment (using just one colour of light) involved changing the **intensity** of the light falling on the metal – by moving the light source closer to the metal. As the light intensity increased, the metal surface *received more energy*.

The leaves in a gold-leaf electroscope move apart when they experience a build up of charge. High frequency light can cause the leaves to part in this way

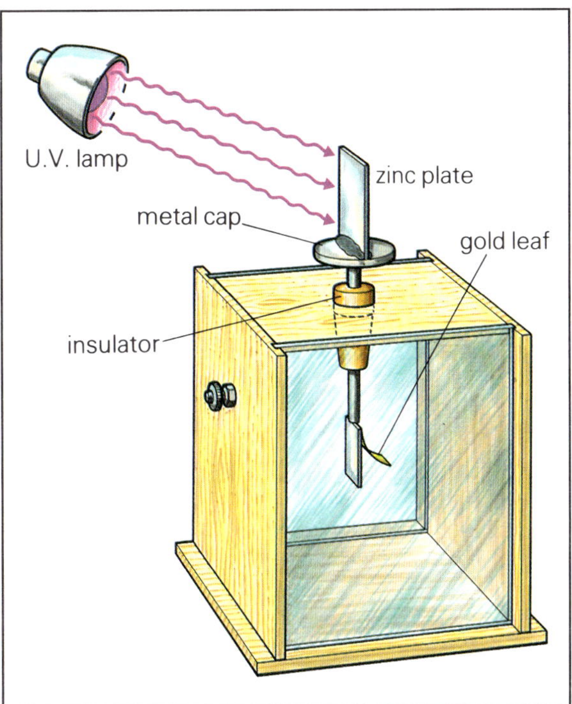

This increased energy could be taken up in one of two ways:

- the *same* number of electrons could be ejected, each having gained *more* energy;
- *more* electrons could be ejected, each having gained exactly the *same* energy as before.

The experiment showed that the ***only result*** was *more* electrons, *all* with the 'standard' amount of energy.

If light was a wave, the electrons should have gained *more* energy from the more intense wavefront. They should have moved *faster* (when ejected from the metal surface) than those ejected by the less intense wavefront (emitted by the more distant light source). But this didn't happen, so the wave theory could *not* explain all aspects of the photo-electric effect. Where next . . . ?

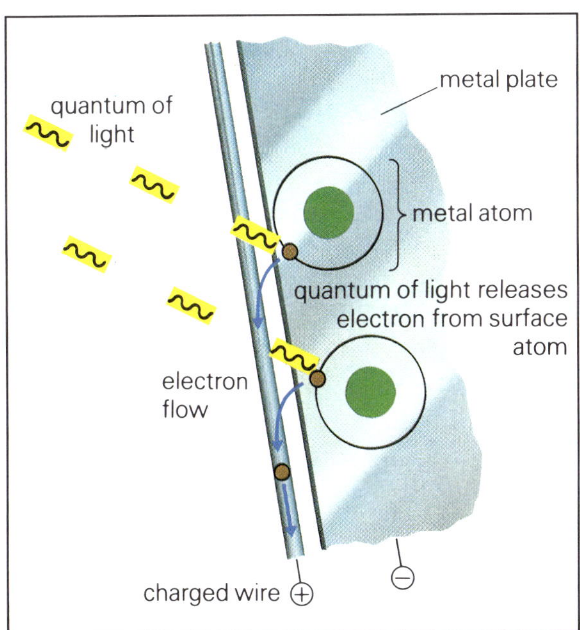

The light is releasing electrons from the atoms in the metal plate

The quantum theory

Max Planck and Albert Einstein both put forward the idea that light was made up of tiny packets of energy called **quanta.** They suggested that *when produced or absorbed* light acted like packets of energy (quanta) – but *when it travelled* in a material or through space, light acted like a wave. When a quantum of energy was absorbed by an atom in the metal surface, the quantum of energy was the precise amount of energy required to make an electron jump free from its 'parent' atom. This explained why the 'intensity experiment' always produced electrons with *exactly the same energy* – no matter what intensity of light was used, the quanta of energy in the light were always the same size. In a way, both Newton's and Huygens' theories contributed to the **quantum theory** – light is made up of tiny packets of energy which can behave like waves!

1 Huygens claimed that light moves by 'aether' passing on ripples of wave energy. How is this similar to the motion of sound waves?

2 Which explains refraction best – corpuscle or wave theory? Why?

3 The photo-electric effect produces electrical energy from light energy.

a Explain how this is used in a remote-control TV.

b How could the effect be used to generate electricity in tropical countries?

Discovering new radiation

Looking at particles

At the same time as investigating the nature of light, scientists in the late nineteenth century were also puzzling over the nature of the atom. John Dalton had earlier proposed a model of the atom as solid and indivisible. This was now under question because experiments on electrical conduction were beginning to show the existence of charged particles *within* an atom. Experiments on the passage of electricity through gases at low pressures, inside sealed **discharge tubes**, showed that charged particles moved along the tube between the two electrodes. The name **cathode** rays was given to these particles. Further experiments showed that when these particles hit an object in the tube, *heat* energy was produced and the object became hot. It was also noticed that some of the energy was converted into *light* energy – the gas in the tube was seen to glow.

Thomson's ideas

At this time (about 1897) J.J. Thomson thought that the particles were charged atoms (**ions**) – previous electrical conductivity experiments had already proved the existence of ions. He tested his hypothesis by trying to deflect them with a magnetic field. In fact, the particles were deflected *much more* than he had expected. They were much smaller than any atom – about 1000 to 2000 times smaller than a hydrogen atom. He called them 'charged corpuscles'. Eventually they became known as **electrons**.

His new model for the atom was based on these findings. It consisted of a positive jelly-like surrounding substance containing negative 'currants' or electrons. It was popularly known as the '*Plum Pudding Atom*'!

Glowing back together!

Thomson's ideas about electrons explain the glow or fluorescence produced in the discharge tubes. Positive ions – positively charged atoms – are produced when the negative electrons are attracted to the positive electrode (**anode** ⊕). As the ions move one way (towards the cathode because they are now positively charged), they collide with electrons moving the other way. The result is a *recombination* to produce an *uncharged* atom which stops moving – and the energy of the moving particles is released. The energy of the electron jumping back into its orbit in the atom is *converted* into electromagnetic radiation. The colour of the light produced was found to depend on the gas used.

The process of ionisation and recombination produces continuous 'cold' light. TVs and fluorescent strip lighting are everyday applications of the properties of cathode ray tubes.

Thomson with the discharge tube which he used to gather evidence for his 'Plum Pudding' Atom.

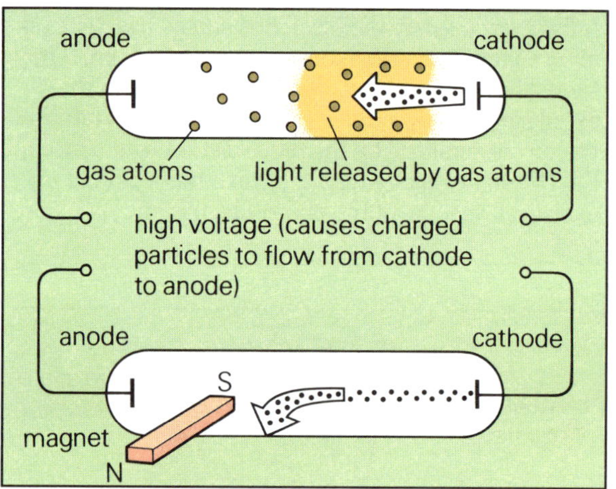

If the charged particles collide with gas atoms, the gas will give out light energy. A magnet can deflect the beam of particles – so they must be charged!

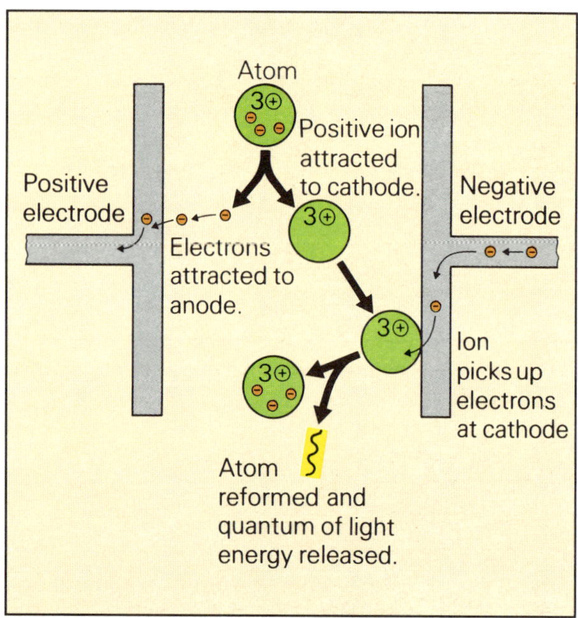

YOU CAN READ MORE ABOUT IONS ON SPREAD 8.12.

And then there were X rays!

Other scientists also wrestled with the problems that faced Thomson at the same time. In a search for answers they reproduced many of his investigations with gas discharge tubes. During one of these experiments the German scientist Röntgen accidentally placed chemically-coated plates near his apparatus. The chemical coating was specially prepared so that it could **fluoresce** (give off light). He noticed that when a plate was near one of the ends of the tube, the plate began to glow. When he placed his hand between the tube and the plate, he saw a shadow of the bones in his hand on the plate!

The unknown (x) ray

Röntgen's further investigations revealed much about what this invisible radiation could do but not much about what kind of radiation it was. It was named the **X ray** – X for unknown – because of this. The name has stuck since then.

What do you think are some of the properties of X rays?

Röntgen tested various materials to see if his newly discovered 'X' rays penetrated them to produce fluorescence on the treated plate. He also used his eyes to try to 'see' X rays!

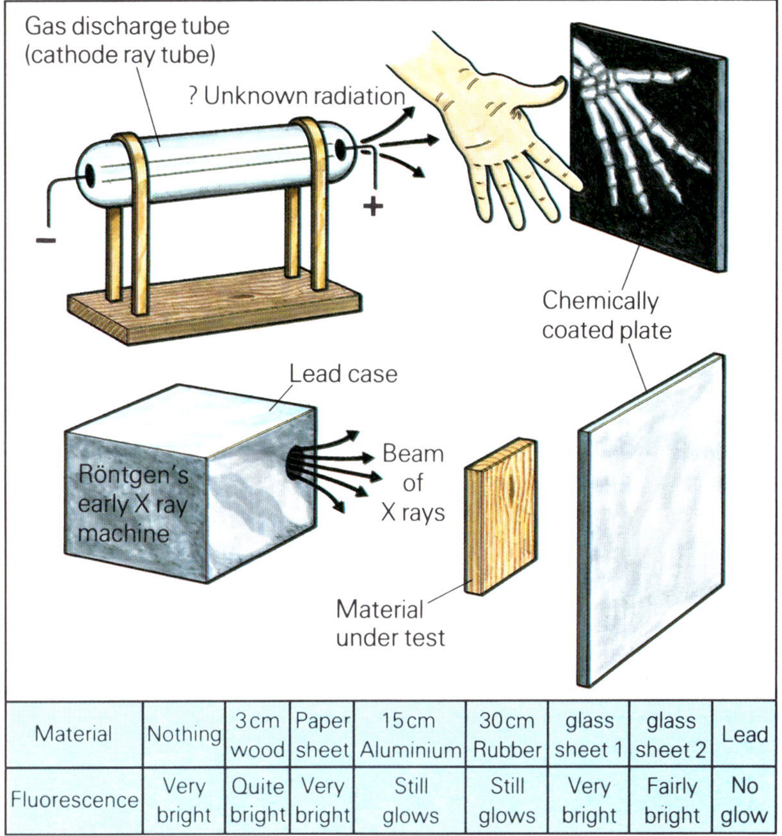

Material	Nothing	3 cm wood	Paper sheet	15 cm Aluminium	30 cm Rubber	glass sheet 1	glass sheet 2	Lead
Fluorescence	Very bright	Quite bright	Very bright	Still glows	Still glows	Very bright	Fairly bright	No glow

Using X rays

X rays are used extensively in industry and medicine. In fact, because of their penetrative effect, only weeks after the discovery of X rays hospitals were trying to use them to look at the injuries of patients with broken legs or internal damage. You can imagine how helpful this was for doctors at this time! Unfortunately, many of the people who used the first X ray machines later died from **cancer tumours** of the hands, face and eyes. X rays were found to cause damage to growing cells of the human body and cause the cells to become cancerous – unless adequate protection was worn and used. But this was discovered too late – *after* the early use of X rays had flourished.

Airport security today is aided by the use of X ray equipment which can 'see' into your luggage. The X rays penetrate the outer layers giving a picture of what is inside!

1. What was the atom like according to the scientist Dalton? What evidence was there that Dalton's ideas were wrong?

2. Why was Thomson's model for the atom called the 'Plum Pudding' model? How does this model explain the production of ions inside a cathode ray tube?

3. A fluorescent tube produces light even though it is cold. How can this happen?

4. Why do you think Röntgen's experiments produced X rays while Thomson's apparently did not?

5. What are the properties of X rays that make them
   a so useful
   b so dangerous?

Diodes, valves and semi-conductors

Self switching light bulbs

Thomas Edison, a nineteenth century scientist, carried out further investigations on the relationship between light and electricity. He made studies of a simple filament lamp by introducing another metal plate which he used as an electrode. His observations showed that a small current would flow from the filament to the metal plate sealed in the tube but only under certain conditions. He found that a current flowed across the gap only when the plate was positively charged compared to the filament. This effect (called the **Edison effect**) was explained 20 years later by another scientist called Richardson. When the filament was hot enough, negatively charged particles (**electrons**) were thrown out from the surface of the filament. This is known as **thermionic emission**. The cloud of electrons produced could be attracted across the space inside the bulb to the positively charged electrode (anode) away from the negatively charged filament (cathode).

Why do you think current would not flow if the electrodes were oppositely charged?

Positive	Negative	Result
Metal Plate	Heater filament	Current flows
Heater filament	Metal Plate	No current

Edison's experimental results.

The 'Edison effect' bulb – if a positively charged plate is placed close to a heated filament wire inside a bulb the electrons are drawn away from the negatively charged filament. This arrangement came to be known as a diode because two electrodes were used.

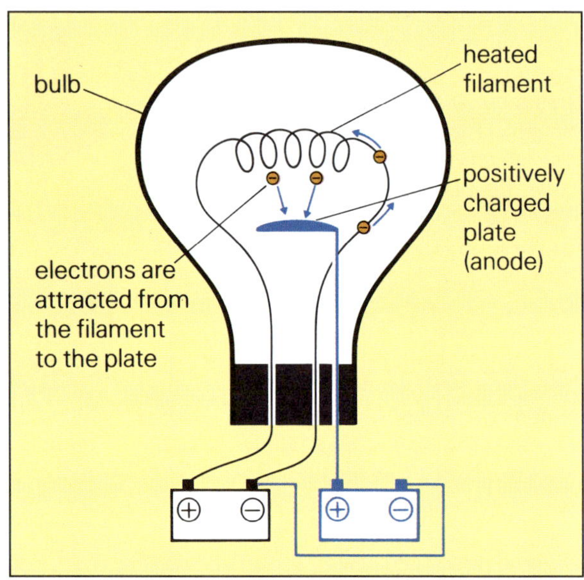

This model of what takes place inside the Edison diode shows how as the atoms in the filament gain more energy from heating the electrons are given enough energy to escape.

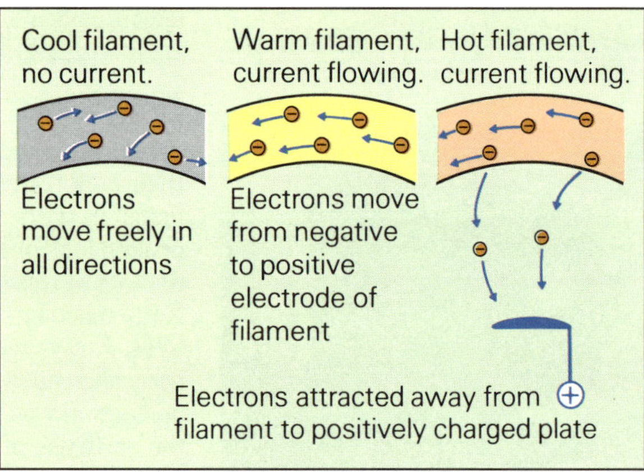

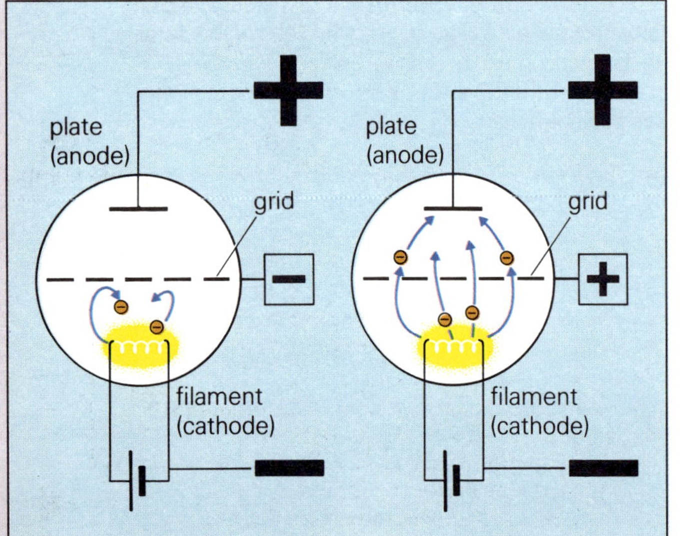

In the triode, changing the grid from negative to positive allows electrons to flow from cathode to anode.

The valve

The two-electrode bulb (**diode**) became known as a **valve** because it could *control* the flow of charge. Other electrodes were added to provide even better control. The **triode** (three electrode) valve contained a *metal grid* (or *gate*) that could control the flow of charge very finely. When the gate was positively charged compared to the filament (cathode), electron flow would be greater. If the gate became negatively charged, then electron flow would be reduced.

The triode valve was used mainly as an **amplifier** making small electrical signals much larger in old fashioned radio sets and similar devices.

Controlling the size

Using simple diode and triode valves, radio receivers could be made which converted an extremely small radio signal and produced the sound message it carried through a loudspeaker. The major design problems of the first of these were the amount of electrical energy needed to heat the filaments and the size and weight of the radio receiver needed. One modification soon found was coating the filament of the valve with materials that gave off electrons very easily when heated . . . but other ways of reducing the size of the controlling valves were needed!

. . . even further

Electrical current passes through some materials better than others. While metals are usually good conductors non-metals are not. Some substances such as silicon are neither good nor bad and are called **semi-conductors**. In semi-conductors the resistance to electrical current can vary. As they get hot or if light shines upon them, there is enough energy to release electrons from the atoms of the semi-conductor to allow current to flow.

Scientists realised that such materials could be used to control electron flow. By adding impurities such as aluminium or phosphorus then the silicon's electrical conductivity can be changed. For example, phosphorus provides more easily movable electrons while aluminium provides more places or holes for electrons to move to.

The flow of electrons can be controlled in the same way that a diode valve controls flow, if slices of silicon 'doped' with these impurities are put together. Current will flow one way across the junction but not the other. This controlling device is called a **semi-conductor diode** – it takes up a microscopic amount of space compared to the old fashioned style diodes or valves.

The junction of p type (p for positive) and n type (n for negative) semi-conductor acts like a diode valve. Current will not flow from n to p when n is positive but will flow from p to n when p is positive.

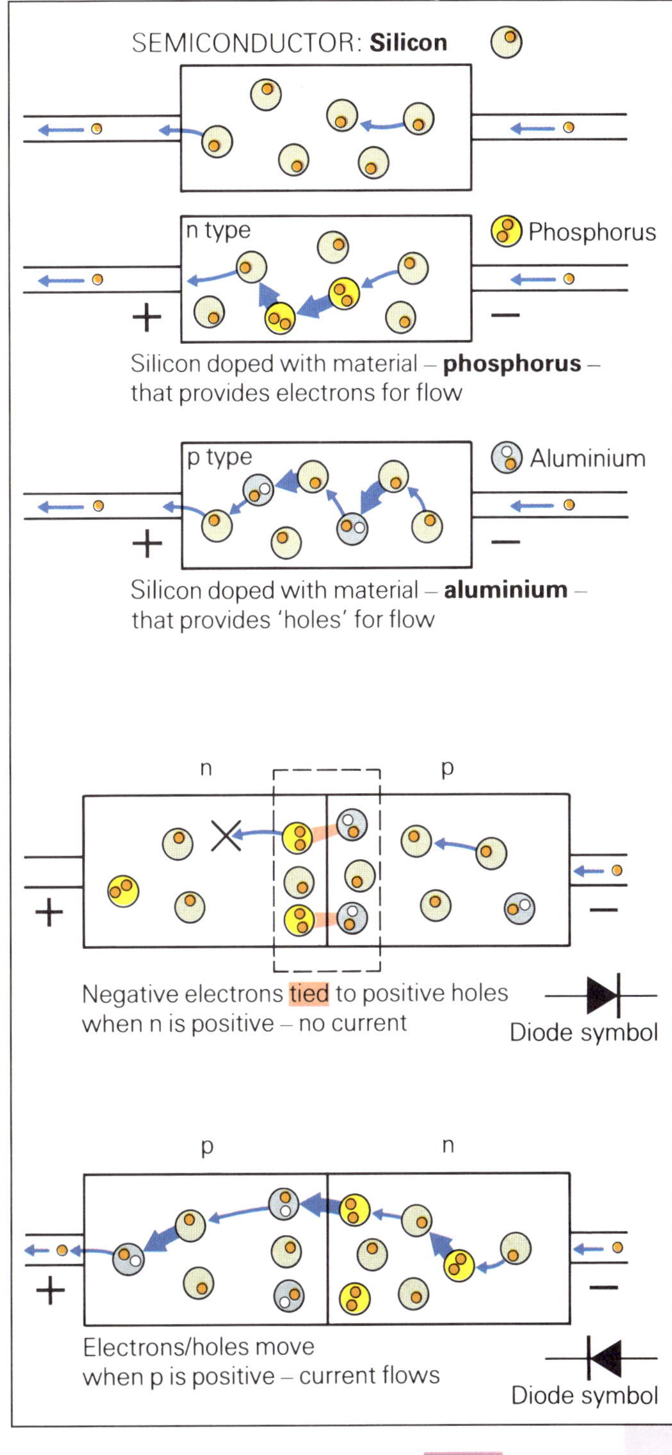

1 When a cotton thread is held near a light bulb it is attracted to the light bulb by an electrostatic charge. How does the idea of thermionic emission help explain this?

2 In Edison's investigation electrons would only flow one way. How did Richardson help explain this effect?

3 How does the triode valve act as an amplifier?

4 Valves were used for only a short time of about fifty years. What were the problems with valve radios and how were these problems solved?

5 How can a diode semiconductor act like a diode valve?

Radio waves and communication

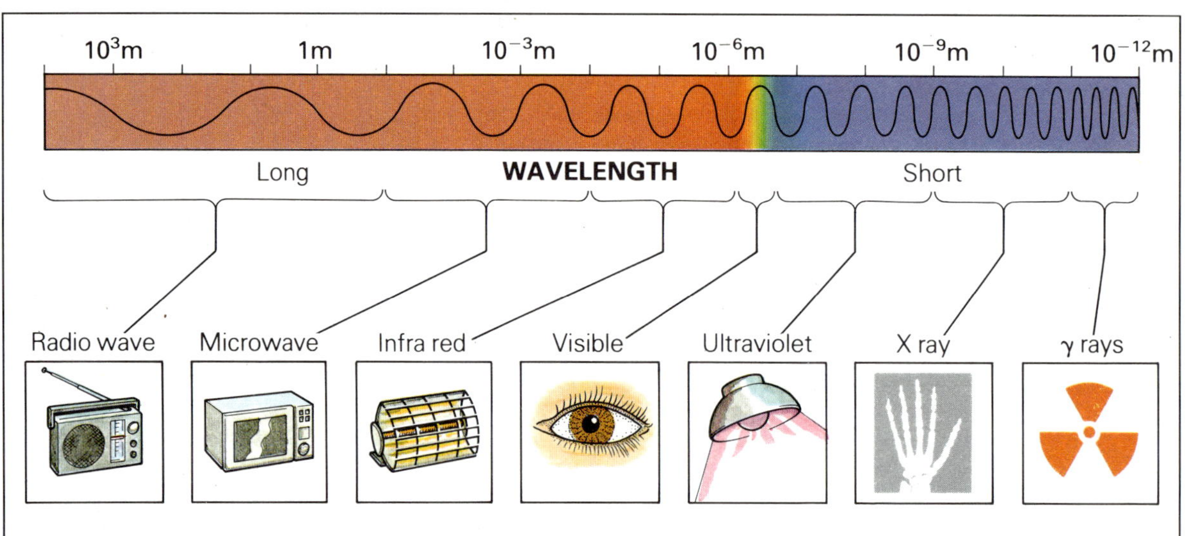

The family of electromagnetic waves – closely related but with important differences.

The electromagnetic family

Electromagnetic waves are emitted from atoms when the atoms are given energy. The energy given to the atoms can be heat energy, magnetic energy, nuclear energy or electrical energy. This causes the atoms to become 'excited' and they give out energy, often in the form of electromagnetic waves. The type of electromagnetic wave – whether infra red, ultraviolet, X ray or radio wave – depends on the material and the amount of energy given.

Hertzian waves

In 1884 a German scientist called Hertz attempted to produce waves of energy using the electrical energy of a spark. He was convinced that electrical energy, magnetism and light were connected in some way. He was also convinced that the electromagnetic spectrum actually existed although he called it the 'undulatory series'. He managed to produce radio waves with enough energy to produce a distant spark between two electrodes connected to a metal ring. The coil in his experiment was really the first radio **transmitter** while the ring was the first radio **receiver.**

A member of the family

Hertz also wanted to show that the waves he had produced had similar properties to those of light waves and that they were in the same series or family. He proved that the waves could be *reflected,* that they travelled at *the same speed as light waves* and that they could also be *refracted.* Thus the electromagnetic family grew to include radio waves. Radio waves were found to have a much longer wavelength than visible light waves. They were used to produce a worldwide radio communication system.

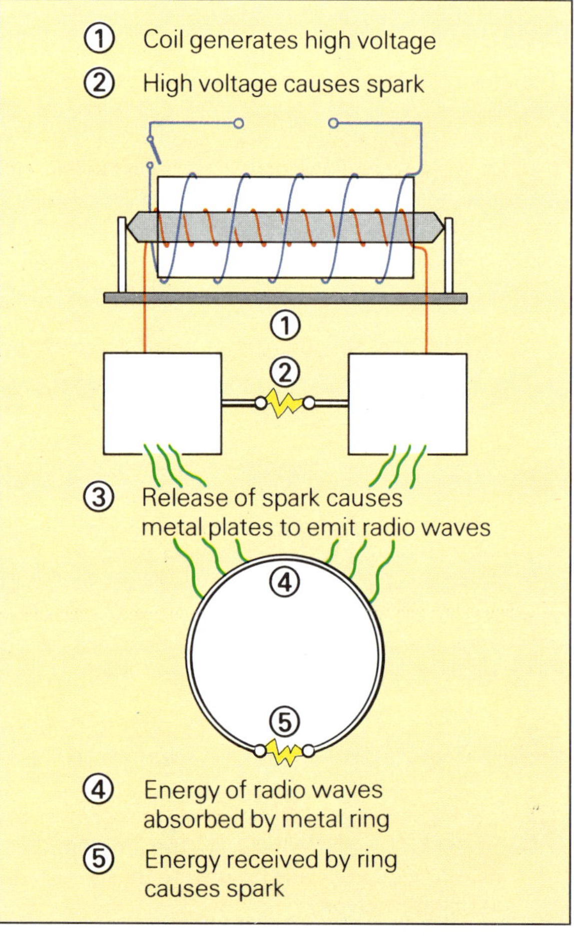

The first radio transmitter and receiver based on Hertz's original experiments.

Bouncing radio waves

The amount that radio waves can be refracted or even reflected is of considerable use in **communication.** The first waves produced for communication purposes were known as **longwave.** These waves could be received hundreds and thousands of miles from the transmitters. But if these waves were just like light waves how could they travel around the curvature of the Earth for thousands of miles? Just like light waves they are in fact refracted and reflected by the Earth's atmosphere and surface. The atmosphere at high altitudes contains layers of different gases. Each layer has a different **refractive index** (*see 7.8*) for each different wavelength of radio wave. Long radio waves are easily refracted until they are eventually reflected off the underside of one of the layers (**total internal reflection**).

Longwave and **mediumwave** communication can however be a little hit and miss. The layers of different gases in the atmosphere can change rapidly, especially late in the evening as some of the layers disappear. As the amount of refraction at each layer changes, the distances that radio waves travel and the amount of energy carried in the waves change rapidly . . . making broadcasting all a bit fuzzy!

Longwave radio waves are bounced around the Earth through continued refraction and reflection.

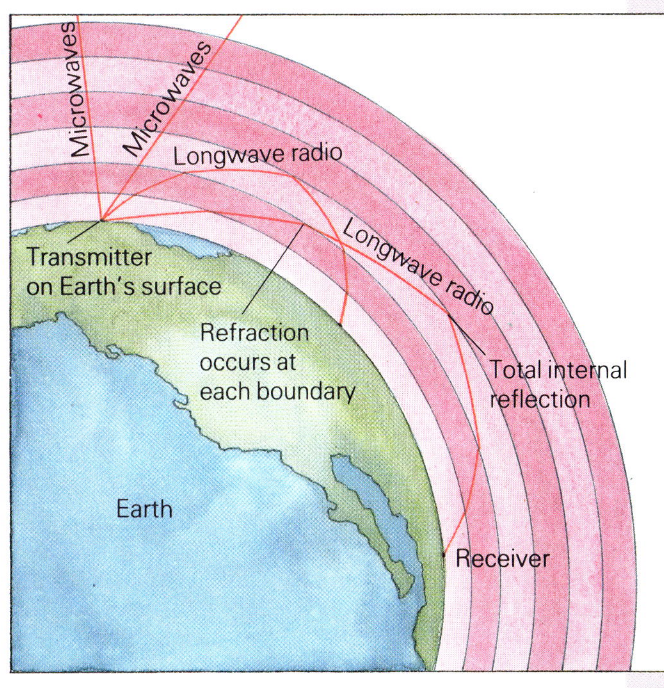

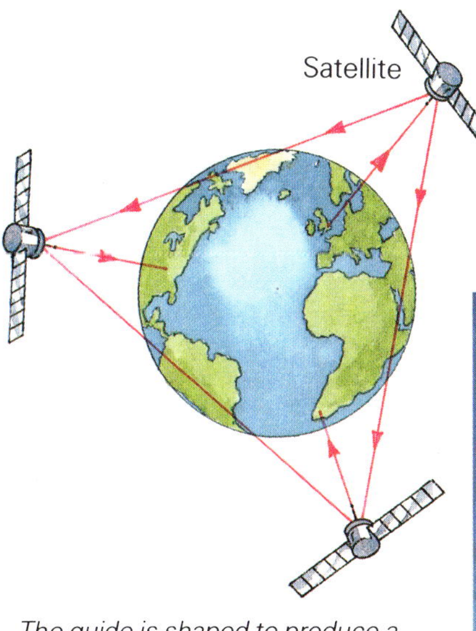

*Microwaves guided between the Earth and satellites in an orbit fixed relative to Earth (**geostationary**) provide instant 'high quality' radio communication.*

The guide is shaped to produce a beam of microwaves in certain directions . . . no widespread wavefronts are produced so less energy is lost

Microwaves – not just for ovens!

Shorter waves (**microwaves**) are not refracted as much by the atmosphere. These waves travel in straight lines from transmitter to receiver. To operate, transmitter and receiver must be in a direct line and at a maximum distance of about 40 miles apart. Many microwave transmitters have shaped **waveguides** to direct the waves. Using receiver/transmitter stations to relay the microwaves, communication links have been established across the country. Using satellites to increase the 'line of sight' microwaves are now used instead of longer radio waves for worldwide radio communication.

1 What are the sources for the different kinds of electromagnetic waves?

2 How do you think Hertz proved that 'Hertzian' waves were members of the electromagnetic spectrum?

3 How were the many properties of 'long' radiowaves used to provide communication links around the world?

4 What are the disadvantages of longwave radio communication?

5 How are satellites essential for radio communication around the world? Why are microwaves used nowadays for worldwide communication?

7.15 Waves, energy and communication

THE WEEKLY REPORTER
Sunday 29th 1906

Reports are now available on the terrible earthquake that took place on the west coast of America on Thursday 19th April. The earthquake caused buildings to collapse, ruptured a fuel pipe and the resulting explosion caused windows to shatter in homes hundreds of yards away.

People are searching for survivors in the building rubble and 200 are feared dead. Rescue workers are using their hands, helped by bulldozing machinery, to dig through the rubble to find those still missing. Hope of survivors diminishes every day. If no more survivors are found by Sunday, the search will be abandoned, and heavy machinery will be used to clear away the rubble.

Read the information given in these two newspaper articles. Look at the way the information is produced and relayed.

1 How are the two accounts of the earthquake, and the ways they are reported different?

2 Try to explain these differences. Use other examples to help your explanation.

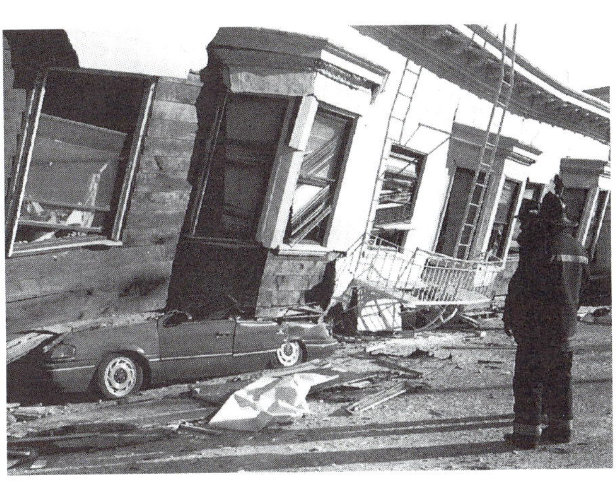

WORLD NEWS

Thursday 13th May 1995

Reports are coming in on the terrible earthquake that hit the west coast of America yesterday evening at 9 pm. The earthquake caused buildings to collapse, ruptured a fuel pipe and the resulting explosion caused windows to shatter in homes hundreds of metres away.

People are searching for survivors in the building rubble and 200 are feared missing. Rescue workers are using infra red detectors to identify the heat from the bodies of the survivors, and 45 people have already been found alive. Workers are also using parabolic microphones to detect the sound of survivors buried deep below the rubble. It is hoped that everyone who is still alive will be rescued. The search will continue until no traces of life are found.

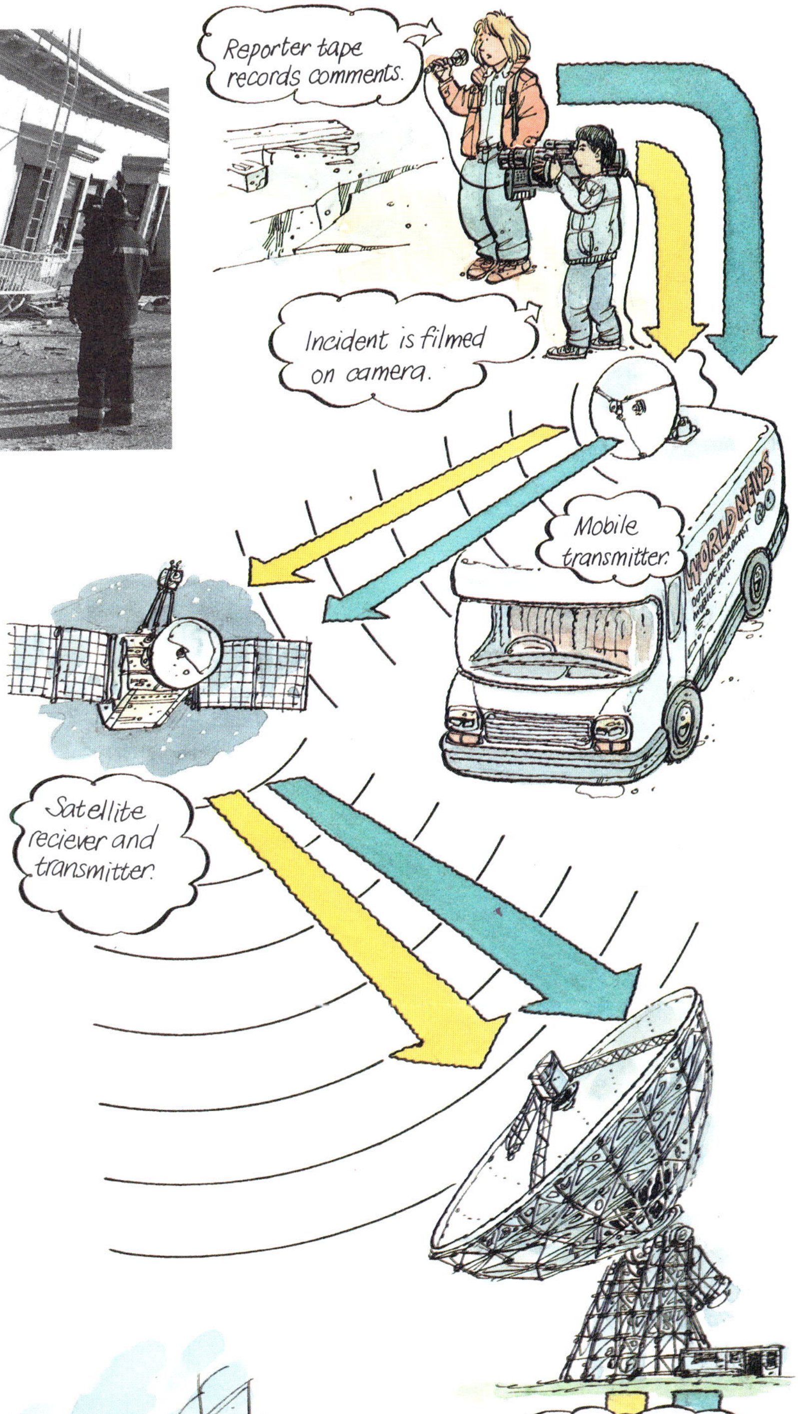

Reporter tape records comments.
Incident is filmed on camera.
Mobile transmitter.
WORLD NEWS
Satellite reciever and transmitter.

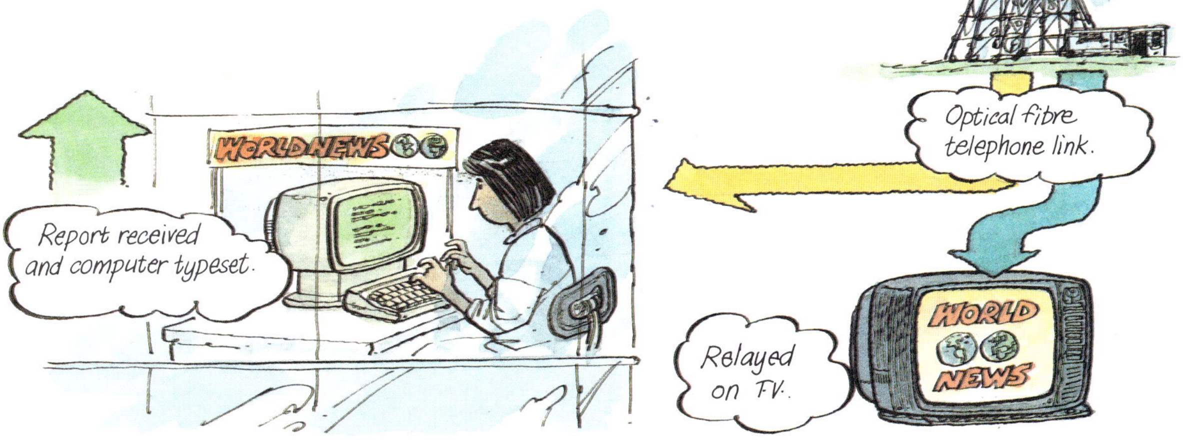

Optical fibre telephone link.
WORLD NEWS
Report received and computer typeset.
Relayed on T.V.
WORLD NEWS

Index

For additional information, see the following modules:

1 Energy
2 Making the most of machines

Photo acknowledgements

These refer to spread number and, where appropriate, the photo order:

Aviation Picture Library (J.A. Brown) *7.12/2;* EPA (A. Teitelbaum) *7.15/2;* Vivien Field Picture Library *7.12/1;* Sally & Richard Greenhill *7.8;* Trevor Hill *7.1/4, 7.7;* NHPA (G. Bernard) *7.2/1, 7.2/2;* Popperfoto *7.15/1;* Science Photo Library (J. Watts) *7.1/1,* (M. Rain) *7.1/3,* (M. Bond) *7.1/5, 7.10/1,* (H. Scheebeli) *7.5,* (H. Morgan) *7.9/1,* (Dr H. Rose) *7.9/2,* (Dr F. Espenak) *7.9/3,* (Dr C. Liguory) *7.9/4,* (L. Mulvehill) *7.10/3,* (P. Plailly) *7.10/2;* Sporting Pictures *7.1/2.*

Picture Researcher: Jennifer Johnson

8 STRUCTURE AND BONDING

The properties of materials depend on their structure and bonding. Many properties can be explained by using simple models to represent different types of structure and bonding. This module will help you to understand these models and to use them to explain and predict the properties of materials.

Relevant National Curriculum Attainment Target: (6), (7), (8)

8.1 Different types of models

A visit to the hairdresser's . . . .

You might visit the hairdresser's quite regularly. A hairdresser uses lots of different substances on hair. Each substance has its own properties, so it has a specific purpose. A model, preparing for a photographic session, might need all the treatments shown below. You might have had more than one of them yourself!

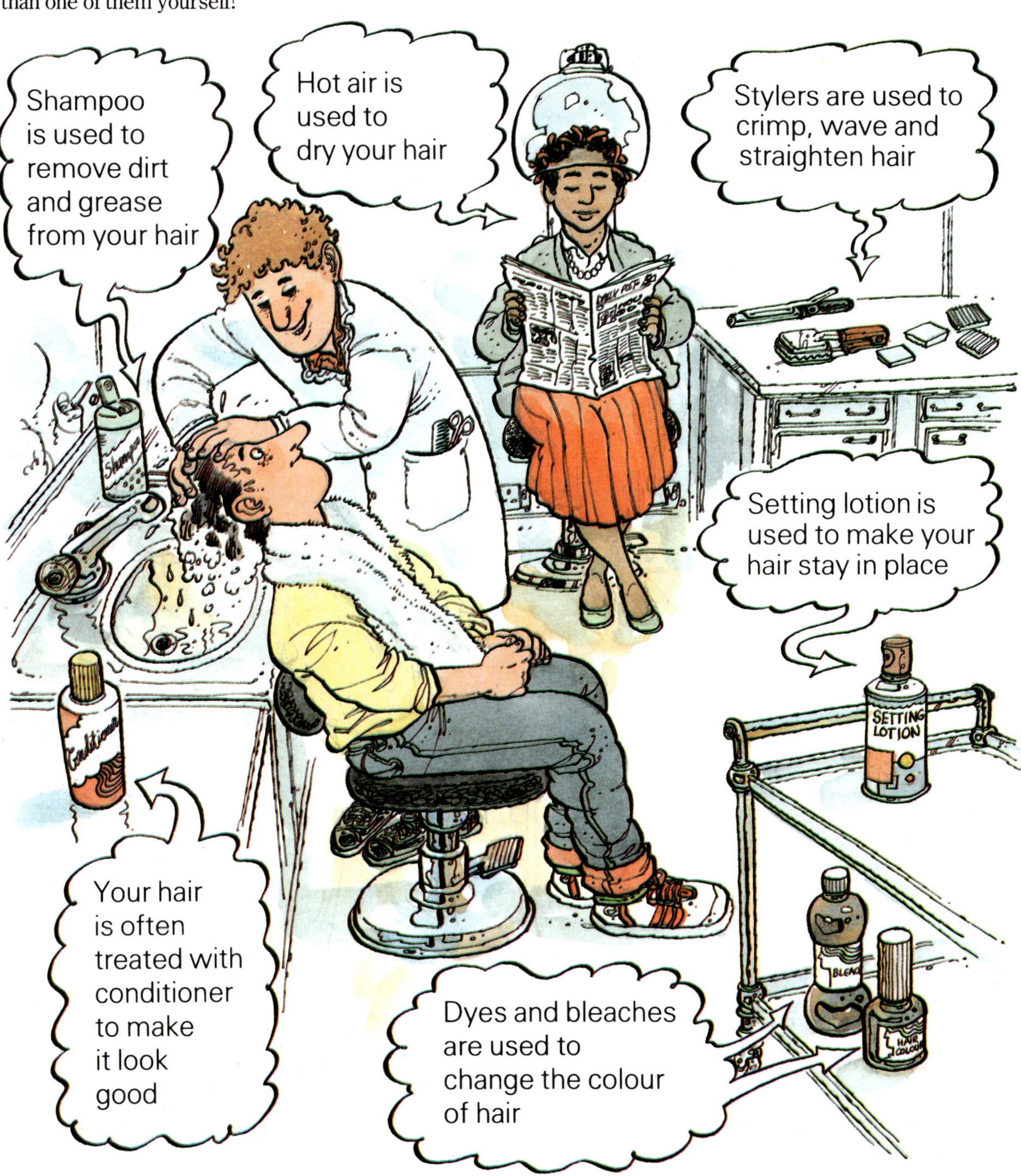

Have you ever wondered why these different substances have so many different properties?

.... is not as 'Cut and Dry' as it seems

When you begin to think about it, there's a lot more going on in the hairdresser's than it at first appears.

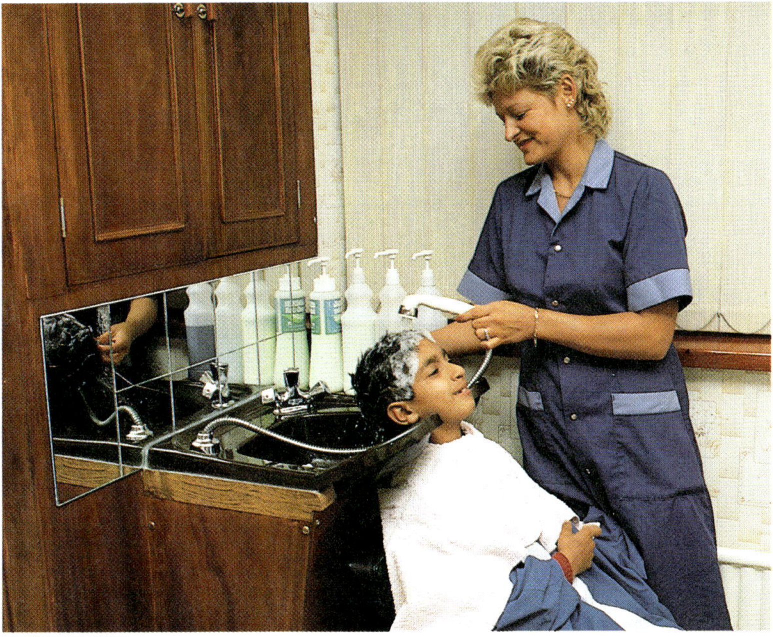

How are shampoos able to make oil and water mix?

Why are some things soluble in water, but others are not and leave a 'scum' behind?

Grease in your hair doesn't just evaporate – so why does the solvent in varnish evaporate so easily?

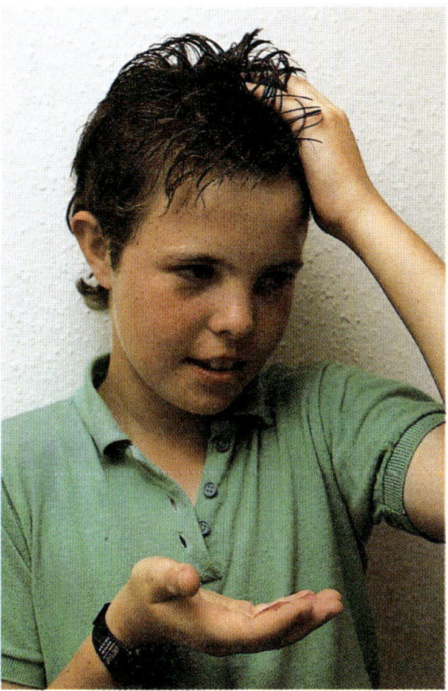

Your hair is very flexible – why do gels and mousses make it stiffer?

A shampoo which suits one person may not suit another. How do manufacturers try to persuade people that their product is better than any other on the market? What sort of things do you look for when you are buying a shampoo?

In order to understand how materials behave – their **properties** – scientists need to have some understanding of their structure and bonding. The **structure** is a *model* to explain how the atoms in the material are *arranged*. The **bonding** is a *model* to explain how the atoms are *held together*. To find out more about structure and bonding, read on.

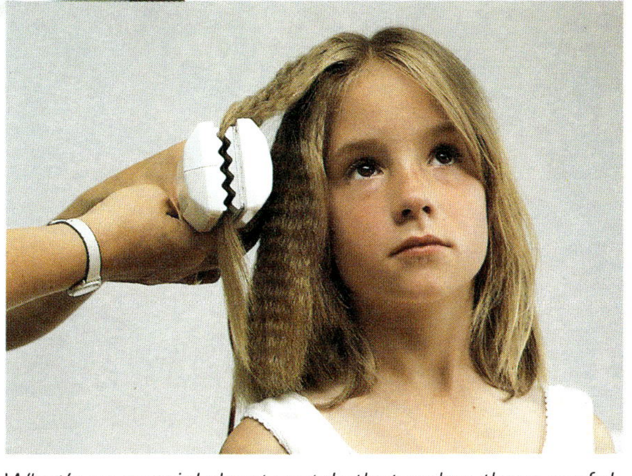

What's so special about metals that makes them useful for crimping hair?

8.2 Molecules

Atoms – the 'master builders'

Everything on earth, including you, is made up of tiny particles called **atoms**. Although there are millions of different substances on Earth, they are made from only about 90 different types of atoms. Atoms are the 'master builders', capable of joining together in many different combinations to produce the world you live in.

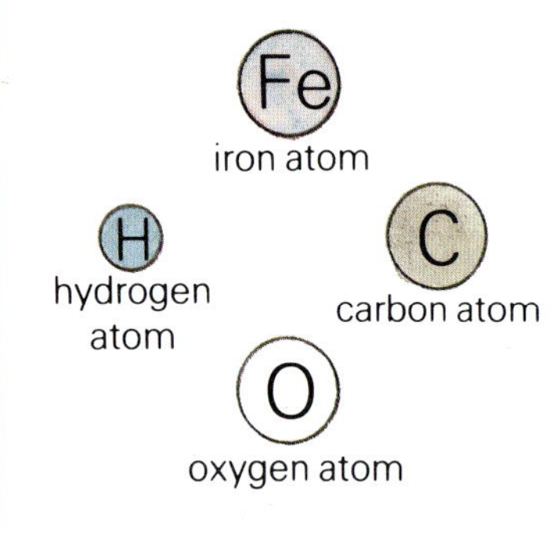

Each atom is represented by a name and a symbol

Iron is an *element*

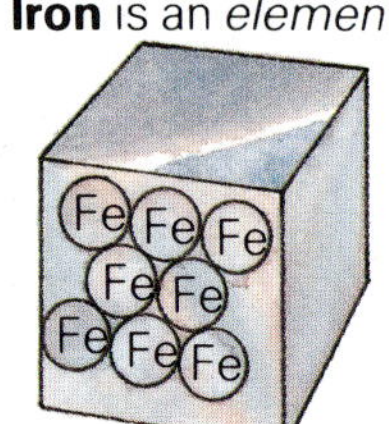

If a substance contains only one type of atom it is called an **element**. Most elements are metals but a few are non-metals.

Sand (silicon oxide) is a *compound* containing the atoms silicon and oxygen

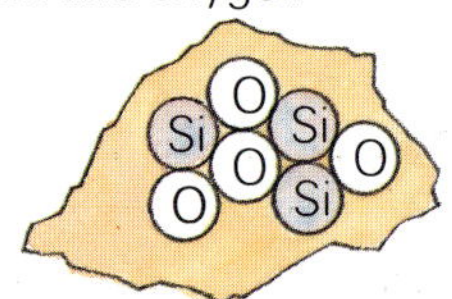

Some atoms of elements can join together to form new substances. If a substance contains different types of atoms joined together it is called a **compound**.

Combining atoms

The simplest combination of atoms is a small group or cluster called **molecules.** These are formed by atoms of non-metal elements joining together. The atoms in a molecule are held together by strong forces of attraction. The forces of attraction between atoms are called **bonds**. This diagram shows how different atoms are held together by the strong forces of attraction (strong bonds) inside molecules.

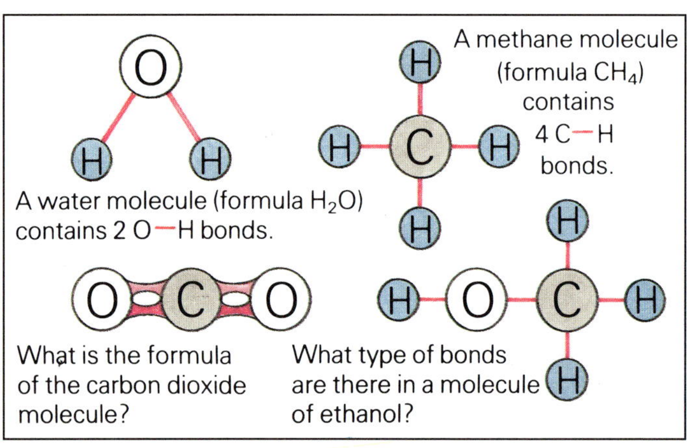

A water molecule (formula H_2O) contains 2 O—H bonds.

A methane molecule (formula CH_4) contains 4 C—H bonds.

What is the formula of the carbon dioxide molecule?

What type of bonds are there in a molecule of ethanol?

Type of bond:

- C—O in ethanol
- C—H in ethanol
- C—H in methane
- O—H in ethanol
- O—H in water
- C=O in carbon dioxide

Relative bond strength: 1, 2

The formula of a compound is like an 'ingredients label'. It tells you how many atoms of each element are in the compound.

Forces within a molecule

When molecules are used to make new materials, the atoms have to be broken away from the molecule. So the bonds holding the molecule together have to be broken. Atoms which are difficult to separate have a high **bond strength.** If you know the strength of different bonds in a molecule, you can *predict* the chemical properties of that material.

Look at the data on bond strengths. Which bond is the most likely to break first in the ethanol molecule?

Forces between molecules

Most molecules are very small – even the tiniest amount of a molecular substance contains millions of individual molecules. The bonds (forces of attraction) *within* a molecule are very strong. But the forces of attraction *between* molecules are usually very weak. These weak forces of attraction *between* the many molecules which make up a substance are called **intermolecular forces**. They are very important in determining the **physical properties** of materials. For example, the *greater* the intermolecular forces of a substance, the *higher* its boiling point.

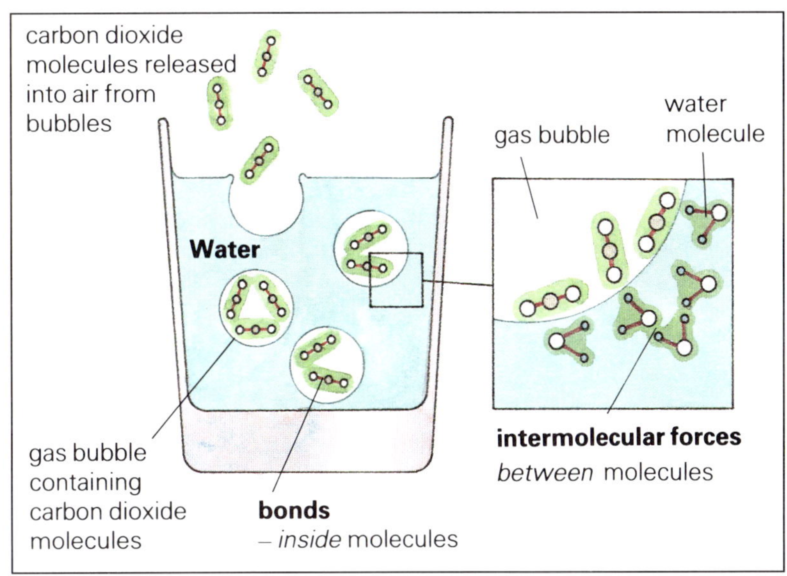

This diagram shows the carbonated water used to make fizzy drinks. What does it tell you about the size of the intermolecular forces in a liquid compared with those in a gas? How do you think the intermolecular forces in a solid compare with those in liquids and gases?

There is one carbon atom at the centre of each tetrahedral arrangement of carbon atoms. It is bonded to the four carbon atoms around it.

DIAMOND

tetrahedral arrangement of carbon atoms

Diamond *is a macromolecule, containing many carbon atoms joined together by bonds. In order to melt diamond, you would have to break lots of these strong bonds.*

Giant molecules

There are some substances that have atoms joined together by bonds but do not consist of individual molecules. They are made up of one very large molecule containing *millions* of atoms joined together by bonds. These giant molecular structures are called **macromolecules.**

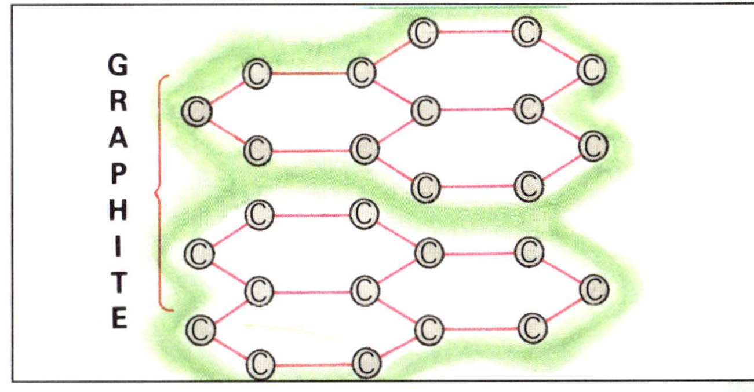

Graphite is another macromolecule made up entirely of carbon atoms. How do the forces in it differ from diamond?

1 A group of molecules called **alkanes** have the general formula C_nH_{2n+2}.
What is the formula of a molecule of an alkane with:
a 3 carbon atoms? **b** 10 H atoms?

2 Look at the data on bond strengths. Which two atoms form bonds of different strengths in different molecules?

3 Water and carbon dioxide are produced as hot gases in a car's exhaust. Which one is more likely to react with the iron in the car's exhaust? Give a reason for your answer.

4 Graphite is used as a lubricant because layers of its molecules can slide over each other. Why are they able to slide over each other? Why is diamond *not* used as a lubricant?

8.3 Polymers

'Setting off' a reaction

'You can't make an omelette without cracking eggs' . . . and you can't make a reaction happen without breaking bonds! Fluorine and oxygen are both elements that take the form of gases made up of molecules. Both elements will react with hydrogen – oxygen reacts so fast with hydrogen that the reaction can cause an explosion. But fluorine reacts even faster with hydrogen – causing an even bigger explosion!

This is because it is *easier* to break a bond in a fluorine molecule than to break a bond in an oxygen molecule. This is why fluorine is a *more reactive* element than oxygen. Chemists use their knowledge of bonds to help *predict* which molecules will react together to form new substances.

Students investigated the reactivity of two closely-related compounds: *ethane* and *ethene*. Both are gases made up of molecules, and both are **hydrocarbons** (molecules containing only the atoms *hydro*gen and *carbon*). The types of bonds in the molecules and their relative strengths are shown here.

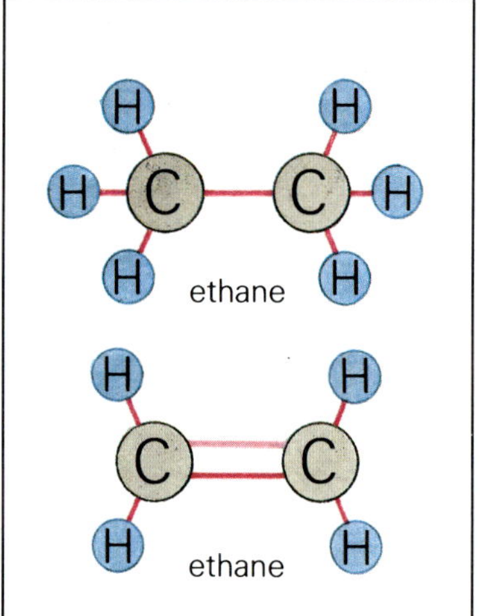

Which molecule do you think will be the more reactive?

The students added orange bromine water to test tubes of each gas. If the bromine (in the bromine water) reacts with another molecule, it loses its orange colour. To make the test as fair as possible, they added 30 drops of bromine water to each tube.

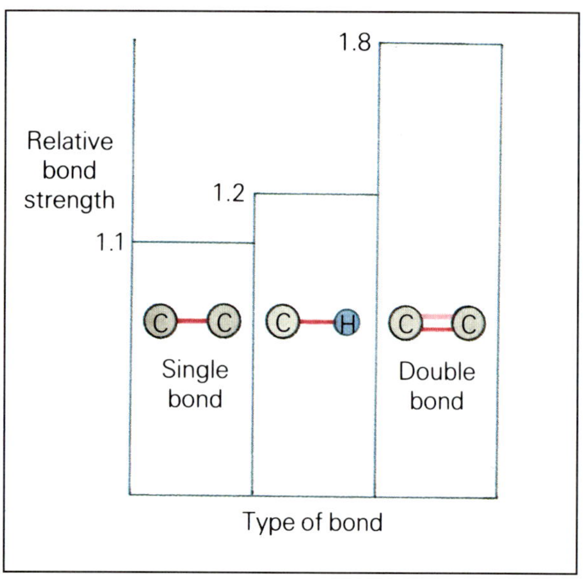

	Observations with bromine water
Ethane	Bromine water remained orange
Ethene	The first 12 drops of bromine water went colourless. The remaining drops stayed orange

You can see from the results that carbon-carbon double bonds in ethene are more reactive than the carbon-carbon single bond in ethane. But the data on bond strengths shows the double bond to be the stronger of the two, *so you would expect it to be less reactive!*

How do you think chemists explain these results?

Which bond will break first in a reaction? If the strongest bond has a relative bond strength of 1, what will be the bond strength of the weak bond?

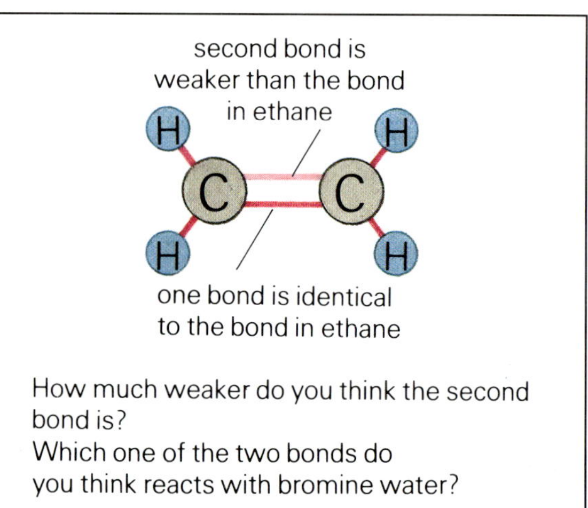

How much weaker do you think the second bond is?
Which one of the two bonds do you think reacts with bromine water?

Making use of reactivity

Reactive molecules containing double bonds can be very useful. Under certain conditions, molecules of this type can be made to join together. Such molecules are called **monomers**. When they react together, monomers form long chains called **polymers**. Plastics, synthetic fibres and fabrics are examples of polymers. Many plastics contain many thousands of carbon atoms which have joined together to form a carbon chain (or backbone). Some plastics have other atoms 'mixed in' as part of their backbone.

Which bonds have to break before the monomers join together?

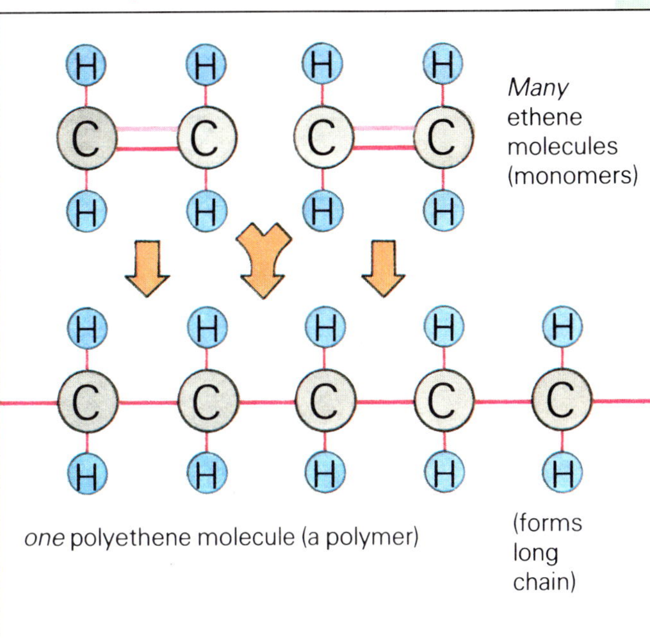

Plastics

There are two different types of polymer plastics that can be made, depending on the types of monomers used to make the plastic.

Thermoplastic polymers have *strong* bonds between the atoms in each polymer chain, but *weak* intermolecular forces between the polymer chains. Thermoplastics are flexible and easy to shape by breaking the weak forces between the chains. Heating a thermoplastic causes the polymer chains to break free from these weak intermolecular forces. This means thermoplastics melt quite easily and so have low melting points.

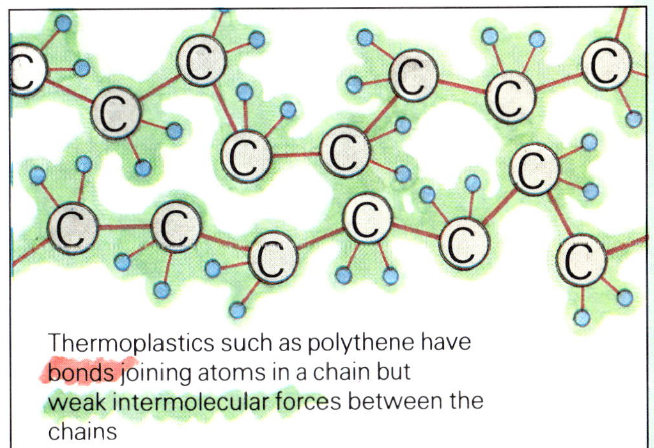

Thermoplastics such as polythene have bonds joining atoms in a chain but weak intermolecular forces between the chains

Thermosetting polymers have different properties from thermoplastics. This is because their *structure* and *bonding* give rise to different intermolecular forces.

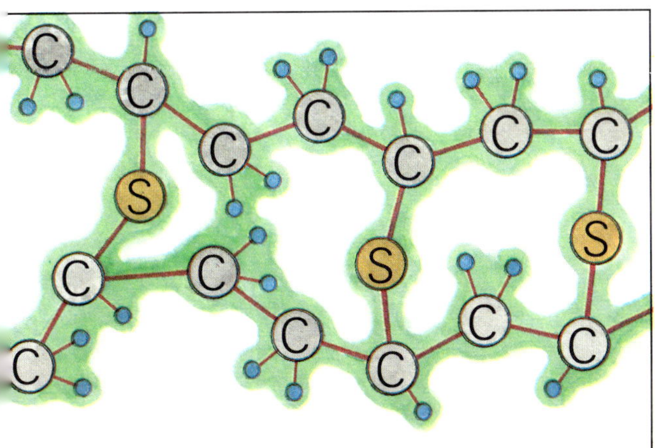

This diagram shows ***vulcanised rubber*** *– rubber which contains sulphur atoms between the chains. Thermosetting polymers, such as vulcanised rubber, are much stiffer than thermoplastics. The more sulphur atoms there are between the chains, the stiffer the polymer becomes.*

1 What are the formulas of ethane and ethene?

2 State two other factors the students (opposite) needed to do to make the tests on the gases fair.

How did they know the C–H bond in ethene does not react?

3 State two properties of thermosetting polymers that will be different from thermoplastics.

4 Draw the polymer (with a backbone 6 carbons atoms long) that can be made from 3 monomers like this:

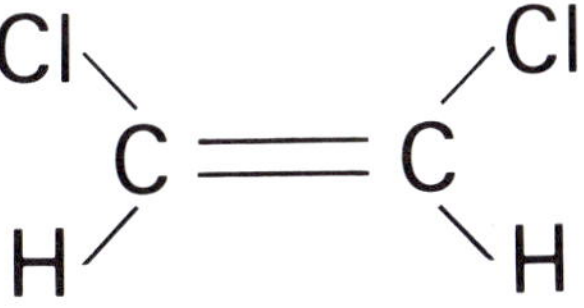

5 Explain why the vulcanised rubber used in a car tyre needs to contain less sulphur than that used to protect a car battery.

YOU CAN READ MORE ABOUT PLASTICS ON SPREAD 2.11

Mixing molecules

A 'sorting' charge

Have you ever built up a static electricity charge on a plastic comb? After being rubbed on hair or a jumper, a comb can pick up tiny bits of paper. The paper is attracted to the charge on the comb. The picture shows you what happens when a rubbed comb is brought close to a stream of liquid from a burette.

What does this tell you about how the molecules of water and oil respond to an electrical charge?

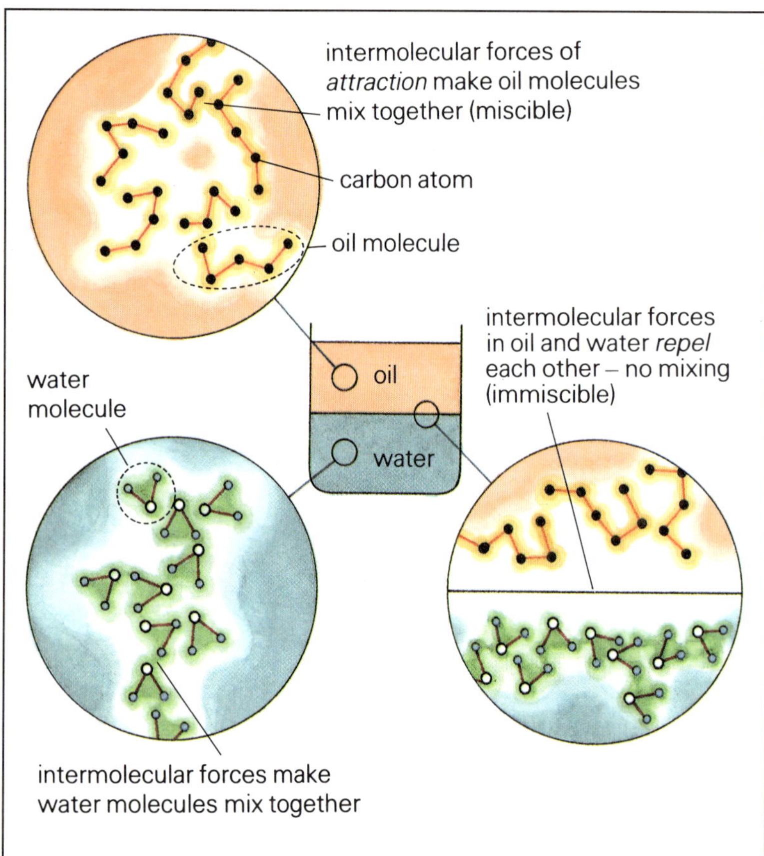

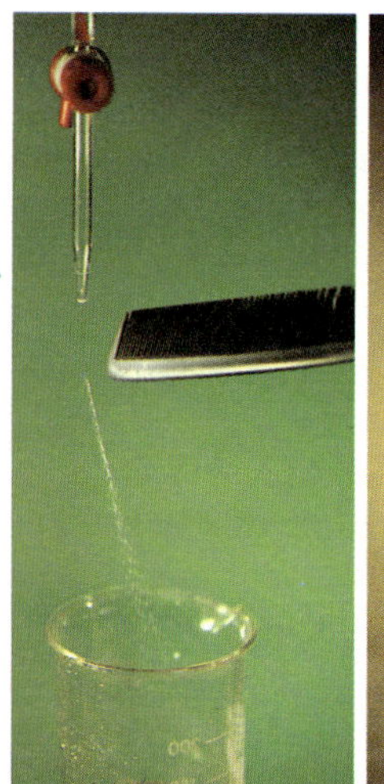

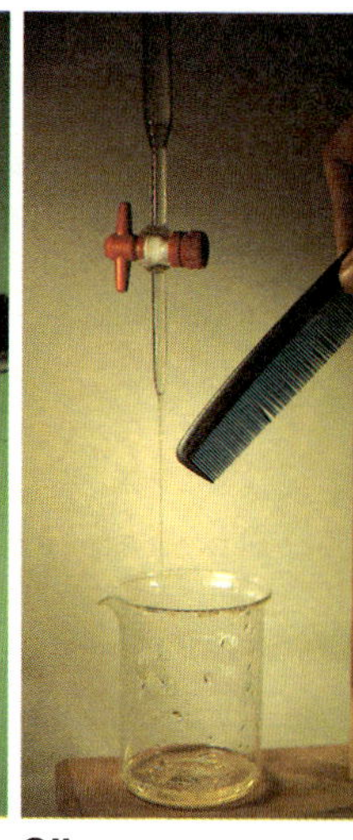

Water **Oil**

Their molecules behave differently when near a charged object.

Mix in or separate out?

Water molecules are different to oil molecules in other ways. Water molecules are **miscible** (mix completely) with each other. When they mix, water molecules form only one **phase** (no separate layers of liquid). This is because '*like*' molecules *attract* '*like*' molecules. In a similar way, oil molecules are completely miscible with *other* oil molecules.

Look at the diagram. How does it help to explain why water and oil are completely **immiscible**, forming two separate phases?

Emulsions

If the oil and water phases are mixed together, they will quickly separate out into their two phases. However, if another substance is added, they can form a mixture which does *not* separate out. The general name given to a stable mixture of two phases is a **colloid**.

When a colloid consists of two phases which are *liquids*, it is called an **emulsion**. In order to form an emulsion, you need to add an emulsifier. **Emulsifiers** are substances added to both phases (such as oil and water) to make them mix. Emulsifiers are widely used in food such as mayonnaise – a mixture of cooking oil and raw eggs (mainly water). In fact, the emulsifier in home-made mayonnaise is already present in the egg yolk!

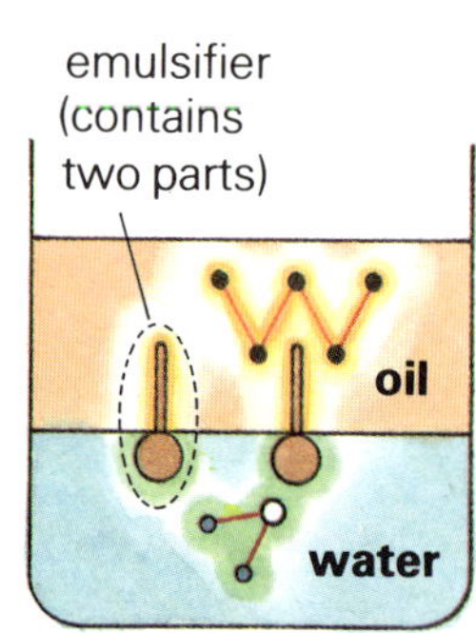

An emulsifier can link oil and water together

Emulsifiers

Oil and water don't mix because each type of molecule **repels** the other – and attracts only its own type. Emulsifiers *reduce* the forces of repulsion between the oil and water molecules. They are able to do this because emulsifiers contain *two* parts: *one* part has a 'liking' for the oil; the *other* part has a 'liking' for the water. As well as in foods, emulsifiers are often used in household cleaners – such as washing powders and washing-up liquids. The emulsifier used in cleaners is called a **detergent**. The diagram shows how a detergent acts as an emulsifier in removing oil and grease from fabrics.

① Detergent added to water with dirty fabric.

detergent molecule

water

grease/oil

fabric

② Oil-liking part of detergent attracted to grease.

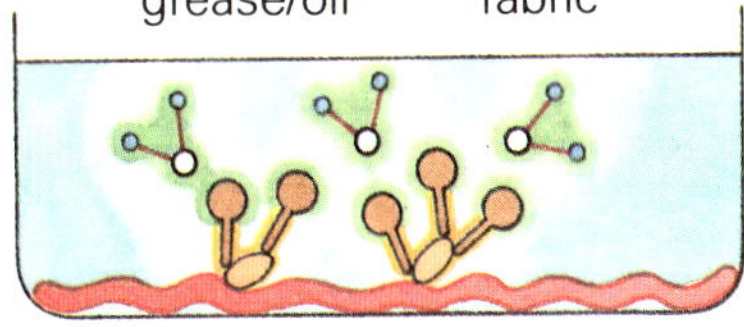

③ Shaking frees grease and detergent from fabric.

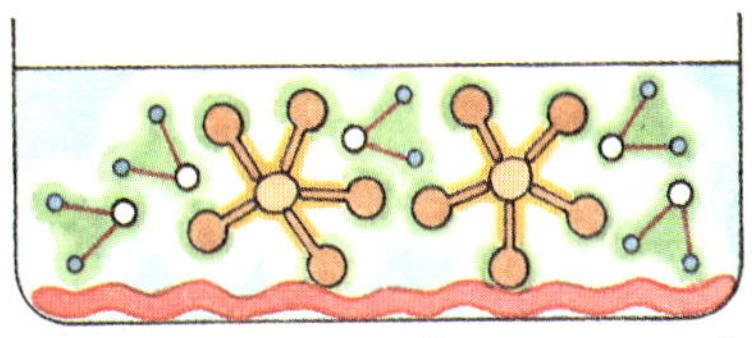

④ Water-liking part of detergent allows grease/detergent combination to mix with water.

*Once the grease/detergent mixes (becomes **miscible**) with the water, it can be rinsed away – leaving the fabric clean.*

Types of emulsions

There are *two* different types of oil and water emulsions. In one type of emulsion, the oil is dispersed as small particles in the water. This is called an **oil-in-water (O/W)** emulsion. Foundation creams and hand creams are examples of O/W emulsions.

What do you think a **W/O** emulsion is?

One way of testing the type of emulsion is by adding **dyes**. *Methylene blue* is a *water-soluble* blue dye. *Sudan 3* is a *oil-soluble* red dye. A mixture of the two dyes was sprinkled onto separate dishes containing butter and milk. The results obtained are shown here. What type of emulsions are milk and butter?

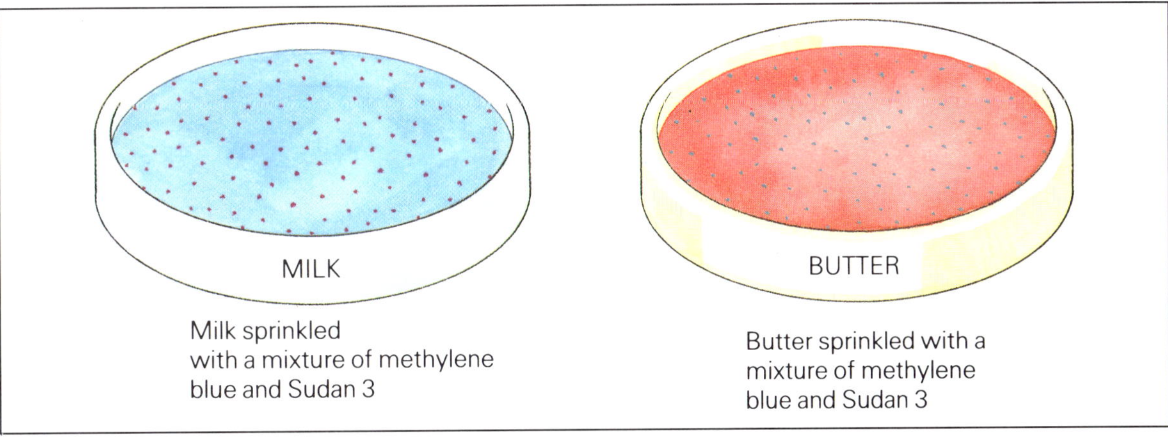

Milk sprinkled with a mixture of methylene blue and Sudan 3

Butter sprinkled with a mixture of methylene blue and Sudan 3

1 Why are oil-based mixtures used to clean car engines – but water-based ones are not?

2 Ethanol has a carbon 'backbone' – just like oils. A stream of ethanol from a burette is attracted by a charged comb. What would happen if ethanol were mixed with: **a** water; **b** oil?

3 Most cosmetics are emulsions. What type of emulsion (W/O or O/W) would be best for: **a** dry skin; **b** oily skin?

Give reasons for your answers.

4 Many perfumes are emulsions containing largely water, with the 'active' ingredient in the oil phase. If a mixture of methylene blue and Sudan 3 were added to a perfume in a dish, draw a picture of what you would expect to observe.

5 'Cold' creams are W/O emulsions. Draw a picture showing how an emulsifier helps the water to be dispersed in the oil.

6 Do you think cosmetics should be made from animal oils and waxes? Write a letter to a local paper explaining your views.

8.5 Molecules in solution

Useful solvents

When thirsty, you can choose from lots of soft drinks. Yet they are all similar, because they are mixtures of one (or more) substances dissolved in a particular liquid. Such mixtures are called **solutions.** The ingredients list of a soft drink will show you that the particular liquid is water; one of the dissolved substances is usually a simple sugar (such as glucose). Glucose is called a **solute** because it can dissolve in a liquid. Any solute needs a liquid to dissolve in before it can form a solution. A **solvent** is the name given to any liquid which can dissolve a solute. Water is a common solvent and forms **aqueous** solutions. There are other liquids (besides water) that can be used as solvents – these are called **non-aqueous** solvents. Because our body chemistry is based on having water as a solvent, non-aqueous solvents are usually poisonous.

molecule of adhesive

solvent keeps reactive adhesive molecules apart

solvent now evaporates

solvent molecule – volatile, but container prevents evaporation

solid adhesive left, reacting to form strong bonds

Arriving at a solution!

Glucose is added to drinks as a sweetener and also to give you energy. The glucose is present as millions of tiny glucose molecules. When all the glucose has dissolved, each part of the solution tastes equally sweet. This is because when solutions have been made, they produce **uniform** or **homogeneous** (evenly mixed) mixtures. Look at picture ① below. The intermolecular forces in the water and the sugar are very similar, so they are attracted to each other. How does this diagram help you to understand the phrase *'like dissolves like'*?

If you keep adding sugar to the water in a cup, eventually no more sugar will dissolve. Even crushing the sugar into tinier particles (or stirring the mixture even more) will not make any difference. At this point the solution is said to be saturated. A **saturated solution** is one in which *no more solute will dissolve* (at that temperature). The only way to be sure that a solution is truly saturated, is to make sure that there is always some undissolved solute present.

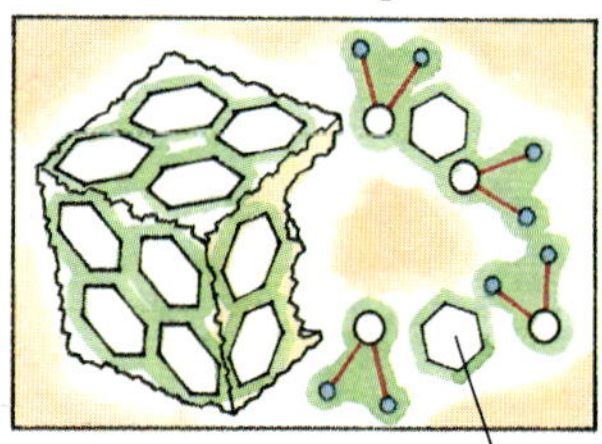

① When a sugar molecule is attracted by a water molecule, it breaks away from the solid and becomes **dissolved.**

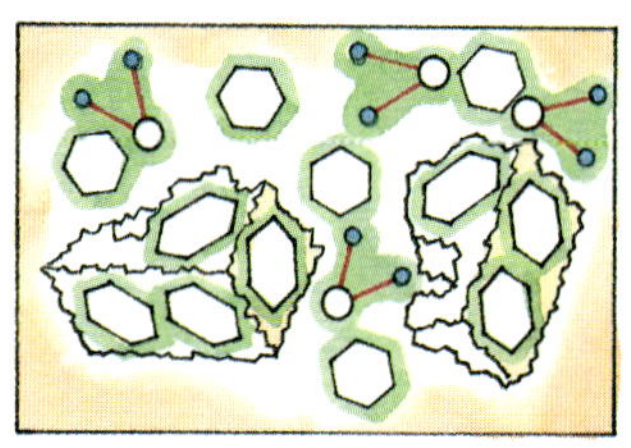

② Once a sugar cube breaks into smaller pieces, there is more contact between the sugar and water molecules. So the sugar dissolves faster.

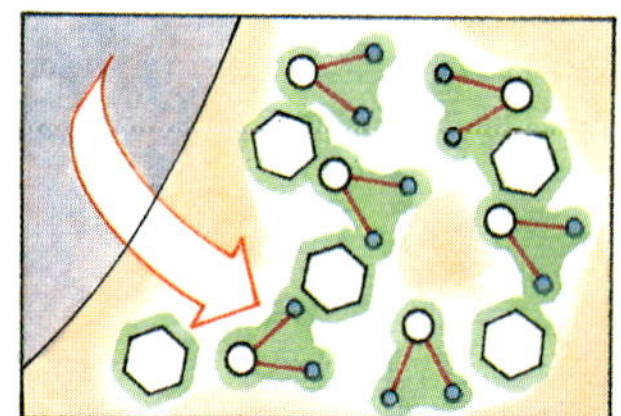

③ How does this model explain why stirring makes sugar dissolve *even faster*?

Solubility

The food and drug industries produce many solid substances (such as sugar and aspirin) which contain **impurities** – these have to be removed before the food or drug can be sold. Often the food or drug is less soluble in water than a more soluble impurity. (An everyday example of differing solubilities is the way in which 'instant' coffee dissolves quickly in a cup, but the same mass of sugar dissolves more slowly.)

To remove a soluble impurity from a less soluble solid, just add a solvent (such as water). The impurity will quickly dissolve into the solvent, leaving the less soluble food or drug at the bottom of the container. The impurity will now be in solution and can poured away; filtering and drying the food or drug leaves you with your desired solid – now without its impurities!

The amount of substance that can dissolve in a certain amount of solvent (at a given temperature) is called its **solubility**. The solubility of a solute in water is usually given as the *amount of solute in grams* that can be dissolved *in 100 grams of water* at a given temperature. A graph that gives information about the amount of solid that dissolves in a solvent at different temperatures is called a **solubility curve**.

Amount of solid (g)
20
18
16
14
12
10
8
6
4
2
0
10 20 30 40 50 60 70 80 90 100
Temperature (°C)
Impurity
Drug
The drug and impurity are insoluble in this region
The drug is insoluble in this region
Drug and impurity are soluble in this region

Solubility curves for a drug and its impurity. What happens to their solubilities as the temperature increases?

Crystallisation

To remove an insoluble impurity from a highly soluble solid, you need to use a technique called **crystallisation**. The solid and impurity are mixed with water and heated. *As the temperature increases,* more and more of the soluble solid dissolves in the hot solvent. An insoluble impurity will not dissolve, and is left at the bottom and filtered off. The solution of soluble solid (solute) and hot solvent is then cooled. As the temperature falls, so does the solubility. Less solute can now be held in solution by the solvent. When the solute can bo longer be held in solution, solid **crystals** of the solute are formed.

Look at the diagram. How does the purity of the drug change after crystallisation?

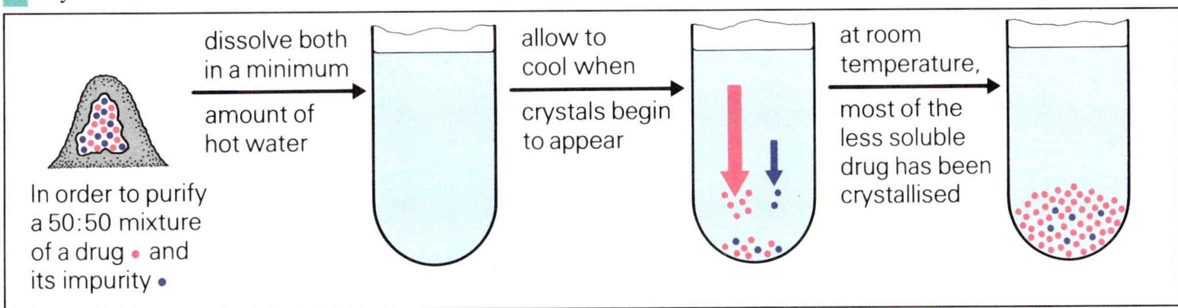

1. Why should non-aqueous solvents be kept out of the reach of children?

2. Draw a model to show what has happened when sugar has **completely** dissolved in water.

3. Why does each part of a *cup* of tea taste exactly the same but a *pot* of tea left to brew gets stronger?

4. Use the solubility curve to calculate the amount of the pure drug that can be dissolved in 500 cm^3 of water at 60°C.

5. If 20 g of the pure drug in Q4 was dissolved in 100 cm^3 of water at 90°C, how much would crystallise if the solution were cooled to:
   a 50°C; **b** 10°C?
   c Why do you never obtain all the 20 g of the drug by crystallisation?

8.6 Physical changes

Holding together

Many of the materials around you are made of molecules. Sugar is a crystal of *solid* molecules, water contains *liquid* molecules and air is a mixture of *gaseous* molecules. There is always a **force of attraction** between molecules. The *size* of this force determines whether a material is a gas, liquid or solid at room temperature. This force of attraction is greatest when the molecules are close together and tightly packed.

In winter after being sprayed out, the liquid water forms a solid ice 'cone' around this fountain. What happens to the free-flowing water molecules as they freeze? Why do they form a solid?

From solid to liquid . . .

When **solids** are heated, they *expand* and the molecules get further apart, so the forces of attraction between molecules become less. As heating is continued, a point is reached when the forces of attraction are too weak to hold the molecules in a rigid pattern. The molecules begin to move freely around each other, and so the solid changes into the **liquid state**. The temperature at which *all* the molecules no longer hold their position is called the **melting point.** Since different molecules have different forces of attraction, each pure substance has a specific melting point – and this property can be used to help identify each substance. The diagram shows you what happens when a solid such as naphthalene is heated to its melting point.

If a solid is melted and then allowed to cool, the change in temperature can be recorded at regular intervals until it becomes a solid again. A graph, called a **cooling curve**, can then be plotted.

Look at the cooling curve for naphthalene. What is happening when the temperature remains constant?

Solids and gases, look at the difference – carbon dioxide can form a white solid (at the bottom of the jar), but as a gas it moves freely.

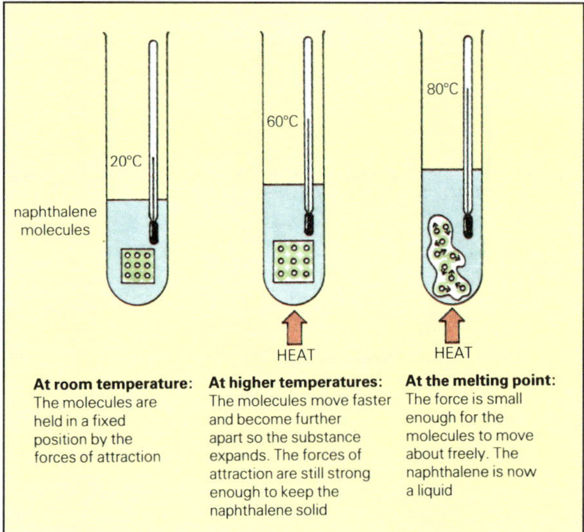

20°C
60°C
80°C
naphthalene molecules
HEAT
HEAT
At room temperature: The molecules are held in a fixed position by the forces of attraction
At higher temperatures: The molecules move faster and become further apart so the substance expands. The forces of attraction are still strong enough to keep the naphthalene solid
At the melting point: The force is small enough for the molecules to move about freely. The naphthalene is now a liquid

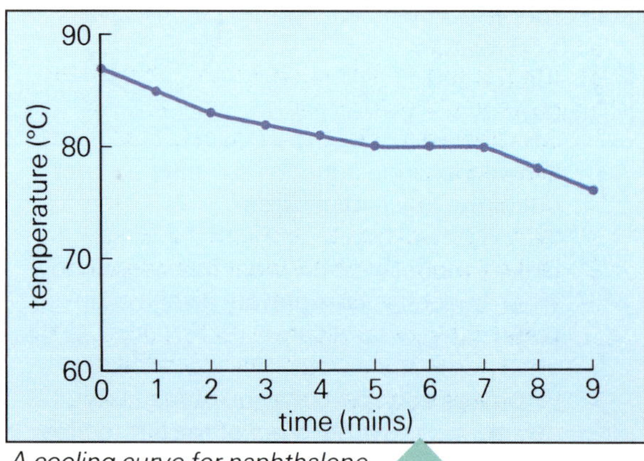

A cooling curve for naphthalene.

①

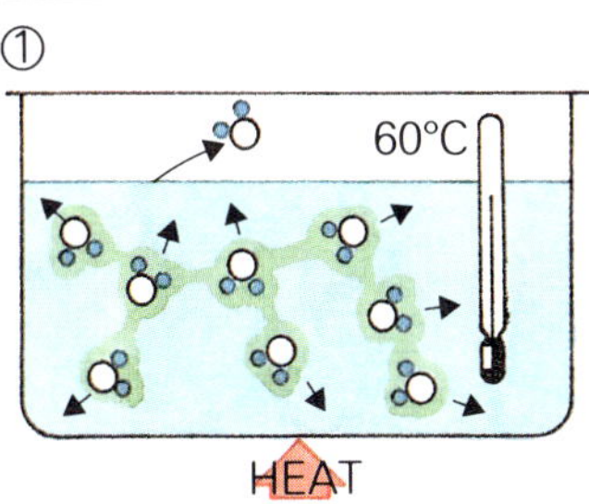

②

80°C

HEAT

③

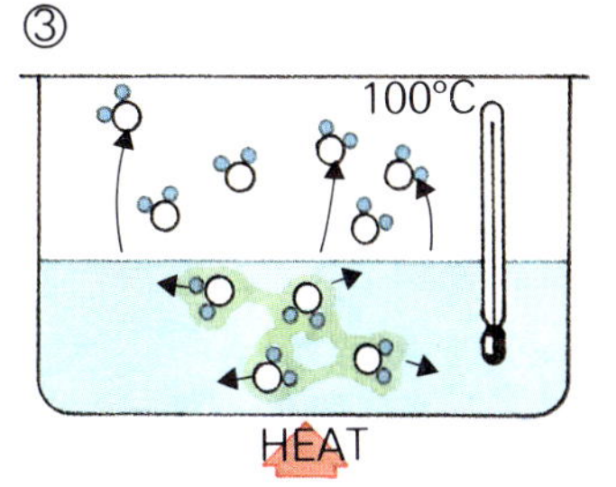

① When water is heated, *most* of the energy is used to make it hotter. The rest of the energy is used to give a few molecules sufficient energy to overcome all their attractive forces and become gases.

② For the same amount of heat, the rate at which gas is produced increases with increasing temperature (up to the boiling point).

③ At the boiling point, water molecules in the liquid state cannot move any faster. So the temperature of the *liquid* water cannot go any higher.

All the heat energy is used to overcome the forces between all the remaining molecules of liquid water. This changes the water molecules into the gaseous state (steam).

. . . from liquid to gas

Although the force of attraction between the molecules of a substance in the liquid state is smaller than when it is a solid, it is *large enough to keep the molecules close together*. In the **gaseous state** the force of attraction is so small (compared to liquids) that almost all the forces of attraction have been overcome – and the molecules are free to move on their own.

Falling apart – changing state

When a molecular substance changes state (from a solid to a liquid, or a liquid to a gas) energy is needed to *overcome* the forces of attraction between molecules. The *greater* the force of attraction between molecules, the *more* energy is needed. The process can be reversed but, in so doing, energy is released. Because the molecules are *chemically the same*, they have changed state – an example of a **physical change**.

Look at the picture below. What does it show you about the amount of energy needed or released when a substance changes from a solid to a liquid (or vice versa)?

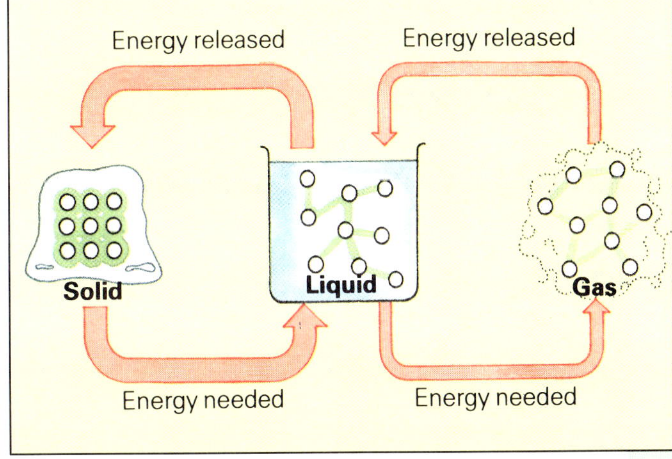

1 Why does a material contract when it gets colder?

2 Look at the cooling curve graph. Sketch the curve you would obtain if the naphthalene was heated to 87°C more quickly than it was allowed to cool.

3 Why is steam produced more quickly by boiling water when it is heated more quickly?

4 Look at the lower diagram on this page. Why are different amounts of energy released when a gas condenses and a liquid freezes?

5 Look at the data on the boiling points and melting points of some substances made of molecules.

Material	B.P. (°C)	M.P. (°C)
water	100	0
ethanol	80	−116
ammonia	−33	−77

a Which material has:
- **i** the lowest melting point?
- **ii** the biggest difference between its melting and boiling points?

b Why is the boiling point of liquid ammonia greater than the melting point of solid ethanol?

YOU CAN READ MORE ABOUT CHANGING STATES ON SPREAD 2.9.

8.7 Physical properties of gases

Investigating pressure and volume

A group of students used the apparatus shown to investigate how the pressure of a gas depends on its volume (when its temperature is constant). A footpump was used to increase the pressure of a column of air trapped above oil in the glass tubing. The pressure exerted on the air was measured from the gauge; the volume of the column of air was measured using the scale by the side of the glass tubing.

They recorded all their results in a table. Each student had their own idea about how pressure and volume were related. Which idea do you agree with?

Plot P against V since this is what we were measuring

When P goes up, V goes down so plot P against 1/V

Plot both P and V against P since their product remains constant

Pressure (KPa)	100	125	200	250	400
Volume (cm^3)	50	40	25	20	12.5

Doubling and halving

From the results, you can see that if you *double* the pressure, the volume is *halved* – and vice versa. Gas pressure is caused by gas particles (molecules *or* atoms) bombarding the walls of the container.

How does the picture help to explain why the pressure is halved when the volume is doubled?

If the volume of air is halved, the molecules collide with all sides twice as often – so the pressure doubles.

***Boyle's Law** explains the change in volume as bubbles of gas rise to the surface of a liquid.*

The relationship between the pressure and volume of a gas can be summed up by **Boyle's Law:**

For a fixed amount of gas (at constant temperature), the product of pressure and volume is constant.

This is often expressed by the equation

$$P_1V_1 = P_2V_2$$

where P_1 and V_1 are the 'old' values of pressure and volume respectively;
and P_2 and V_2 are the 'new' values of pressure and volume.

Investigating pressure and temperature

If a gas is heated in a sealed container, it cannot expand – but its pressure increases. Pressurised containers such as aerosol cans are marked with warning signs about exposure to sunlight and temperatures above 50 °C because a build-up of pressure in the can could cause it to explode.

The students investigated the change in pressure due to temperature increases by using two identical round-bottomed flasks. Each flask contained air at a particular pressure. At the start of the investigation (at room temperature), one flask contained air at atmospheric pressure. The other flask had some air sucked out using a vacuum pump, leaving air at a lower pressure than Flask 1 (at room temperature).

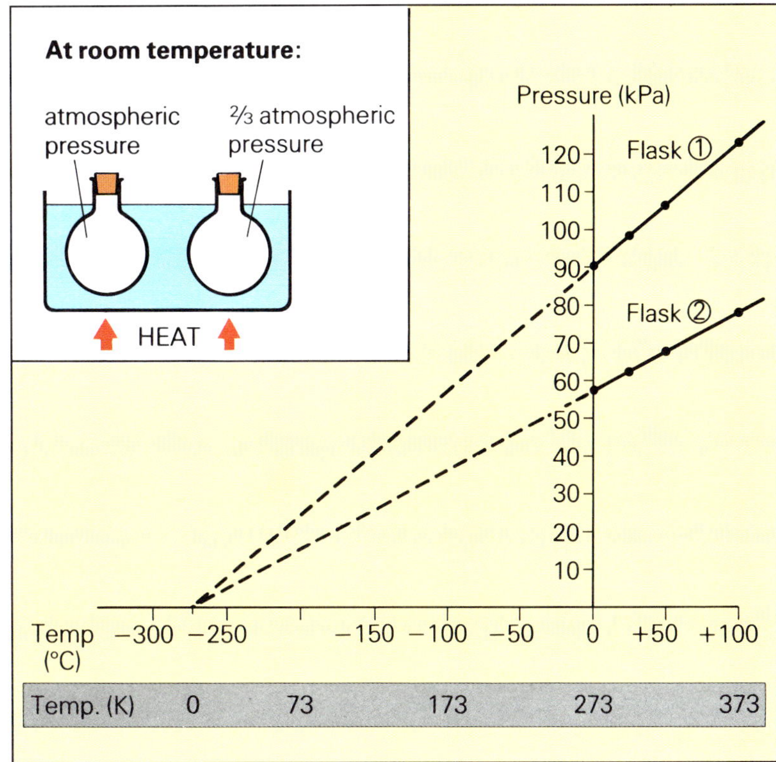

The flasks were connected to a pressure gauge, then put in a water-bath. On heating, changes in temperature and pressure were noted. The graph of the results they obtained is shown above.

Can you suggest why the pressure of a gas is not zero when the temperature is 0 °C?

Pressure (kPa)	Flask ①	33	66	99
	Flask ②	20	40	60
Temperature (K)		100	200	300

For a fixed amount of gas (at constant volume), pressure divided by temperature (in Kelvin, K) is constant.

Absolute zero and the Kelvin scale

If the pressure of the gas at 0 °C is not zero it means the gas must still be moving and colliding with the sides of the container. In order to find the temperature at which the gas particles stop moving (so their pressure is zero), you have to draw back the line until it cuts the temperature axis. If you look at the lines on the graph above, you can see that this temperature is −273 °C. It is called **absolute zero**. It is often useful to measure temperatures from this point (to help with calculations). When temperatures are measured from absolute zero, the new temperature scale is called the **Kelvin scale**.

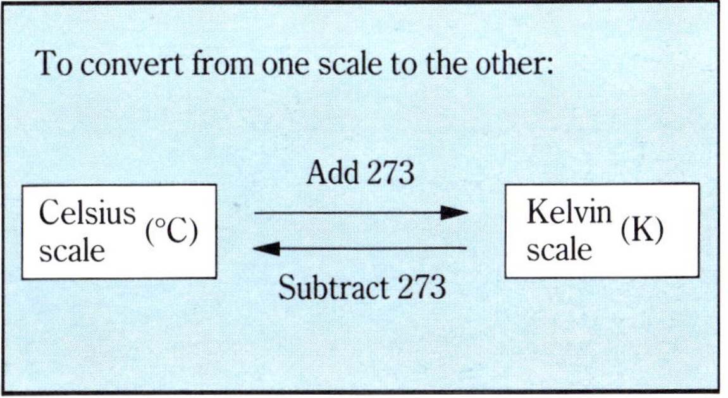

1. Sketch the graphs:
   a P×V against V; **b** V against 1/P
   at constant temperature.

2. Explain what happens to the pressure of a gas if the number of gas molecules is doubled, but the temperature and volume remain the same.

3. Look at the picture of the diver. What is the volume of the bubble when the pressure is 200 kPa?

4. Explain (in terms of the motion of molecules) why the pressure of a gas (at constant volume) increases with the temperature.

5. Look at the graph above. What is the pressure in both flasks at **a** 0 °C; **b** 100 °C?

8.8 Chemical changes

Getting a reaction

In the Middle Ages, alchemists tried to obtain gold from cheap metals, but failed. The reason for this was simple – since gold wasn't contained in one of the starting materials (reactants), they couldn't get gold as one of the products!

Hydrogen and oxygen are simple chemicals. When hydrogen gas burns in oxygen gas, water is formed because the oxygen and hydrogen **react** together. The simplest way of representing this **chemical reaction** is to use a *word equation* as shown here.

Hydrogen and oxygen both exist as pairs of **atoms** *bonded together* as **molecules**. Water is made up of molecules containing *two* hydrogen atoms bonded to a *single* oxygen atom. You can represent the reaction by drawing the molecules taking part. You can see that starting with 1 molecule of oxygen (O_2), you will form 2 molecules of water (H_2O) when the oxygen combines with 2 molecules of hydrogen (H_2). Although this is a very clear way of describing a reaction, it is rather longwinded.

	Reactants		Products
Word equation	Hydrogen + Oxygen	→	Water
Draw molecules	H–H, H–H, O=O	→	H–O–H, H–O–H
Symbol equation	$2H_2 + O_2$	→	$2H_2O$
Check: Do atoms balance?	4H + 2O	→	4H + 2O

Look at the 'Check' step. There are 4Ⓗ atoms and 2Ⓞ atoms on both sides, so the equation is balanced.

Balanced equations

Another representation uses **chemical symbols** to show what happens in reactions. When you do this the equation is called a *symbol equation*. This gives the *same* information as drawing the molecules, but in a much shorter form.

In *all* reactions, the type and number of atoms present is the same *before* and *after* the reaction. This means a chemical (symbol) equation includes the same type and number of atoms on each side – and the equation is said to '**balance**'.

There are two more examples of chemical equations below. Can you balance them?

	Reactants		Products
Word equation	Ethanol + _?_	→	Carbon Dioxide + _?_
Draw molecules	H–C–C–O–H (ethanol), O=O, O=O, O=O	→	O=C=O, O=C=O, H–O–H, H–O–H, H–O–H
Symbol equation	C_2H_6O + 3 _?_	→	? _?_ + $3H_2O$
Check: Do atoms balance?	2C + 6H + ? _?_	→	? _?_ + 6H + 7O

	Reactants		Products
Word equation	Nitrogen + _?_	→	Ammonia
Draw molecules	N≡N, H–H, H–H, H–H	→	NH₃, NH₃
Symbol equation	N_2 + ? _?_	→	2 __
Check: Do atoms balance?	2N + ? _?_	→	_?_ ? + 6H

Releasing energy . . .

As well as making new materials, most chemical reactions release energy. You eat food to provide you with energy. The energy from food keeps you warm and allows you to do everything from just breathing to running. The energy is released by a chemical reaction called **respiration**.

. . . by breaking and making bonds

In a chemical reaction the atoms are rearranged by making new **bonds**. Energy is first *used* to *break* the bonds in some of the molecules. This forms 'free' atoms that are then able to join together (in a different arrangement) to make new molecules.

Energy is *released* to form new bonds when the 'free' atoms join together. Some of this energy is used to break the bonds in *other* molecules – providing the energy for the reaction to continue. The overall energy change arising from the reaction is the *difference* between *the energy needed* (for bond breaking) and the *energy released* (by bond making). An energy profile can be drawn for any chemical reaction, showing this difference in energy. This difference is called the **enthalpy change** of the reaction and is given the symbol **ΔH.**

When fuels are burnt in oxygen, they release a lot of energy. Most common fuels consist of **hydrocarbon** molecules (containing only atoms of hydrogen and carbon). The table shows you the amount of energy released by burning 1 m^3 of different fuels (all gaseous hydrocarbons). This amount of energy is called the **calorific value** of the fuel.

In batteries, chemicals release electrical energy which can be changed into light or sound or movement or . . .

*An energy profile for the combustion of methane. When methane burns in oxygen, E_{OUT} is greater than E_{IN}, so $E_{IN} - E_{OUT}$ is negative. When **ΔH is negative**, the reaction is **exo**thermic and **releases energy** as heat (and light).*

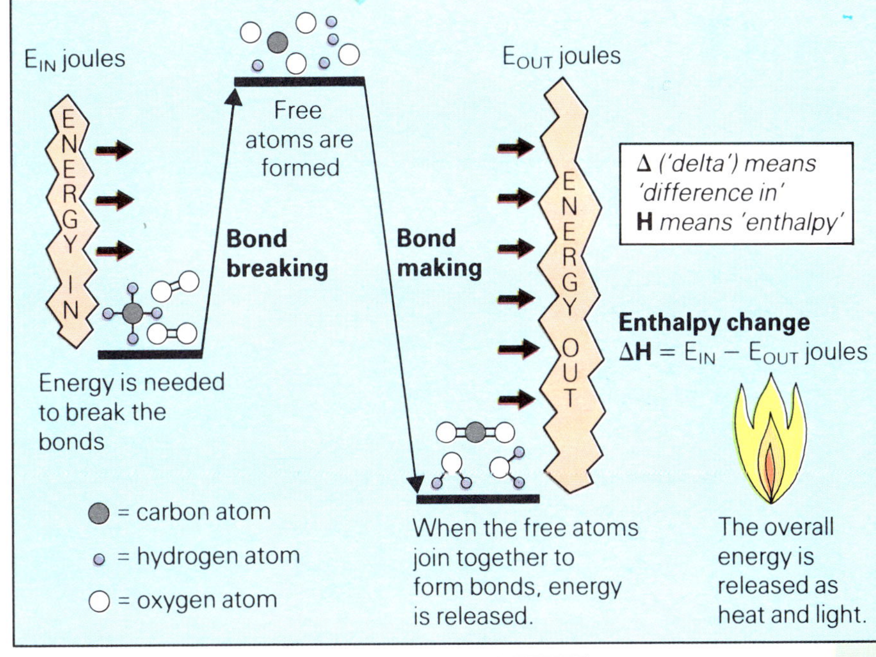

Carbon atoms in 1 molecule of fuel	1	2	3	4
Calorific value **MJ**/m^3	38.5	67.5	96.5	125.5

1 Balance the following equation:

$$C_3H_8 + O_2 \rightarrow CO_2 + H_2O$$

2 Give one example of an energy change involving: **a** heat; **b** light; **c** electrical energy.

3 Write an equation for the combustion of methane shown in the energy profile above.

4 Draw an energy profile for an **endothermic** reaction where **ΔH** is **positive**.

5 The EEC has suggested the U.K. replace the **B**ritish **T**hermal **U**nit for measuring the energy of gas. What would you replace it with?

6 Look at the table above showing calorific values. What would be the calorific value of a fuel with 6 carbon atoms?

7 The Gas Board charges about £15 for 38.5 MJ of energy. If they supplied you with 20 m^3 of methane (CH_4), what would your gas bill be?

Early models

The idea that matter is made up of tiny particles is not new. Almost 2500 years ago, the Greek philosopher Epicurus suggested that it would not be possible to go on dividing a piece of matter indefinitely. In 1808 a Manchester school teacher, John Dalton, resurrected the age-old idea of the Greeks. He imagined different elements to be made of different types of very small indestructible spheres. He called these spheres **atoms** after the Greek word *atomos* which means *indivisible*.

Dalton imagined all the atoms of one element to be the same size and mass. When atoms combined to form compounds, he believed they remained unchanged.

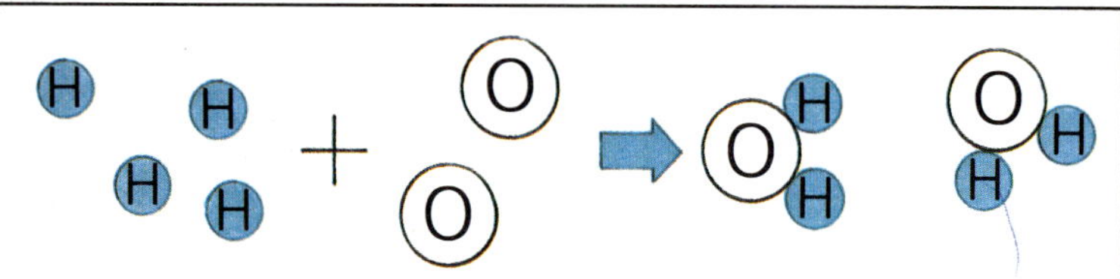

The Greeks imagined that atoms had different shapes and sizes – and that some atoms had 'hooks'.

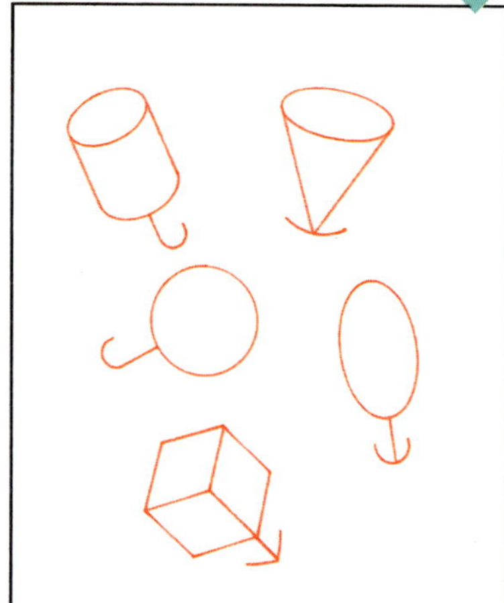

The model falls apart!

Towards the end of the nineteenth century, other particles were discovered which came from atoms. The atom was not after all indivisible. These particles were called **sub-atomic particles**. J.J. Thomson was the first person to discover a sub-atomic particle. The year was 1897 and he called it the **electron** after the Greek word *elecktra* which means *charge*.

The electron has a very small mass compared to the rest of the atom. It also has a negative charge (in contrast to the uncharged atom).

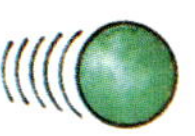

Positive 'drops' of matter with same mass as atoms had been discovered by Goldstein in 1886.

These discoveries led J.J. Thomson to propose a new model for the atom

Thomson imagined the atom as a **cloud of positive charge** with **negative electrons** spread throughout like 'plums in a pudding'

The proof of the pudding . .

In 1911, Ernest Rutherford, a New Zealand scientist working at Manchester University, decided to test Thomson's model experimentally. It was well known that *like charges repel one another* – the greater the concentration of charge, the greater the repulsion. Rutherford decided to use positive particles, called α **(alpha)** particles as high speed 'bullets' which would be repelled by the positive cloud.

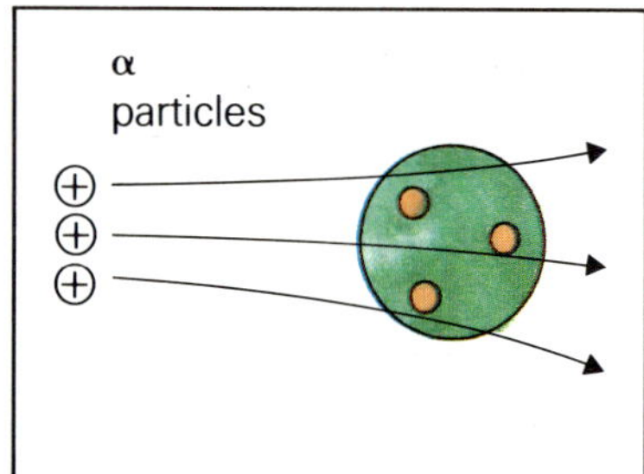

If Thomson was correct, positive 'bullets' would pass through with slight deflections due to the atom's widespread positive cloud.

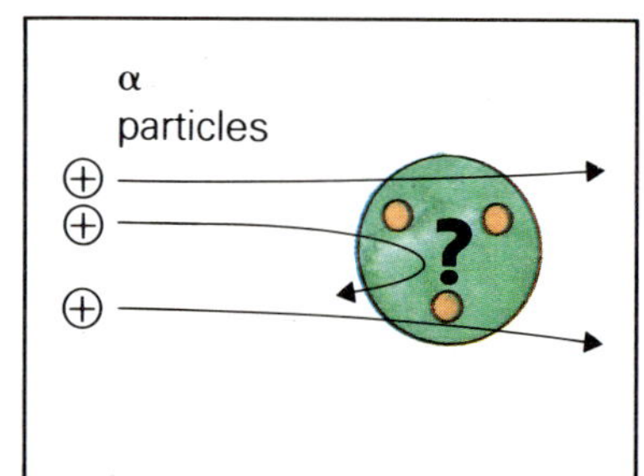

Rutherford was surprised – the deflections were much larger than expected. Some 'bullets' even deflected straight back!

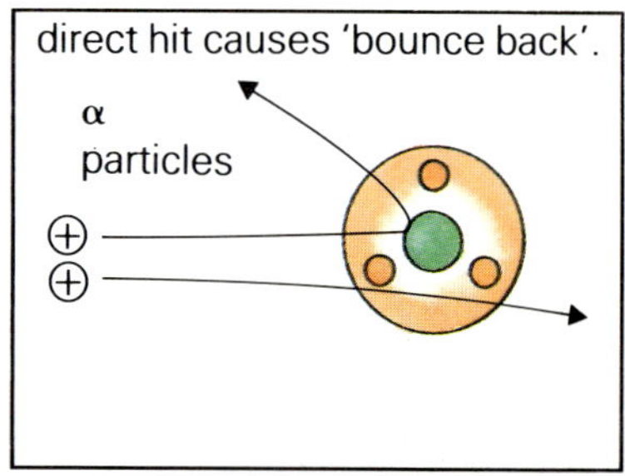

Rutherford realised there must be a high concentration of positive charge just at the ***centre*** *of the atom.*

Classifying atoms

Rutherford was able to show that the positive charge at the centre of the atom was due to positively charged particles. He called these particles **protons**. The charge on the proton is *equal* in size but *opposite* to the negative charge on the electron – however the proton is about 2000 times heavier than the electron.

All the atoms of one element have the *same number* of protons – this number is very important because it tells us which **element** an atom belongs to. The number of protons in an atom of an element is called its **atomic number**. Since an atom is electrically neutral (it has no overall charge) *the number of protons is always equal to the number of electrons.*

6 electrons
6 protons
6⊕

All carbon atoms have 6 protons in the nucleus and 6 electrons. It has an atomic number of 6.

9 electrons
9 protons
9⊕

All fluorine atoms have 9 protons in the nucleus and 9 electrons. *What is its atomic number?*

The element sodium, Na, can be written

Mass N° → **23**
Atomic N° → **11** **Na**

$^{23}_{11}\text{Na}$

It has 11 protons, 11 electrons and 12 neutrons.
The atomic structure of sodium is

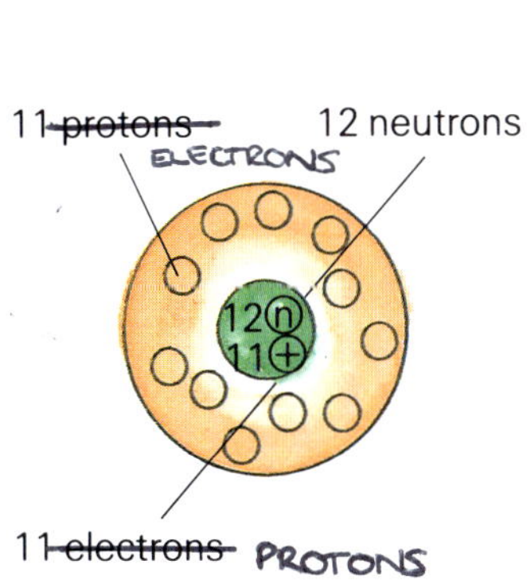

The mass of atoms

Although most atoms of an element have the same mass, in 1918 Aston found that a few atoms of an element had different mass. Since these atoms reacted *chemically* in *the same* way as normal atoms, they must have the *same atomic number* (which means they each have the same number of protons). So, what was causing the difference in the mass?

Chadwick answered this in 1932 when he discovered neutral particles with the same mass as protons. They were called **neutrons** and (like protons) they were found in the **nucleus** of the atom. To identify an atom fully, a number was needed from which the number of neutrons could be found. This number is called the **mass number**.

Mass number = Number of protons + Number of neutrons

An atom of a particular element must still have the same number of protons and electrons but it may have various numbers of neutrons. Atoms with the same number of protons and electrons but different numbers of neutrons are called isotopes. **Isotopes** are *chemically the same* as the normal atoms of an element, but have a *different mass number.*

So far, so good – but Rutherford's model (though helpful) is not the most accurate atomic model. To find out more, see the next page.

1 In what ways were the Greeks' ideas the same or different to Dalton's?

2 How many positive units of charge must there be in Thomson's model of an atom shown opposite?

3 Draw Rutherford's model of the atom showing the path of an *undeflected* particle.

4 How does Rutherford's model of the atom explain the fact that only a few particles were deflected backwards?

5 Complete the following Table

Particle	Relative Mass	Relative Charge
electron	?	−1
proton	1	?
neutron	?	?

6 Phosphorus has 2 isotopes $^{31}_{15}\text{P}$ and $^{30}_{15}\text{P}$

a Explain why they are isotopes.

b What is the atomic number and mass number of each isotope?

c Work out the number of protons, neutrons and electrons in each isotope.

8.10 Covalent bonding between atoms

Electrostatic forces . . .

Forces make things move – you often see mechanical forces (such as pushes and pulls) making an object move. However there are *other* types of forces such as magnetic forces and **electrostatic forces** (forces between charged particles). Electrostatic forces push or pull, depending on the type of charges involved.

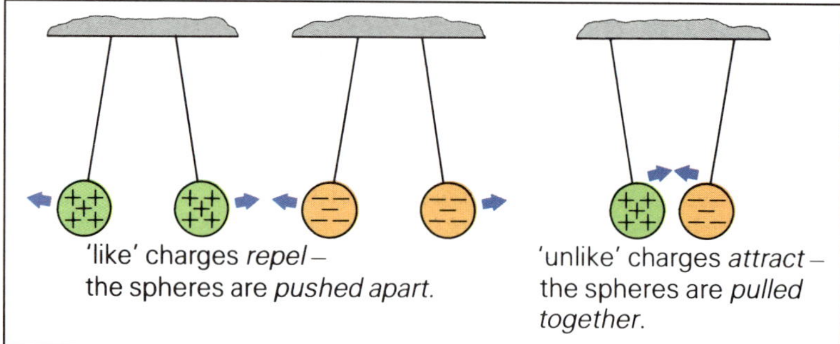

'like' charges *repel* – the spheres are *pushed apart*.
'unlike' charges *attract* – the spheres are *pulled together*.

. . . make chemical bonds

Some atoms of non-metallic elements join together to form molecules. The atoms are held together by strong forces of attraction called **chemical bonds.** These chemical bonds are caused by electrostatic forces. Atoms of elements have no overall charge, but do contain charged particles. **Protons** are *positively charged* particles that are found in the small **nucleus** at the centre of the atoms. **Electrons** are *negatively charged* particles that *move around* the nucleus.

The simplest example of atoms joining together to form a molecule is the combination of two hydrogen atoms.

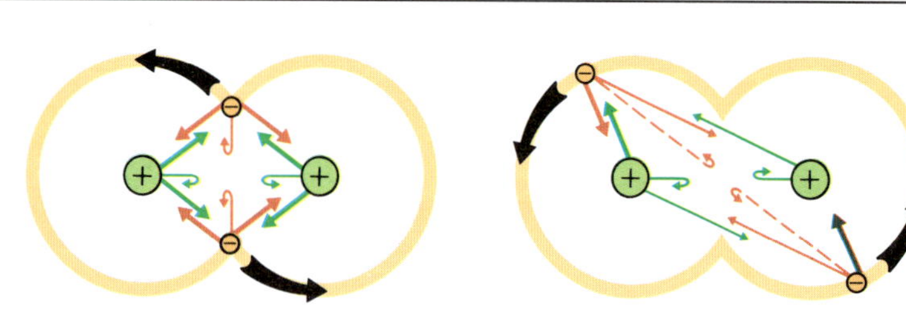

Hydrogen atoms join together to form **molecules** because there are 4 forces of attraction ( ) but only 2 forces of repulsion (&).

Even when the electrons move around the atoms, the 4 forces of attraction are still greater than the 2 forces of repulsion.

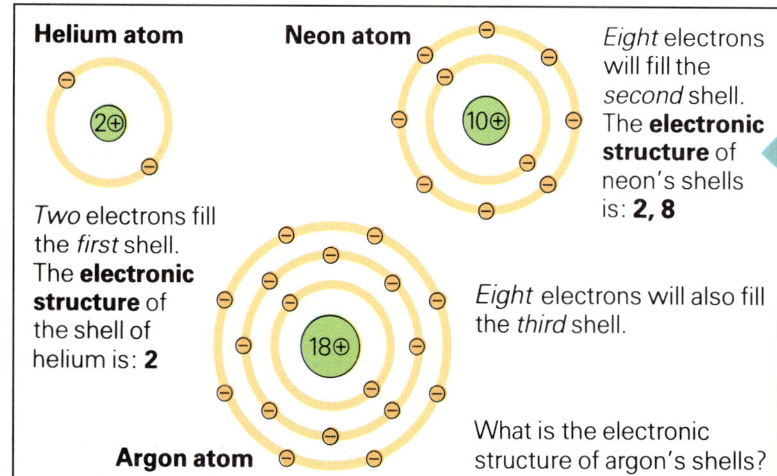

Two electrons fill the *first* shell. The **electronic structure** of the shell of helium is: **2**

Eight electrons will fill the *second* shell. The **electronic structure** of neon's shells is: **2, 8**

Eight electrons will also fill the *third* shell.

What is the electronic structure of argon's shells?

Filling shells

Not all elements have atoms that will join together to form chemical bonds. **Helium**, **neon** and **argon** are a group of atoms that don't form bonds. Chemists call them the **inert gases** – because they are so *unreactive*. In order to explain the inability of some atoms to join with others, chemists proposed that electrons were arranged in **shells** around the nucleus. Each shell has a *limit* to the number of electrons it can hold. Electrons go into the shells in a certain *order*. The **inner shells** (those closest to the nucleus) are always filled *first*. The diagrams show you the number of electrons that can fit into the first three shells.

An atom with *all* its shells full cannot fit any more electrons into these shells. *As a result, it does not form bonds with other atoms.*

Bonding to different atoms

Atoms become more *stable* if they can find a way of filling their outer shells. An atom with an unfilled outer shell of electrons can **share electrons** with another atom which has an unfilled outer shell – this sharing means that both atoms end up with filled shells. The bond formed by the sharing of outer shell electrons is called a **covalent bond**. Fluorine (electronic structure *2,7*) forms one covalent bond when it reacts with a hydrogen atom (electronic structure *1*).

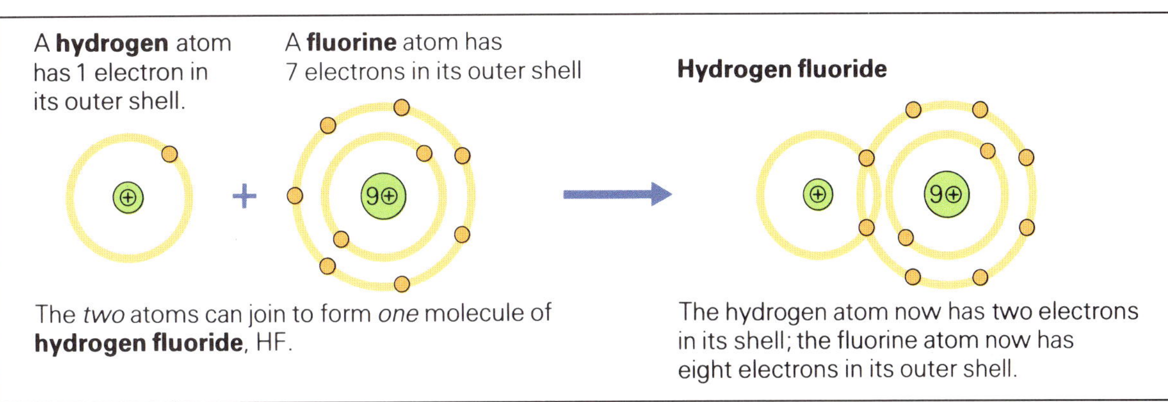

A **hydrogen** atom has 1 electron in its outer shell.
A **fluorine** atom has 7 electrons in its outer shell
Hydrogen fluoride
9⊕
+
9⊕
The *two* atoms can join to form *one* molecule of **hydrogen fluoride**, HF.
The hydrogen atom now has two electrons in its shell; the fluorine atom now has eight electrons in its outer shell.

Not all the outer shell electrons have to be involved in the sharing of electrons. These electrons do not take part in bonding. Oxygen (electronic structure *2,6*) forms *two* covalent bonds with *two* hydrogen atoms.

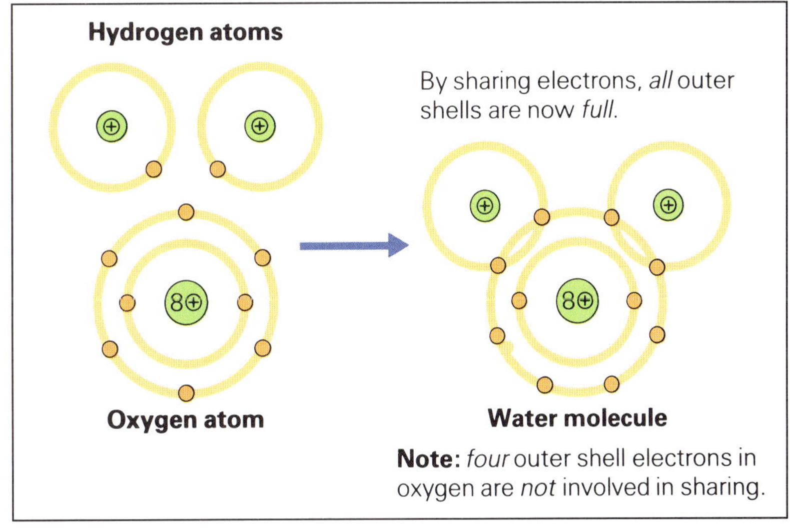

The nitrogen atom has an electronic structure *2,5*. How many covalent bonds do you think it will form when it reacts with hydrogen atoms? How many hydrogen atoms will become bonded to the one nitrogen atom?

1 What is the electronic structure of the following atoms? (Number in brackets = *total* number of electrons.)
a boron (*5*); **b** phosphorus (*15*); **c** magnesium (*12*); **d** chlorine (*17*).

2 **a** Which one of the atoms in Q1 has the same number of outer shell electrons as fluorine?
b Draw the atomic structure of the atom in **a**.
c How many covalent bonds would you expect this atom to form with hydrogen?

3 The valency of an atom is the number of electrons supplied by the atom for sharing to form a covalent bond. What is the valency of:
a hydrogen; **b** fluorine; **c** oxygen?

4 Nitrogen (*7*) and phosphorus (*15*) have similar chemical properties.
a Suggest a reason for this.
b Name 2 other elements from this spread that you might expect to have similar chemical properties to each other. Why?

5 Draw a diagram to show how electrons are shared to achieve full shells when the following atoms join together to form molecules:
a A carbon atom (*15*) and 4 hydrogen atoms (*1*);
b A nitrogen atom (*7*) and 3 fluorine atoms (*9*);
c How many electrons in each atom are not involved in bonding?

Ionic bonding between atoms

Filling shells . . .

The atoms of metals and non-metals join together in a different way to the covalent bonding between non-metal atoms. *You will need to be familiar with the main ideas about atomic structure to understand how this happens.* (These ideas are explained more fully on Spreads 8.9 and 8.10).

. . . by losing and gaining electrons

Metal atoms have only a few electrons in their outer shells. When metals react with non-metals, the easiest way for metal atoms to obtain a full outer shell of electrons is to *lose electrons*. When metal atoms lose electrons, they are left with more protons than electrons. As a result, the atom is no longer neutral – it is now *positively charged*. A charged atom is called an **ion. Metals** *lose electrons to form* **positive ions.**

The electrons lost by the metal atoms are *gained* by the *non-metal* atoms. When a non-metal atom gains electrons, it has more electrons than protons so it becomes *negatively charged*. **Non-metals** *gain electrons to form* **negative ions.**

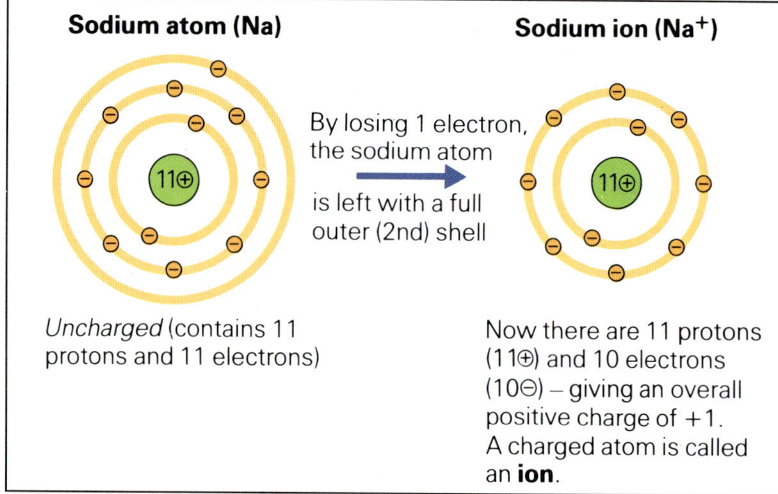

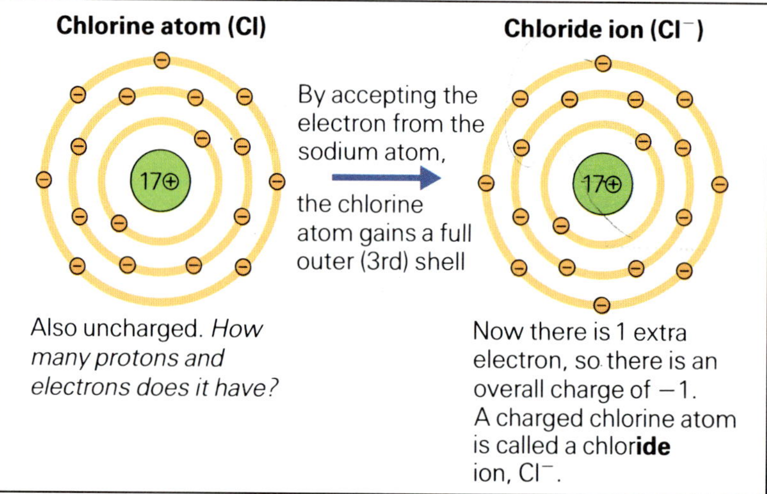

is left with a full outer (2nd) shell
Uncharged (contains 11 protons and 11 electrons)
Now there are 11 protons (11⊕) and 10 electrons (10⊖) – giving an overall positive charge of +1.

Chlorine atom (Cl)
Chloride ion (Cl^-)
17⊕
17⊕
By accepting the electron from the sodium atom,
the chlorine atom gains a full outer (3rd) shell
Also uncharged. *How many protons and electrons does it have?*
Now there is 1 extra electron, so there is an overall charge of −1.
A charged chlorine atom is called a chlor**ide** ion, Cl^-.

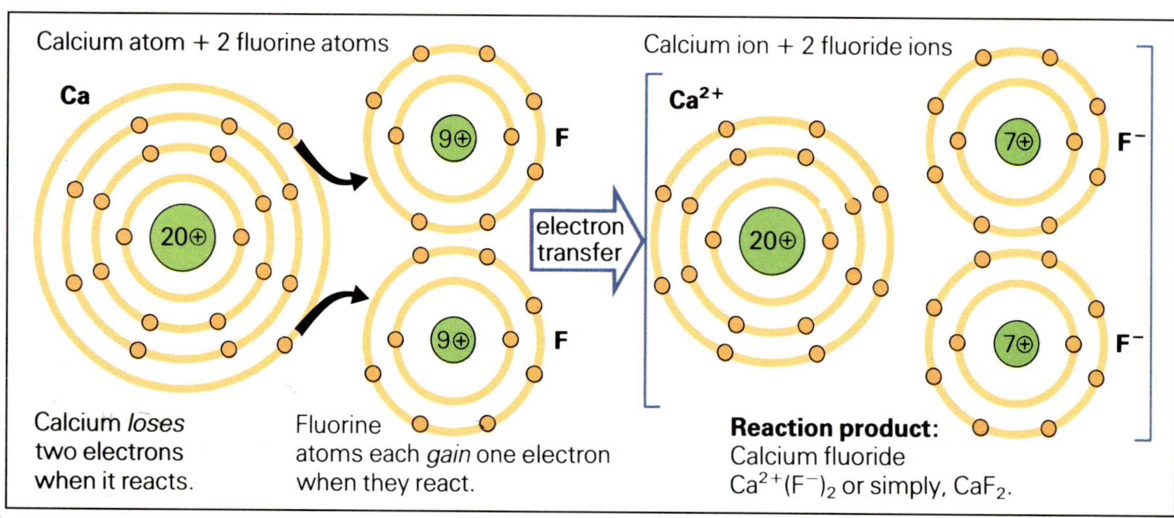

Reaction product:

$Ca^{2+}(F^-)_2$ or simply, CaF_2.

The number of electrons lost by the metal atom is equal to the number gained by the non-metal atom(s) with which it reacts.

Charges on the ions

For elements with up to 20 electrons, the number of electrons transferred from the metal to the non-metal depends on the electronic structure.

Different metals with the *same* number of electrons in their outer shells will each normally lose the *same number* of electrons. The size of the positive charge on the metal ion indicates the number of electrons that have been lost.

Similarly, different non-metals with a particular number of electrons in their outer shells will each gain an identical number of electrons. The size of the negative charge will indicate the number of electrons that have been gained.

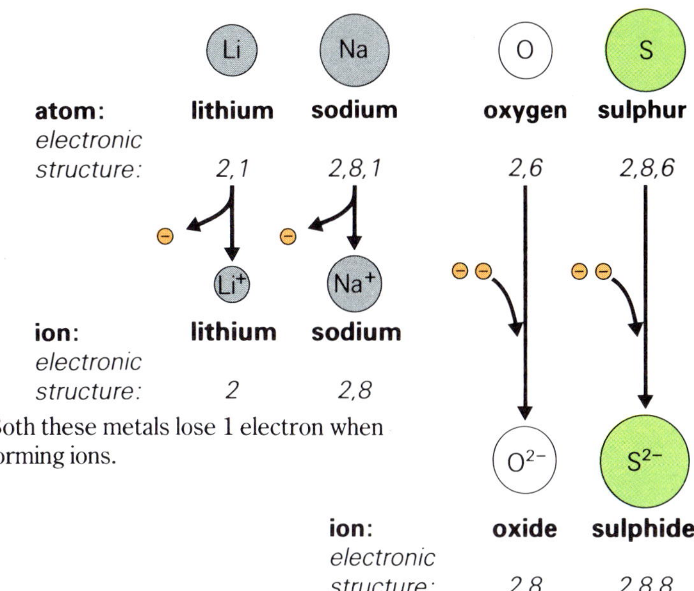

Both these metals lose 1 electron when forming ions.

Both these non-metals gain 2 electrons when forming ions.

Forces of attraction

There is a force of attraction between the oppositely charged ions. This *strong* force acts as a chemical bond, holding the ions together. This type of force between oppositely charged ions is called an **ionic bond**. Unlike most molecules, the ions are not found in small groups but as a **giant structure** in a framework or **lattice**. The greater the charge on the ions, the larger the force of attraction between the ions. A lot of heat energy is needed to overcome these strong forces of attraction – so ionic compounds usually have high melting points. The greater the force of attraction between the ions, the greater the melting points of the **compound** made up of the ions.

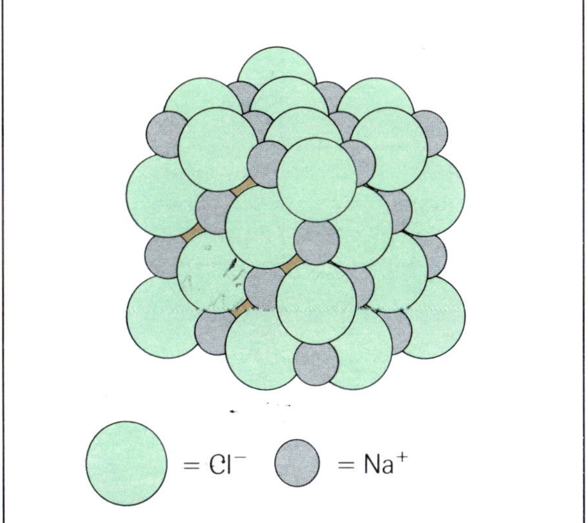

Sodium chloride – table salt – is made up of sodium and chloride ions arranged in a lattice.

In the following questions, the number in brackets refers to the number of electrons in each atom.

1 By drawing the atomic structures show the transfer of electrons that takes place when Ca(*20*) reacts with O(*8*). What is the name and formula of the product?

2 From the following list of symbols of elements; P(*15*), K(*19*), N(*7*), Mg(*12*), F(*9*), choose:
- **a** the atom which forms an ion of charge +2;
- **b** the atom which forms an ion of charge −1;
- **c** the atoms which form ions with the same charge.

3 What shape do you think sodium chloride crystals are?

4 Aluminium oxide is made by reacting aluminium(*13*) with oxygen(*8*). Their electronic structures are:
Al: *2,8,3*; O: *2,6*
- **a** What is the charge on each ion?
- **b** Aluminium oxide is used to line furnaces. What property makes it an ideal material and why is it better than NaCl?

5 In what ways is ionic bonding similar to covalent bonding?

Ionic solutions

Positive ions		Negative ions	
+1	K^+ potassium, Na^+ sodium	−1	NO_3^- nitrate, OH^- hydroxide, Cl^- chloride
+2	Mg^{2+} magnesium, Pb^{2+} lead	−2	O^{2-} oxide, SO_4^{2-} sulphate, CO_3^{2-} carbonate
+3	Al^{3+} aluminium		
Metals form positive ions		**Non-metals** (separately or in groups) **usually form negative ions**	

Ions do it their way!

You may drink milk because it contains calcium, and use toothpaste that contains fluoride because both are good for your teeth. But as pure elements fluorine and calcium are highly reactive and would do you more harm than good. However when they are present as **ions** – calcium ions and fluoride ions – they can help to keep your bones and teeth healthy. So, ions can behave differently to the elements from which they are formed – they have their own properties, such as an ability to dissolve in water. Some common ions and their respective charges are shown here.

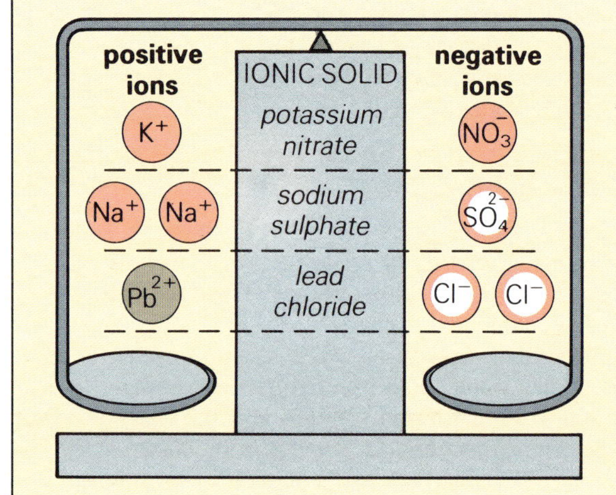

The charges of the ions in the ionic solid cancel each other – they balance!

Charged ions, but neutral compounds

Positive or negative ions don't occur on their own. If they did the milk or toothpaste would be electrically charged and you'd get an electric shock! There are always oppositely charged ions present; these cancel the charges out. In a solid, the oppositely charged ions are packed closely together and form strong forces of attaction called **ionic bonds** (*see 8.11*). Some toothpastes contain solid aluminium hydroxide as an abrasive to help to remove plaque. In aluminium hydroxide there are three hydroxide ions (OH^-) for every aluminium ion (Al^{3+}), so the charges cancel out.

Soluble or insoluble?

Most toothpastes contain about 20% water by weight (so that the paste can be squeezed easily out of the tube!) The fluoride is usually provided by a compound such as sodium fluoride, and this dissolves in the water. If aluminium hydroxide is to act effectively as an abrasive it is important that it does *not* dissolve. Whether an ionic compound dissolves in water depends on the type of ions present. Some combinations of positive and negative ions are more soluble in water than others. Use these solubility rules when you want to find out if an ionic compound is soluble.

SOLUBILITY RULES

1. Any solid is **soluble** if it contains
   - sodium ions
   - potassium ions
   - nitrate ions

   } See (circle) above
   - chloride ions – *except silver or lead chloride*
   - sulphate ions – *except calcium, barium or lead sulphate*

2. Any solid is **insoluble** if it contains
   - oxide ions
   - hydroxide ions
   - carbonate ions

   } *except for sodium or potassium compounds.*

What happens on dissolving?

If an ionic compound is water-soluble, it dissolves in water to form a solution containing **aqueous** (dissolved) **ions**. When sodium chloride dissolves in water it forms a solution containing aqueous sodium ions, $\mathbf{Na^+}(aq)$, and aqueous chloride ions, $\mathbf{Cl^-}(aq)$.

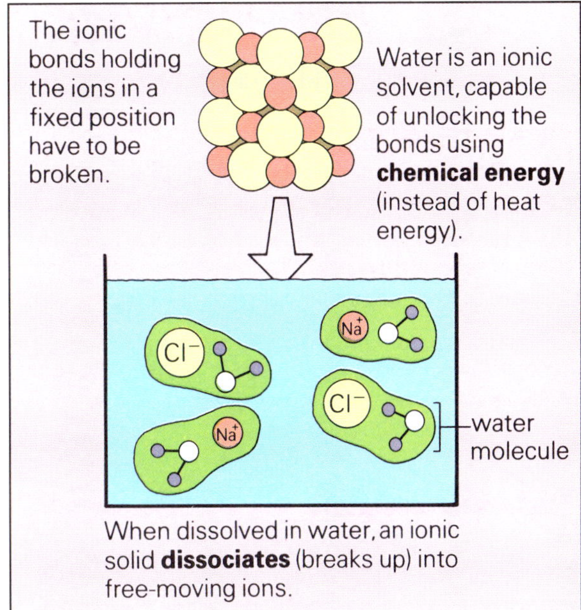

The ionic bonds holding the ions in a fixed position have to be broken.
Water is an ionic solvent, capable of unlocking the bonds using **chemical energy** (instead of heat energy).
Cl^-
Na^+
water molecule

When dissolved in water, an ionic solid **dissociates** (breaks up) into free-moving ions.

Reversing the process

If two aqueous solutions containing free ions are mixed, they can immediately produce an insoluble solid in the mixture. The insoluble solid is called a **precipitate**.

Precipitation is a chemical reaction that sometimes occurs when two solutions of ions are mixed. The word equation for the reaction shown below can be written

Sodium carbonate + Magnesium sulphate → Sodium sulphate + Magnesium carbonate (↓)

The downward arrow indicates that this product is formed as a precipitate.

If sodium carbonate solution and magnesium sulphate solution are mixed, . . .

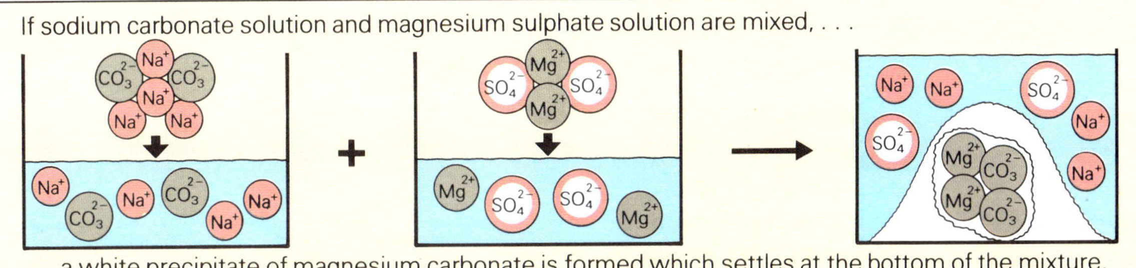

. . . a white precipitate of magnesium carbonate is formed which settles at the bottom of the mixture. What does the solution now contain?

Problem: *Prepare magnesium hydroxide by adding water to, and then mixing, two of the solid reagents labelled A to E.*

A = potassium hydroxide
B = magnesium carbonate
C = lead hydroxide
D = magnesium sulphate
E = sodium hydroxide

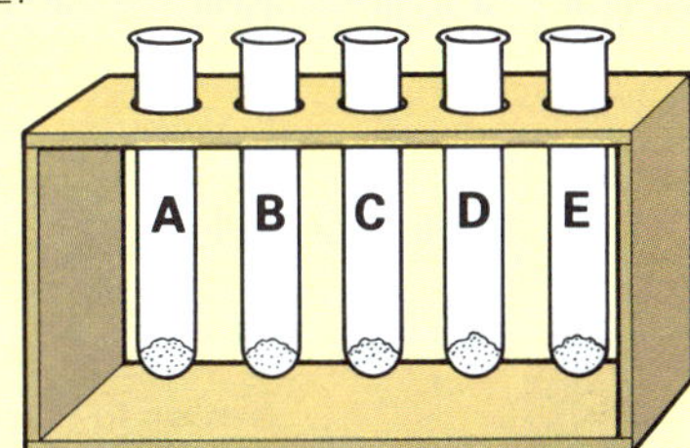

Joseph tried mixing A & B;

Lin decided to mix D & E;

Mark chose to mix C & D.

Who do you agree with? What other mixtures would have worked?

1 Draw the ions present in:
a calcium nitrate; **b** lead hydroxide.

2 Use the solubility rules to explain why:
a aluminium hydroxide is insoluble;
b sodium fluoride is soluble.

3 If you suspected tap-water from old lead pipes was contaminated with lead ions what solution could you add to the tap-water to identify the lead? Why?

4 Refer back to spread 8.5 and explain the difference between a molecule and an ionic compound dissolving.

5 **a** Suggest two solutions you could mix to obtain a precipitate of aluminium hydroxide.
b What technique would you use to separate the precipitate from the rest of the mixture?

6 **a** Name the precipitate formed by mixing solutions of sodium sulphate to barium chloride
b What is present in solution afterwards?

Electrolysis

Electrical conductors

The electrical energy that your TV uses is carried by **electricity** – the flow of electrons. Electricity flows through metals very easily. Such materials are good **electrical conductors.** They are, however, *chemically unchanged* when carrying electricity.

Electricity passes through electrical conductors as a flow of electrons all around a circuit. The metal wire remains chemically unchanged, but the compounds in the battery are chemically changed.

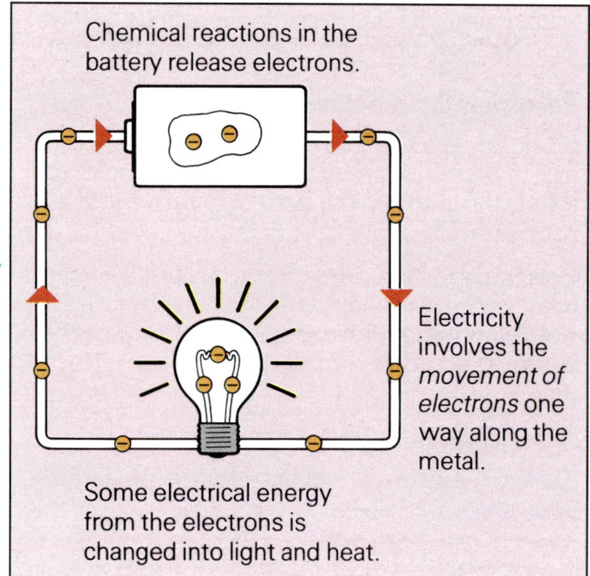

Electrolytic conductors

When melted, some compounds will conduct electricity. Rods called **electrodes** allow electrons to enter and leave such compounds. When electricity flows through such a compound (like lead bromide), some of the electrical energy *decomposes* (breaks down) the compound – this is *a chemical change.* The use of electricity to cause chemical change is called **electrolysis**. Compounds that can behave in this way are called **electrolytic conductors** or **electrolytes.**

Reactions at electrodes

Molten lead bromide is an ionic compound containing *free-moving* ions.

The positive ions are attracted to the cathode (which has a negative charge). The Pb^{2+} ion has 2 electrons *less* than the Pb atom. To change Pb^{2+} into a Pb atom, the lead ion must *gain* 2 electrons. These 2 electrons come from the surface of the cathode. This is represented by writing an **ionic equation**:

At the cathode: $Pb^{2+} + 2e^- \rightarrow Pb$

The negative ions are attracted to the anode. The Br^- ion has one electron *more* than the Br atom. To change Br^- into a Br atom, it must *lose* 1 electron. This electron is lost to the surface of the anode. The **ionic equation** for this reaction is:

At the anode: $Br^- \rightarrow Br + e^-$

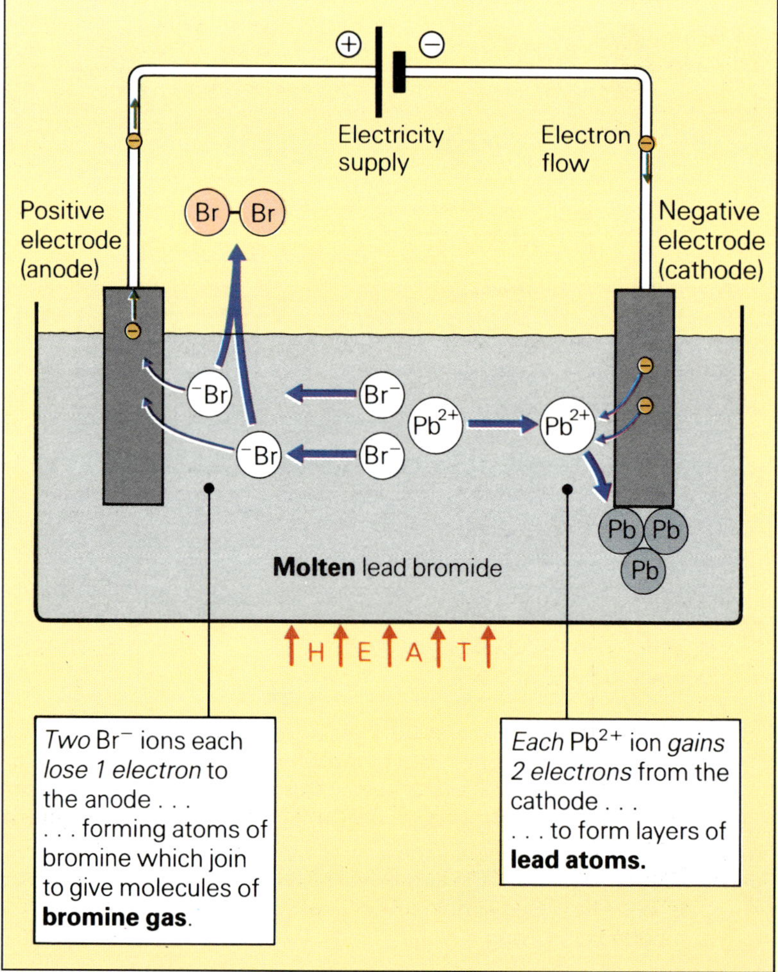

Aqueous electrolytes

If an ionic compound dissolves in water, it dissociates into free-moving ions (*see 8.12*). If carbon electrodes are placed in the solution, the **positive ions** are attracted to the *cathode*; the **negative ions** are attracted to the *anode*. The flow of electricity *through the solution* is caused by this *movement of ions* to the different electrodes. A chemical change takes place at the electrodes – so *aqueous solutions of ionic compounds* are also **electrolytes.** However, with *aqueous* electrolytes, the water molecules can also take part in the chemical changes.

*Using reactivity tables, you can predict the **products** of electrolysis at the cathode (right) and anode (below).*

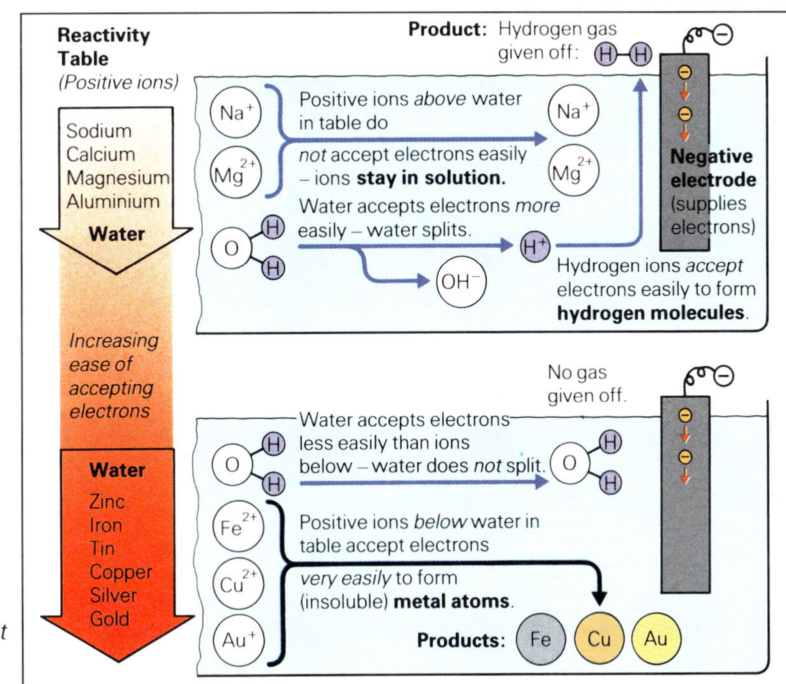

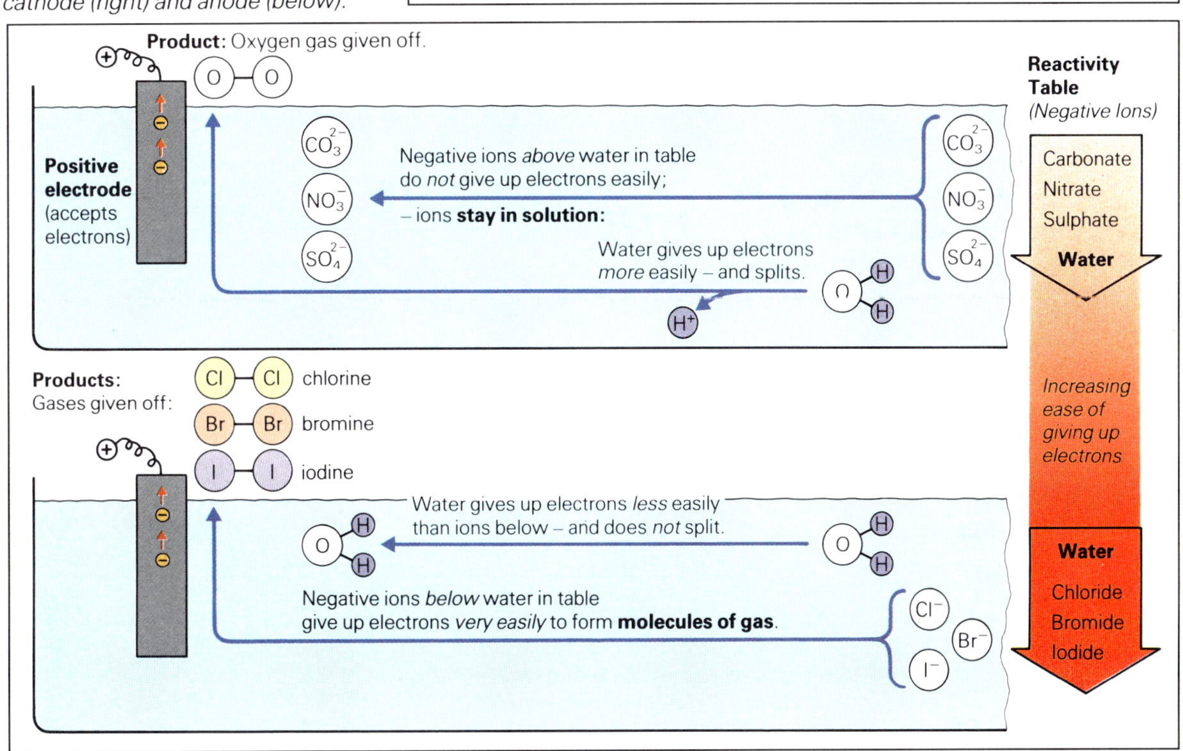

1 How does the conduction of electricity in metals differ from that in electrolytes?

2 The chemical process of **reduction** can be defined as the *addition of an electron*.
- **a** When molten lead bromide is electrolysed, does reduction take place at the anode or cathode?
- **b** **Oxidation** is the opposite of reduction. Define oxidation in terms of electron changes.

3 *Molten* sodium chloride (NaCl) is electrolysed industrially.
- **a** What forms at each electrode?
- **b** Write ionic equations for the reactions at each electrode.

4 Predict what is formed at each electrode when these *aqueous* solutions are electrolysed (using carbon electrodes):
- **a** magnesium bromide **b** copper chloride
- **c** sodium carbonate.

8.14 Metallic structures

Slipping and sliding . . .

Metals consist of **giant structures** containing many millions of atoms. The atoms are packed closely together in **layers**. If you apply a large enough force, the layers are able to *slide* over each other. This is called **slip**. When the layers of atoms slip, the metal takes on a new shape. This helps to explain why, compared to many other materials, metals are easily shaped (**malleable**) and capable of being drawn out into long wires (**ductile**).

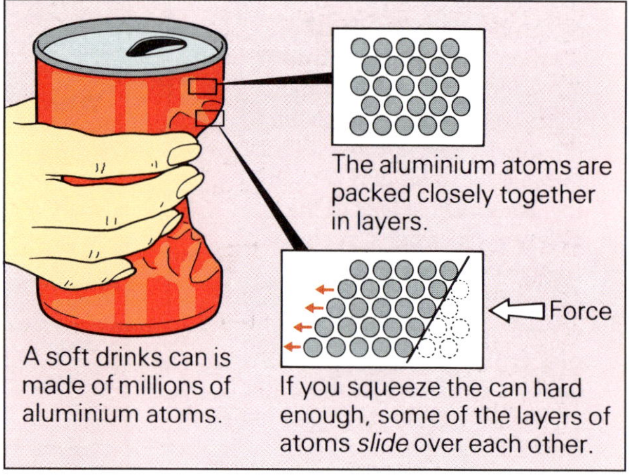

The aluminium atoms are packed closely together in layers.

Force

A soft drinks can is made of millions of aluminium atoms.

If you squeeze the can hard enough, some of the layers of atoms *slide* over each other.

. . . to the breaking point

If the force on the metal is increased, eventually a point is reached when the atoms are *pulled apart* (instead of sliding over each other). When this happens the metal breaks.

The giant structure of metals consists of layers of atoms. In these atoms, some of the outer electrons are *free to move about* from atom to atom. The nucleus of atoms is positively charged and (although the 'free' electrons move around), there is still an **attraction** between the 'free' electrons and the nucleus of each atom. This attraction is called a **metallic bond**. Electrons act like a 'glue', holding the positive ions together.

Metals which contain the *same* number of 'free' electrons can be grouped together. Look at the models of sodium and potassium. What happens to the strength of the metallic bond if the number of 'free' electrons stays the same, but the size of the atoms increases?

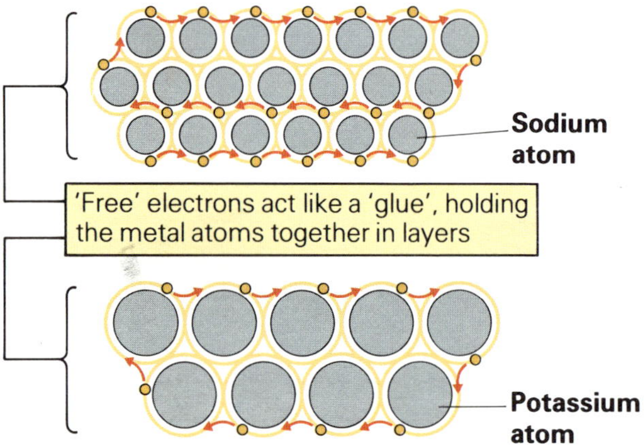

Sodium atom

'Free' electrons act like a 'glue', holding the metal atoms together in layers

Potassium atom

Free electrons	Potassium: *1*	Sodium: *1*
Melting point	Potassium: *63°C*	Sodium: *98°C*
Strength	Potassium is *weaker* than sodium	
Atom size	Potassium is *larger* than sodium	

Other properties

Metals are also very good at transferring heat or electrical energy from place to place. They are said to be **good conductors of heat and electricity**. The transfer of both types of energy is caused by the free moving electrons. The table below shows you the **thermal** (or heat) **conductivity** of different metals; the higher the value, the better the metal is at conducting heat.

How does this table help to explain why aluminium is a better conductor than sodium?

Thermal conductivity ($Wm^{-1}K^{-1}$)	135	150	220	240
Metal	Sodium 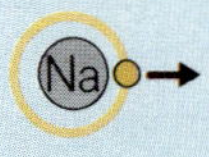 (Na)	Beryllium (Be) 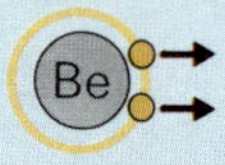	Magnesium (Mg) 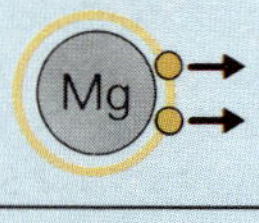	Aluminium (Al) 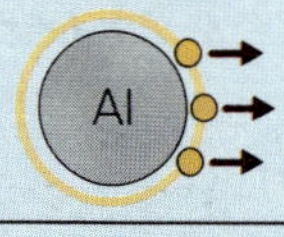
Number of free electrons	1	2	2	3

YOU CAN READ MORE ABOUT CONDUCTIVITY ON SPREAD 2.3.

Stopping the slip

A metal can be made harder and stronger by stopping the layers of atoms from slipping. One way of doing this is to add small amounts of another element. This is called **alloying**. The atoms of the alloying element are different in size to that of the metal and they act as a barrier, stopping the layers of atoms from sliding over each other.

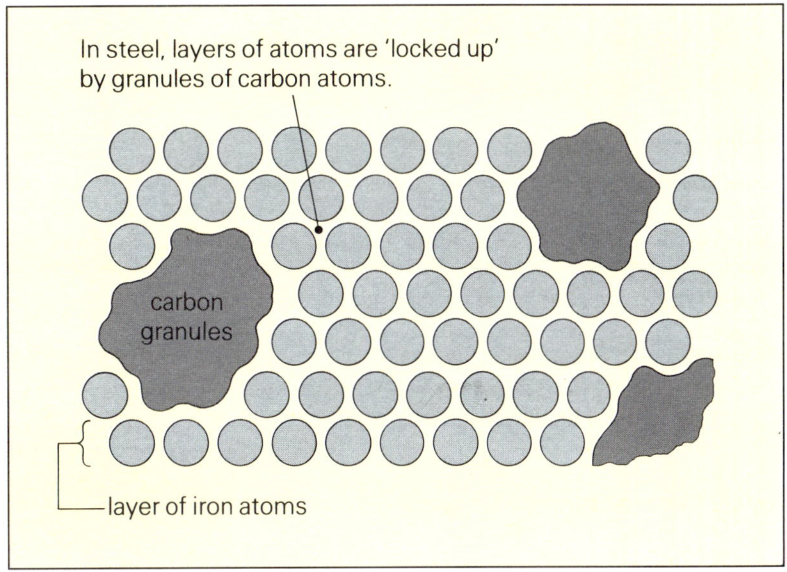

Steel is an **alloy** containing a little carbon mixed with iron.

Grain size

Alloying is not the only way of altering the properties of metals. When atoms are arranged in an orderly manner, they form **crystals**. So metals are crystalline. They are made up of many small crystals or grains. The difference in grain size forms patterns on the surface of the metal. You can sometimes see these patterns on thin metal coatings such as the zinc coating on a metal dustbin or bucket. All metal surfaces have similar patterns but they are usually only revealed by the etching action of acids.

The size of the grains has an important influence on the properties of the metal. In general, *the smaller the grain size, the stronger and harder the metal.* Cooling the molten metal very quickly produces a harder stronger metal with smaller grains.

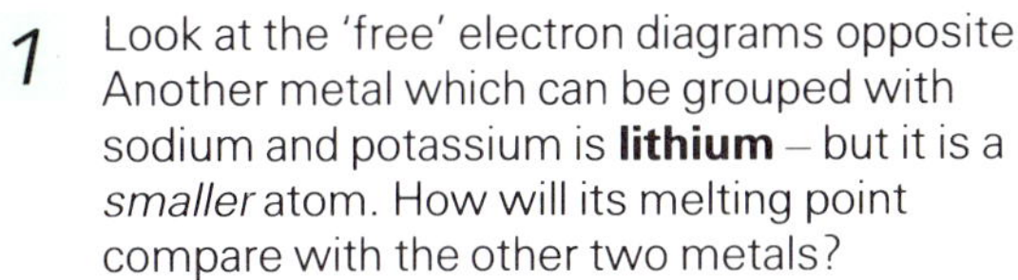

The grain size can also be altered by hammering or rolling. How does this change the properties of a metal?

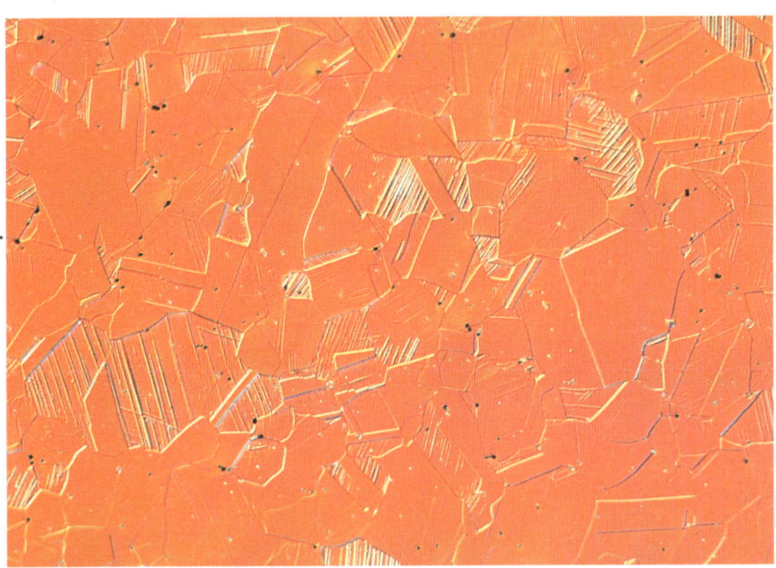
Metals often look smooth, but magnification 25 times shows a rough surface made up of different sizes of grains (crystals).

1. Look at the 'free' electron diagrams opposite. Another metal which can be grouped with sodium and potassium is **lithium** – but it is a *smaller* atom. How will its melting point compare with the other two metals?

2. Explain why:
   a the pattern for electrical conductivities should show the same trend as thermal;
   b potassium is a better conductor than sodium;
   c beryllium is stronger than magnesium.

3. Gold atoms are larger than silver atoms. Which would you expect to be stronger, a gold bracelet or an identical silver bracelet? Why?

4. Draw a model of the alloy bronze made up of 90% copper and 10% tin (a much larger atom). Explain why it is much stronger than pure copper.

5. **Annealing** is a process of cooling metals very slowly. What happens to the grain size when metals are annealed and how will this change their properties?

6. In what ways are metallic, ionic and covalent bonding: **a** similar; **b** different?

YOU CAN READ MORE ABOUT METALS ON SPREAD 2.14.

8.15 Silicon

'What, no chips?'

This is the age of the 'silicon chip', but silicon has played an important part in our lives long before the 'chip' was invented. About 75% of the earth's crust is made up of **silicates** – materials containing the elements silicon and oxygen. There are over a thousand types of silicates: sand, gemstones (topaz and garnet) and many different clays. The *electronic* properties of the silicon 'chip' are often the focus of attention – but instead this spread looks at how useful silicon compounds are, and how their *structure* and *bonding* determine their *physical* properties and uses.

Sand is made up of tiny quartz crystals. The silicon-oxygen bonding makes quartz hard and sand abrasive.

Rigid giant molecules

Sand contains an orderly arrangement of silicon atoms bonded to oxygen atoms to form **silicon dioxide** (silica, SiO_2). The orderly arrangement of atoms leads to a crystalline structure. Pure sand is colourless but iron impurities give it its characteristic yellow or brown colour. Covalent bonds link the atoms into a **giant crystalline molecule**. As a result, sand is *hard* and has a *high melting point*. Its hardness has been put to good use in the building trade to make *hardwearing* concrete and mortar.

Slippery layer structures

Silicon and oxygen atoms can join together to form crystalline **hexagonal plates**. An example of this is found in the mineral **mica**. The plates are like sheets of paper lying on top of each other. *Within* each sheet there are covalent bonds, so fairly strong forces hold the atoms in a sheet. The forces of attraction *between* the sheets are *very weak*. As a result, it is easy to split mica into sheets.

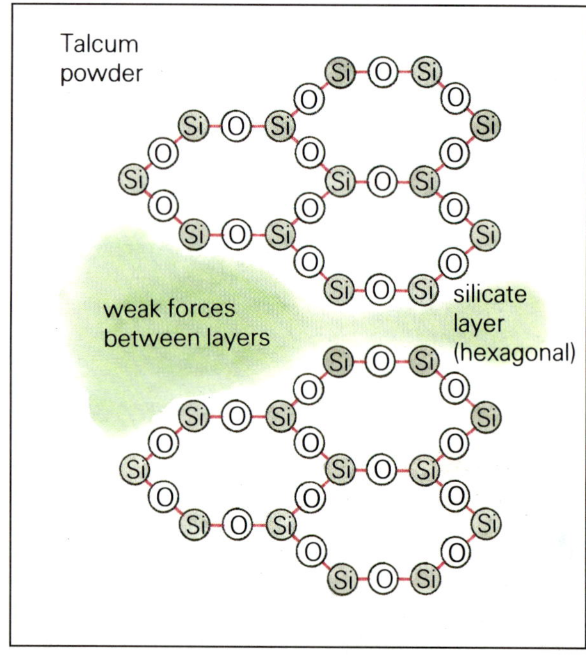

Talcum powder is made of layers of ***silicates*** *– which slide easily over each other.*

Ceramics – fired clays

Clays also consist of plates lying on top of each other (as they do in talc or mica). However, when clay is wet, water molecules are able to get in between the layers and it becomes slippery and *easy to shape*. But if the water evaporates *slowly* the clay loses its slippery feel and becomes hard. The process can be reversed by adding water.

Water molecules act as a lubricant in wet clay – like tennis balls trapped between layers of chicken wire! During firing, the chemical change caused by rapid water loss causes new bonds to form in clay – linking *silicate layers* into a strong *giant molecular structure.*

Wet clay

silicate layer

water molecule

○ : oxygen atom

○ : silicon atom

In ancient times, once people had learnt how to '*fire*' clay, they were able to build long-lasting homes with **bricks** (rather than stone). They were also able to store food in **pottery** containers – keeping it fresher for longer. These people had discovered that the properties of clays could be *permanently* changed by heating strongly ('firing'). Water in the clay is driven off by the strong heating and *new bonds* link the layers of silicates together. Clays that have been 'fired' are called **ceramics** and are *very hard.*

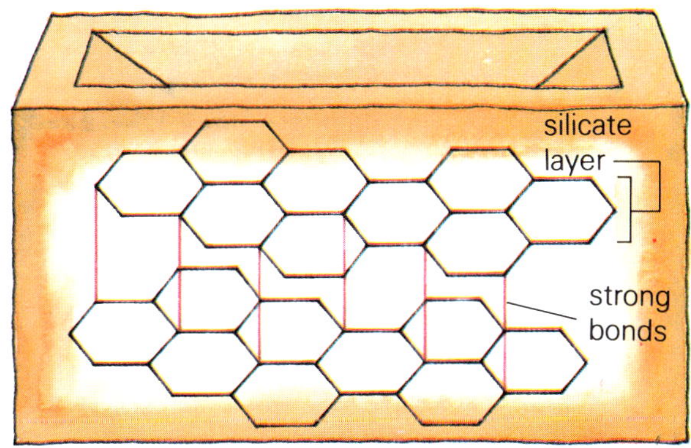

Fibrous chains

There are silicates which consist of layers rolled into a tube (like rolled-up newspaper). The tubelike structure gives such minerals a fibrous appearance. The most common fibrous minerals are types of **asbestos** – which can be made into sheets (just as wood is made into paper). It was widely used as an insulating material in building – until it was discovered that fibres of a certain size irritate the lungs, and can cause a cancer called **asbestosis**.

Changing the chain

Chain structures of silicon and oxygen atoms can also be made with different chain lengths. These substances are called silicones. **Silicones** with *short* chain lengths are *liquids*; but as the chain length *increases*, they become *greases* and *rubbery solids*.

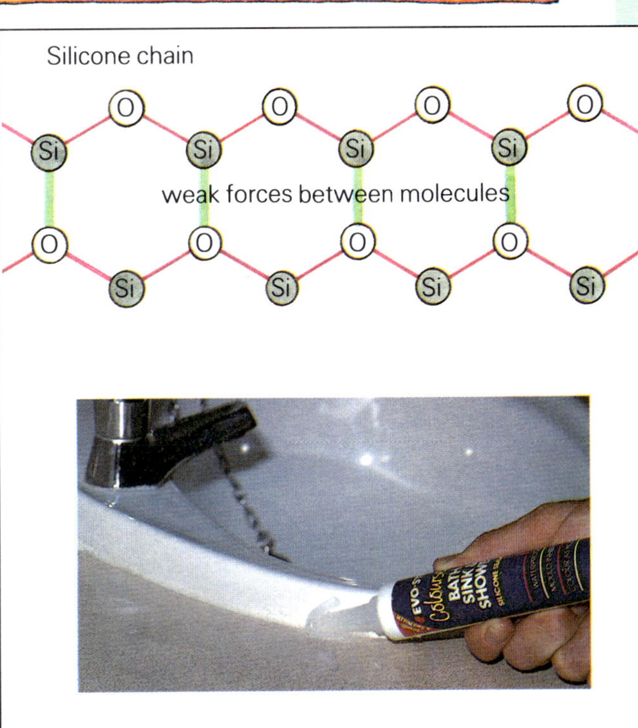

What does this tell you about the forces of attraction between the chains as the chain length increases? Silicones are very useful materials because they *resist most chemicals* and *repel water*. Can you think of any uses for silicones?

Look back through this module. For each of the structures shown here, find one similar structure elsewhere in the module. Compare their properties and uses.

Index

For additional information, see the following modules:

2 Materials
9 Chemical Patterns

Photo acknowledgements

These refer to spread number and, where appropriate, the photo order:

Clare Hayes *8.4* (×2); Trevor Hill *8.1* (×4), *8.8, 8.15/2;* Science Photo Library (A. McClenaghan) *8.6/1,* (A. Hart-Davis) *8.6/2,* (G. Muller) *8.14,* (A. Michler) *8.15/1.*

Picture Researcher: Jennifer Johnson